NON-FICTION

364.1523 Sco84h

Scott, Gini Graham
Homicide :100 years of murder in Am
erica

DISCARDED
by the
Mead Public Library
Sheboygan, WI

4/99

9000832410

W9-ATF-909

832410

Special thanks to Wayne Klatt, who knows true crime like few others, and to the staff at Roxbury Park Books.

532.110

Contents

HOMICIDE:
100 Years of
Murder in America

Gini Graham Scott, Ph.D.

A ROXBURY PARK BOOK

LOWELL HOUSE JUVENILE

LOS ANGELES

CONTEMPORARY BOOKS

CHICAGO

Homicide: 100 Years of Murder in America
is a creation of Roxbury Park Books.

© 1998 by RGA Publishing Group, Inc. All rights reserved. No part of this work may be reproduced or transmitted in any form or by any means, electronic or mechanical, including photocopying and recording, or by any information storage or retrieval system, except as may be expressly permitted by the 1976 Copyright Act or in writing by the publisher.

Roxbury Park is an imprint of Lowell House,
A Division of the RGA Publishing Group, Inc.

Scott, Gini Graham.
    Homicide : 100 years of murder in America / Gini Graham Scott.
        p.   cm.
    "A Roxbury Park Book."
    Includes bibliographical references and index.
    ISBN 1-56565-905-8
    1. Murder—United States—History—20th Century—Case studies.
    2. Homicide—United States—History—20th Century—Case studies.
    I. Title
    HV6524.S36   1998   98-15661
    364.15'23'0973—dc21   CIP

Editor in Chief, Roxbury Park Books: Michael Artenstein
Director of Publishing Services: Rena Copperman
Managing Editor: Lindsey Hay
Additional Research: Wayne Klatt
Index: Michelle Graye

Lowell House books can be purchased at special discounts when ordered in bulk for premiums and special sales. Contact Department CS at the following address:

Lowell House
2020 Avenue of the Stars, Suite 300
Los Angeles, CA 90067

Manufactured in the United States of America

10 9 8 7 6 5 4 3 2 1

screamed for help in the vestibule of a New York City apartment building. More than thirty people heard her shouts, and not one telephoned the police. The murder made many Americans wonder, "What have we become?" The resulting outrage encouraged community involvement in fighting crime, and it was just such an involved community that caught Richard Ramirez, the "Night Stalker," in the 1980s.

Although the 1990s had its own shocking crimes, murder rates around the country dropped as criminology improved and people became more conscious of the real forces behind murder. Although murder might be part of human nature, calculated killings are a serious social problem. *Homicide: 100 Years of Murder in America* concerns itself with killings that shocked the public and defined each of the decades in the twentieth century.

The increase in methods of detection means that we are becoming more aware of crimes than ever before. After all, there is no way of knowing all the murders that were committed in the past. Authorities in ancient Rome did not even concern themselves with individual killings unless they threatened the Empire. More than one book has claimed that serial murder is a new type of crime, although such cases appear in folk literature and have been documented since the fifteenth century. In the eighteenth and nineteenth centuries, a few impulsive killers actually believed they were temporarily transformed into wolves, because their culture believed that such things were possible. Other killers escaped prosecution by just moving on, acting as innocent as Lizzie Borden, or claiming any blood found had come from an animal. It has taken decades for investigators and the courts to establish guilt or innocence by physical evidence alone.

In addition to advancements in criminalistics, communication has become instant, thanks to fax machines, telephones, and the Internet, unlike the days when it took a month or more for police agencies in different locales to notify each other of a crime. As we enter a new century, we may feel confident that if all the detective work and laboratory procedures are strictly followed, there may no longer be such a thing as a perfect crime.

—*Gini Graham Scott*

REFERENCES

Franke, David. *The Torture Doctor.* New York: Avon Books, 1975.

Franklin, Charles. *The World's Worst Murderers.* New York: Taplinger Publishing, 1966.

Golden, Harry. *A Little Girl Is Dead.* New York: Avon Books, 1965.

Nash, Jay Robert. *Murder, America.* New York: Simon & Schuster, 1980.

Rubenstein, Richard E., ed. *Great Courtroom Battles.* Chicago: Playboy Press, 1974.

Swanberg, W.A. *Dreiser.* New York: Bantam Books, 1967.

once a respectable local journalist in Delaware. He had jumped at the chance to head the San Francisco bureau of the Associated Press. However, for some time after his arrival in San Francisco, Dunning carried on a sordid affair with a woman named Cordelia Botkin, whom he had met when his bicycle broke down on his way to work.

Botkin was ten years older than Dunning and not particularly attractive, but her sense of wildness intrigued him after a lifetime of respectability. Botkin despised the oppressive times into which she was born. She left her husband in the central California farming community of Stockton to thrive in the vice dens of San Francisco's Barbary Coast. Before long, Botkin found sex with Dunning insufficient, and the couple engaged in a foursome with Botkin's heavyset son and his forty-year-old mistress in orgies lasting well into the night.

Elizabeth quickly found out about her husband's infidelity. Social convention told her to look the other way, but she had been reared as a proper Victorian lady, the daughter of a U.S. Congressman. She sold her furniture and jewelry for a train ticket back to her family in Delaware. In time, Dunning's irresponsible behavior got him fired, but he was hired as a newspaper correspondent to cover the Spanish-American War.

After he ended his relationship with Botkin, Dunning started writing conciliatory letters to his wife. But Elizabeth was also receiving letters from San Francisco—signed "a friend"—telling her that John had taken up with a pretty Englishwoman and was enjoying a bohemian life of abandon. Elizabeth sent a letter to her husband to confront him, but he denied the supposed new affair and noted that the handwriting looked like Botkin's. From then on, whenever an anonymous letter arrived from California, Elizabeth gave it to her father unopened, and he would put it with the others in a drawer.

Not connecting the chocolates with the letters, opening the package brought back to Elizabeth dear memories of cool summers by the bay and a time when she felt that she and Dunning would be happy forever. But the next day, she, her sister, and their children felt strangely ill. At first, they suffered stomachaches and headaches, and a doctor making a house call dismissed the illness as cholera morbus, probably from eating corn fritters. The children soon were fine. But Elizabeth and her sister kept to the house, and the following day their sharp stomach pains came in spasms and their skin turned yellow.

Their father called in a specialist, who grimly stated, "I believe they have been poisoned."

Elizabeth's esophagus seemed on fire. She began vomiting, her flesh turned clammy, and she had diarrhea mixed with blood. Pennington and his wife tried to assure their daughters that they would be all right, but the couple agonizingly watched as both young women died on the same day, September 12.

Everyone in the family had eaten the corn fritters, but only the ones who had eaten several chocolates became sick. Pennington rushed around the house looking for the empty candy box, and fortunately it still had the wrapping and the handwritten note. Although Elizabeth had not connected the treats with the letters, her father did. He pulled the letters out of the drawer and saw at first glance that the writing was exactly the same.

Dunning received a telegram about his wife's death while he was in Puerto Rico. He went by boat, train, and carriage to be with the family. He sat down in the living room with the anonymous letters, shocked at their lies and at the similarities with the note that had come with the candy. Everything matched what he remembered of Botkin's writing.

Dover police conveyed the family's suspicions to authorities in San Francisco. The police chief there, Isaiah Less, knew well the area where Botkin lived, the seedy section from Broadway to the edge of Chinatown, which was full of small saloons, prostitute cribs, and opium dens. As Less saw it, Botkin must have thought that if she could eliminate her rival, Dunning would return to her.

Of the evidence sent to Less, the handwriting would seem to be his strongest lead, but such was not the case in the California courts. Less had to find another way to prove Botkin's guilt. First, he needed to question her. He tracked down Botkin at the Hotel Victoria, a small place with the lacy trim of its time. He walked down the dim, narrow corridor, and saw Botkin standing outside her door.

He explained who he was and why he was there. "But I'm innocent," the suspect said, "I did nothing." Even so, Less assured her that the police had enough evidence to jail her on suspicion.

Once the woman was locked away, Less returned to the hotel to search her room. Botkin looked like a woman who might overindulge in candy, and he was hoping to find a box matching the one sent to Elizabeth. Instead, he found some wrapping from the George Haas candy company. He pocketed the wrapper and went to a store with the empty candy box that had been sent from Delaware. "Oh yes, that's from our store," said a clerk. When Less described Botkin, the clerk added, "I remember her; she bought a box of candy here."

Then Less chased down the lace handkerchief that had covered the bonbons. After visiting several shops, a salesperson at the elegant City of Paris department store recognized the price tag.

Returning to Botkin's hotel, Less questioned several employees. Some recalled seeing Botkin return with a box of candy from Haas's store and go to her room. "It was surprising," one said, "because she stayed there for several days." When they saw her leave, she was carrying a large box with wrapping paper around it. "It looked like she was taking it to the post office," one said.

Because Less had to build a case out of only circumstantial evidence, he had to pile on every circumstance possible to convince a jury. That meant checking all the drugstores near the hotel on the off-chance that a clerk or employee might remember someone recently buying arsenic. Finally a clerk at a small shop, who at first could not remember anyone, recalled that a couple of weeks earlier a woman had asked for some arsenic to clean a straw hat. She remained in his memory because he had heard of many uses for arsenic but never for cleaning straw hats.

The clerk did not have a registry of sales, but he kept an informal log. One listing was for "Mrs. Bothin" of the Victoria Hotel. Less thought the closeness of "Bothin" to "Botkin" furthered his circumstantial case.

In an unusual spirit of cooperation, the Delaware state attorney general traveled across the country in 1899 to try the case in California. In three hours of closing arguments, noted defense attorney George Knight portrayed Botkin as an innocent, persecuted woman, and claimed "the machinations" of the police had completely fabricated a case against her. Nevertheless, after a brief deliberation, the jury found Botkin guilty of murder in the first degree and recommended life imprisonment. When asked if she had anything to say, Botkin insisted, "I'm totally innocent of this horrible crime." She maintained her innocence until her death in San Quentin prison in 1910.

The House on Murder Hill

The mysteries surrounding Belle Gunness exist to this day. Did she really lure dozens of suitors to their death, earning her the nickname "Lady Bluebeard"? Was she killed in the fire on her farm in northwestern Indiana? Did she get away with murder? Or did she die in a hell of her own making?

Gunness was born in 1859, the daughter of a farmhand and occasional stone mason in a Norwegian fishing village. Tired of drudgery as a tender of cattle and a milkmaid, she sought her fortune in America. The fastest place to make money at the time was Chicago, which was rebuilding itself after the fire of 1871. Gunness soon learned, however, that hard work did not always bring riches in the United States, so she contrived two guaranteed paths to wealth: matrimony and insurance claims.

Gunness married farmer Mads Sorensen not for love but simply because she wanted to live in a nice house. She opened a small confectionery shop twelve years later when she was in her mid-thirties. But a kerosene lamp reportedly exploded and burned down her shop. Then their house burned to the ground, killing two of their four young children. At a time when most people carried no life insurance, all Gunness's children were covered by policies.

In 1900, Mads Sorensen died with symptoms suggesting strychnine poisoning. Gunness assured the doctor that she had given her husband only a powder to help him recover from his cold. The death certificate listed natural causes.

She used the $8,500 insurance money in the fall of 1901 to buy a forty-eight-acre farm on a hill a mile outside La Porte, Indiana. For a former milkmaid from Norway, it was an impressive spread, featuring a striking brick mansion. The mansion was luxuriously furnished by its former owner, a one-time madam named Mattie Altic.

A few months later, in 1902, Belle married a Norwegian farmer, Peter Gunness. He did not live out the year. The coroner found Peter lying face down in the parlor with a broken nose and a hole in the back of his head. In the kitchen, a bowl of brine and a sausage grinder were found on the floor. Belle explained that her husband was helping her make sausage. She claimed not to be present when the accident took place but that she found Peter in the kitchen holding his head and moaning. Peter got up, walked a little, and then collapsed. Gunness told the coroner that Peter might have knocked the brine off the stove with the heavy grinder toppling onto him as he fell. The coroner attributed the death to an accident, but neighbors had their doubts.

Gunness lived the outward life of a respectable widow. Although Belle weighed two hundred eighty pounds and had a distinctive row of golden teeth, she began posting ads in newspapers: "A rich and good-looking woman, the owner of a big farm, desires to correspond with a gentleman of wealth and refinement. Object matrimony. Scandinavian preferred."

Postal workers joked about the flood of mail she received because, despite her name and the ad, Belle was anything but good-looking.

Her neighbors continued to grow suspicious. They noticed a stream of gentlemen callers. But few of these suitors showed up at the station for a train to return home. Others vanished as well.

In 1906, Gunness's foster daughter, Jennie Olson, disappeared, and Gunness told the curious that the young woman had gone to a finishing school in California. Then a would-be wooer, Andrew Helgelien, arrived with a handsome coat. No one saw Helgelien again, but the neighbors wondered why Gunness would sometimes go out wearing his coat.

The neighbors were putting two and two together and getting four, six, and ten.

Belle's farm was slowly acquiring the whispered nickname of "Murder Hill." Had someone gotten a really good look at the house, a lot of questions might have been answered. But no one got the chance. On April 29, 1908, flames lit up the night sky in La Porte. Farmers came by wagon and automobile to view the spectacle. No one heard any screams, and no one saw Gunness escape. The striking mansion of mysteries burned to the ground.

The next day, the local sheriff and several men returned to the site of the fire with rakes to poke through the smoldering ruins behind the windbreak of trees. In the cellar, they uncovered three small bodies and one of a headless woman. The victims apparently were in a bed that fell through a flaming floor. The police surmised that the juvenile bodies were those of Gunness's three children, who ranged in age from five to eleven. The other body weighed much less than Gunness but, considering its condition, could have been hers. As for the head, perhaps a falling beam had decapitated the body. However, the head was never found, although police discovered a scattering of gold teeth.

The sheriff arrested a handyman Gunness had fired two months before, Ray Lamphere, on the grounds that Ray wanted revenge or was jealous over one of Gunness's suitors.

The case would have ended there if the digging had. But on May 3, Andrew Helgelien's brother, Alse, showed up after a bank clerk sent him a clipping about the fire. Alse and Andrew had immigrated from Norway and worked on a ranch in South Dakota, saving most of their money. But Andrew left for Indiana to court a rich widow. Afterward, Alse discovered that Andrew had withdrawn $4,500 to help pay Gunness's mortgage. Alse conveyed his concerns to Gunness, but she wrote back that his brother had returned to Norway—without telling him. Earlier she told neighbors that Andrew had gone to Chicago.

The sheriff coordinated twenty deputies and civilian volunteers as they dug up the grounds. There they found sacks of body parts believed to have been Andrew's. Nearby, they found the remains of a young woman, who was assumed to be Gunness's foster daughter, Jennie. Digging on, they found the skeletal bodies of a woman and two men.

Unable to believe that Gunness could be so evil, the sheriff assumed that she had merely helped hired-hand Lamphere kill or dispose of the victims. Indeed, newspapers were promoting this theory as "cupidity." Perhaps Jennie was slain out of fear that she would tell about earlier murders.

A former would-be suitor, Carl Peterson of Waupaca, Wisconsin, came forward with old letters from Gunness.

"I wanted to marry her," he said, "but when she asked for more money than I had and I asked her if she could consent to be a poor man's wife, she backed down."

With every day bringing more indications of guilt, the sheriff notified all police departments near seaports that Gunness might be on her way back to Norway.

From the local postmaster, authorities learned the names of other correspondents over the past four years, thinking this might help identify the skeletons found near Jennie's body. At the same time, his men discovered four more victims, in the yard and by the barn. Quicklime was poured around the gunnysacks to speed decomposition. It seemed someone that careful in disposing of victims might well escape a fire. Could Gunness have killed a woman to represent her in death, removed the victim's head to fool authorities, and then pulled (or had someone else pull) a few of her telltale gold teeth to scatter as evidence?

Not only the Indiana papers but also the *New York Times* was fascinated by the story. Gunness's sister, Mrs. Nellie Larson, told reporters, "My sister was crazy for money. That was a great weakness. As a young woman, she never seemed to care for a man for his own self, only for the money or luxury he was able to give."

"She must have been a stranger to sympathy and sentiment," a *Times* editorial writer claimed, "devoid alike of pity and fear, unmoved by the sight of blood, and free from any sensibility."

With nine bodies unearthed, theories abounded about Gunness's possible whereabouts. One was that she was killed by a Chicago gang; another had her trying to sneak back to Norway.

Eventually fourteen bodies were found on Gunness's property. The sheriff even had a former gold prospector go through the grounds with sluicing equipment. Still, no one could tell whether Gunness was among the ashes or if she had indeed slipped away from the police. Nor did anyone learn how her suitors were killed. One possible explanation had Gunness drugging her suitors, crushing their skulls, and, as she had butchered hogs, cutting them up and burying their remains. The sheriff estimated that Gunness stole over $30,000 from her victims.

Because Gunness could not be found, Lamphere was convicted of arson and sentenced to twenty-one years in prison, where he died. But Lamphere told a cellmate something that shed light on part of the Gunness myth and added darkness to the rest. The handyman said he had known about Gunness's murders and helped her by burning some of the bodies. Then, he claimed Gunness lured a Chicago woman to her farm, gave her whiskey laced with strychnine, decapitated her, and put the headless body in bed with her own children. She also pulled out some of her own teeth so that the police would think the poisoned woman was her. Afterward, said Lamphere, Gunness burned down the mansion on Murder Hill and fled to the next train station after La Porte. She was supposed to contact him so that they could go off somewhere, but she never did.

The myth Gunness left behind was so strong that there were occasional and probably false sightings of her around La Porte for fifteen years. Did Gunness vanish? Or did she appear in other parts of the country under different names—but with the same murderous intent?

In 1931, when Gunness would have been in her early eighties, Los Angeles Deputy District Attorney George Stahlman said a woman known as Esther Carlson was accused of poisoning an elderly man under her care for his bank account, and that she resembled what Gunness might have looked like then. In addition, she carried photos of children who resembled Gunness's Myrtle, Lucy, and Philip. But Carlson denied being Gunness, and we will never know the truth.

Since the 1970s, some La Porteans and others have gone to the site of the mystery mansion and called upon Gunness's spirit in a seance. In one such seance, one of the girls in the chain of linked hands reportedly screamed. When the lights were turned on, she was dead—her back pierced by knife wounds.

There are also ballads about the Belle of La Porte, such as one concluding:

> *They looked for her in Texas*
> *In sunny Tennessee*
> *They sought her most/from coast to coast*
> *O where, O where is she?*
> *Perhaps she's gone to heaven*
> *There's none of us can say*
> *But if I'm right in my surmise*
> *She's gone the other way.*

REFERENCES

Fido, Martin. *The Chronicle of Crime.* New York: Carroll & Graf Publishers, 1993.

Gnash, Jay Robert. *Bloodletters and Badmen.* New York: M. Evans & Co., 1995.

Langlois, Janet. *Belle Gunness: The Lady Bluebeard.* Bloomington, Ind.: Indiana University Press, 1985.

New York Times, December 29 and 31, 1898, and February 5, 1899.

———, May 6–8, 1908, and November 7, 1908.

The 1910s

Europe headed for the disaster of World War I by refusing to change, but America flourished with the unleashed energy of all that was new and exciting. The second decade of the century saw a growing freneticism in daily life, influenced by the cubist abstract art of Picasso and Paul Klee, the modernism of architect Frank Lloyd Wright, and a fresh wildness in such unconventional music as Stravinsky's *Rite of Spring* ballet and the newly emerging jazz scene.

Most women continued to fill traditional roles, although many found jobs in the cities. As these working women adapted to the bustle of urban life, their trusting nature was easily exploited by the unscrupulous, whether posing as doctors with miracle cures or love-struck suitors.

Crimes were no longer shocking examples of moral collapse but rather exciting newspaper reading. Details only hinted at before were now given explicitly, as in the crimes of Dr. Harvey Crippen. The Michigan homeopath, who worked for a patent-medicine company in London, poisoned his wife, Belle, at the urging of his slender lover, Ethel LeNeve. After pawning Belle's jewelry, Crippen dismembered his wife, buried her remains in a cellar, and returned to America under a false name with his lover dressed as his son. But the police met Crippen at the dock. They caught up with him with unprecedented swiftness because the ship's captain had used Marconi wireless telegraphy to report his suspicion about a passenger who resembled photos of the hunted doctor.

At Crippen's trial, renowned pathologist Sir Bernard Spillsbury explained to the jury how just a scar found in the decaying remains dug up from a cellar was sufficient to prove that the victim was Crippen's wife. Crippen was hanged in England in November 1910, less than a year after committing the crime.

In that same year, Frenchman Edmund Locard—an avid reader of Sherlock Holmes stories in translation—established the "exchange principal," which states that a criminal always leaves or takes something away from the scene of the crime. Rather than the faulty memories and possible lies of witnesses, police science could now rely on clothing fibers, pieces of skin scraped from the victim's fingernails, a strand of hair, or oil on the killer's shoes.

As the police became more scientific, killers became more cunning. And a new element was introduced into many crimes: the thrill of trying to outsmart law enforcement.

Three Women in Black

Manhattan quickly reflected every advancement of this period, along with all the new political theories and social philosophies. But across the Hudson River, East Orange, New Jersey, was still a rural community with its small-town suspicions about newcomers, such as the two women who walked close together on the town's streets. When they moved to the town in mid-November of 1909, everyone assumed they were sisters. The older woman—the one always dressed in black— had a pinched, stern face. The young, sad one was beautiful despite her emaciation, and she had a steady, hacking cough. The two women seldom spoke to anyone, and when they did it was with a light Southern accent. Why did they choose to live in a community where they refused to assimilate?

On the eve of November 28, Sergeant Timothy Caniff received a telephone call from one of the "sisters" asking that a coroner be summoned for what she called an accident in the two-story gray house at 89 North Fourteenth Street. Because the police department did not have a coroner, Caniff dispatched his assistant, Dr. Herbert Simmons, who grabbed his black medical satchel and walked the short distance to the home.

Waiting for Simmons was the tall, thin woman. She was completely in black with a heavy veil over her face and her cape touching the ground. This woman, Virginia Wardlaw, silently led the doctor upstairs and down a hallway to the nude body of her pretty, twenty-nine-year-old sister in a half-filled bathtub with her face submerged between her knees. A washcloth was in the corpse's hand. The doctor lifted the sister's head from the water and saw no bruising, and feeling the skull through her long hair he found no wound or injury. A note pinned to her clothing lying on the floor stated:

> *"Last year my little daughter died; other near and dear ones have gone before. I have been prostrated with illness for a long time. When you read this I will have committed suicide. Do not grieve over me. Rejoice with me that death brings a blessed relief from pain and suffering greater than I can bear."*

With the precise diction of an educator, Virginia explained that the dead woman was in fact her niece, Ocey Snead. The black-draped aunt said that Ocey's first child had died two days after birth the year before, and her husband died a few months later. Her second child, a four-month-old son, was in a Brooklyn hospital because Ocey could not care for him owing to her poor health.

Dr. Simmons was always fascinated by police work, and he kept noticing inconsistencies in the woman's story. Virginia said that she had called as soon as she saw her niece lifeless in the bath, but Ocey had been dead for at least twenty-four hours. And why would anyone commit suicide in a bathtub? Why was there virtually no furniture in the large house? Although Virginia had an explanation for everything, nothing rang true. Simmons called in the case as a possible suicide but asked that a police officer come over.

Sergeant William O'Neill agreed that things were suspicious. For example, he found a long silk gown and pretty shoes Ocey had put away. Yet a barrel served as her dressing table, and evidence on the keg suggested that her last meal was some evaporated milk, cereal, and an orange. The dining room table was fashioned from a plank on a packing box.

The matronly Virginia told the police that she and her niece had moved from New York City so that she might nurse her niece back to health. Virginia said that she slept on the floor and Ocey used a cot upstairs. Virginia briefly answered each question and would say no more. Police Chief James Bell decided to lock her up overnight as a material witness.

An autopsy concurred that Ocey had died from drowning and noted that at the time of her death she weighed no more than eighty pounds. Another doctor in town told of how Virginia had insisted that he issue Ocey a certificate stating that she was in normal health, even though he found the young woman "weak and inclined to bronchitis."

Despite a lack of evidence pointing to foul play, the police were determined to prove that Ocey was murdered. A check of hotel registries in New York City revealed that Virginia had stayed in the exclusive Brevoort Hotel until a spat over the bill. Virginia and Ocey then moved into a house in Brooklyn and soon aroused suspicion. A neighbor who had helped deliver Ocey's baby reported that the thin young woman complained that she was being starved to death.

Then the story became even stranger. A janitor at another house said that Ocey had moved in with her husband about a year and a half before. A few months later, they were joined by three women in black, but the husband was no longer around.

A family physician said he had prescribed some medicine because of Ocey's weakened condition, but one of the other women—possibly Virginia—claimed they had to use all their money to keep up Ocey's insurance policies. The doctor notified the police of possible illegal activity. A lawyer reported that Virginia brought her niece to his office and asked him to draw up her will to include $500 for her baby. The rest of her estate was to go to her eighty-four-year-old, nearly blind grandmother, Martha Eliza Wardlaw. Ocey quietly assented and signed.

The detectives discussed among themselves not so much what they had learned as what they had been unable to find. There were no pens or ink in the home, so how could Ocey have written a suicide note? Virginia said she lit a fire for Ocey's bath, but the stove showed no indication that a fire had been started for weeks. Every officer who worked on the case was sure that Virginia, who supposedly was Ocey's caretaker in her final days, had starved her, thrown her into the bathtub water, and held her down for the insurance money.

Virginia was charged in the desperate hope that more convincing evidence could be found before her trial. The police used a bundle of documents found in the home, including the will, to contact what became a network of police agencies to do the legwork for an investigation that would have been impossible in the previous century. The investigators found that Ocey had been heavily insured with several companies since she was fifteen. All seven policies, totaling $24,000, had nearly reached their borrowing limit.

The investigators learned from Brooklyn attorney Julius Carraba that Virginia and one of her sisters wanted the recent will redrawn on the grounds that it was not properly witnessed. Carraba urged the sisters to get their young niece to a doctor, but the older women said they did not have the money. When the sisters left the office to get a pen, Ocey whispered to the lawyer that she wanted her money left to her son and grandmother, not as her aunts might instruct him. The sisters returned, refused Ocey's suggestion, and the lawyer never drew up a new last testament.

The mystery of the three women in black intrigued newspaper readers. A drugstore owner reported to the police that a woman clad in black had left him a package of documents to hold, but she never picked them up. These documents proved especially helpful in uncovering the family history. The three sisters were the daughters of South Carolina Supreme Court Justice David Lewis Wardlaw. Their family traced its ancestry to the Norman Conquest and included church leaders, merchants, lawyers, bankers, surgeons, public officials, and Confederate officers. Virginia herself was at one time president of Soule Female College in Murfreesboro, Tennessee, where she dominated the lives of her sisters and her niece.

Caroline Martin—Ocey's mother—was the middle sister. She had lived with her husband in a mansion just outside Louisville, Kentucky, until the house was gutted by fire. Neighbors busied themselves with wild speculation about how their son had died: Had Caroline mistreated the boy, who had spinal meningitis, or had he fallen down a flight of stairs? With $22,000 from the insurance, the couple moved to a run-down boardinghouse in Manhattan.

People around the Martins thought that Caroline was obsessed with money, and one neighbor said she would borrow from him to pay insurance premiums for policies on relatives. Caroline told the neighbor she would repay him with her pension when she retired as a school principal. Another neighbor recalled hearing a loud crash followed by groaning. He found Caroline's husband mortally injured on the floor and Caroline seemingly unconcerned on a nearby bed. Their child, Ocey, was crying hysterically and trying to say something, but her mother kept her quiet with a glare and said just one word: "Remember!"

From then on, the three Wardlaw sisters seemed to live only for themselves. They went nearly everywhere together, adopting black as a symbol of their unity and their self-imposed isolation from the changing world. They were known for walking the halls of Soule Female College with increasing eccentricity, sometimes chanting, until money problems forced Virginia to resign.

A similar chain of circumstances occurred when Caroline headed a school in Christianburg, Virginia. She and her sisters wandered the halls in black as if haunting the school. While there, Mary's son John died shortly after his night-clothes caught fire. Perhaps it was an accident, perhaps not. The young man was heavily insured, and prior to his death he had reassigned one of the polices from his ailing wife to his Aunt Virginia. However, the sisters quickly used up the money because they chose not to work anymore for a living— not as long as there was another expendable relative.

Financial problems forced the sisters to move to New York. Despite their fiscal woes, they stayed in expensive hotels such as the Brevoort for as long as they could. The documents that the police found ended here. They were left to search for clues elsewhere.

Police found the youngest sister, Mary Snead, caring for the sisters' frail mother in a basement apartment on West 22nd Street in Manhattan. From Mary, the police learned that Ocey, her niece, had married her son, Fletcher, but he left her and went to Canada. Ocey's mother lied and told her daughter that her husband had died, contributing to Ocey's sadness over the death of her infant son and her other baby being taken away from her. It seemed as if her mother and aunts were forcing her into a suicidal depression.

New York City Police Commissioner Elijah Boeetler noted that the existence of all those policies and loans and other financial papers had all the markings of insurance fraud. Although all the money would go to Ocey's grandmother, Virginia and her sisters were sure the money would be theirs after their mother passed away.

During a grand jury session, an expert testified that Ocey's suicide note was an apparent forgery in that the angle of the pen in the signature was different from the rest of the message, which was actually written with another type of pen tip. When Virginia appeared for arraignment amid a crowd of reporters and spectators in the East Orange city hall and courthouse, she had to be ordered to lift her black veil so that she could be identified for the record.

Investigators were still trying to find Ocey's mother, who had made no contact despite the death of her daughter. They learned that the New York City school superintendent was recommending that Caroline Martin be asked to resign as a principal because she was "mentally incapacitated." The detectives found her in a run-down hotel near New York's theater district, but she refused to open the door for them.

The determined police turned to the reporters to obtain more information. When Caroline slipped out, one of the reporters found a black tin box Caroline left behind with clippings about her daughter's death and a number of receipts. The box also contained three suicide notes written in the same handwriting as the one that was pinned to Ocey's clothes. The notes looked as if they were written for practice, and they remained in the tin box because the methodical Caroline seldom threw away anything.

All three sisters were charged—Virginia and Caroline with murder, and Mary as an accessory. Mary assured reporters that she and her sisters were being sacrificed by "big interests who want to cheat us out of our money." But Virginia, ever the Southern aristocrat, refused to disgrace herself with a trial. She starved herself to death in her jail cell and was pronounced dead on August 10, 1910.

At a sanity hearing, Caroline flew into a rage proclaiming her innocence. The judge concluded that she might be insane to some degree, but her keen mind and remarkable memory showed that she understood the nature of the charges.

In January 1911, Caroline pleaded guilty to a charge reduced from murder to manslaughter and was sentenced to seven years in prison. She arrived at the iron gates in her black veil, dress, gloves, and cape. Although Caroline had nothing more to gain from a show of insanity, she suffered attacks of stupor followed by hysterical outbursts while in prison. She was in a catatonic state when she died in the New Jersey State Hospital for the Insane in June 1913.

The final sister, Mary, was set free when her lawyer successfully argued that there was no state crime of "accessory to manslaughter." She returned with another son, Albert, to a ranch in Colorado and lived the rest of her life in obscurity.

Doctor Death

Dora and Claire Williamson, wealthy British heiresses, arrived in Seattle in February 1911 and immediately went to see Dr. Linda Burfield Hazzard. The sisters thought Hazzard's unusual but internationally known fasting techniques would cure their long-standing stomach and female troubles.

With no government regulations on food or medicines, and professional associations slow to act against charlatans, sanatoriums were sometimes run by dreamers or schemers. The well-off, accustomed to buying everything from mansions to legislation, felt that they could purchase a few more years of life, whether from monkey glands for virility or starvation for health. Hazzard's "cure" was merely a systematized extension of the medieval belief that denying sustenance to the body purified the soul. In a time when many rich alcoholics went to sanatoriums to vomit their way to sobriety, and the Kellogg brothers in Michigan were preaching grain as the salvation of tired bodies, Hazzard's reputation seemed as valid as any.

Dora and Claire had recently inherited a fortune from their Scottish-born grandfather, who had died in Australia. Living near the British health resort of Brighton, the sisters read a brochure from Hazzard and then her book, *Fasting for the Cure of Disease.* The doctor—her only medical training was as a nurse and as a licensed osteopath in Minneapolis— taught that many bodily disturbances came from meat-eating and other nutritional imbalances. Hazzard secured a medical certificate for her treatment and claimed to cure diseases including cancer, psoriasis, heart trouble, tuberculosis, epilepsy, and even insanity.

Medical practitioners labeled Hazzard a quack, but they offered no cures of their own. She plastered over their denouncements with a steady stream of literature against "organized persecution from medical sources" because her work would put thousands of doctors out of business.

Dora and Claire, convinced by Hazzard's preachments that "overeating is the vice of the whole human race," found Dr. Hazzard's office in a brick bank building. As horse-drawn wagons and an occasional automobile rumbled by, Hazzard introduced herself and said a few words about her successes and how she was looking forward to opening her sanatorium, then being constructed on a small island across Puget Sound.

Almost immediately, the sisters were struck by Hazzard's confident manner and the force of her personality. She passionately described the wonderful cures of patients who abided by her regimen of fasting, light broth, enemas, and baths. Hazzard personally gave Dora and Claire a massage, pummeling their naked backs with her fists. Afterward, she suggested three or four weeks of treatment accompanied by vigorous exercises to eliminate the poisons causing their malaise. Hazzard said the women would have stronger uteruses, their stomachs would be soothed, and they would feel more vigorous.

The treatment began with visits to Hazzard's office in the Seattle bank building five times a week. The sisters would return to their small apartments nearby to compare their progress. Instead of feeling stronger, they gradually felt weaker. But because the sisters were sure they were becoming cleaner and more balanced, the weakness became a light-headed euphoria instead of a concern. Seeking continual reassurances during their days of groaning pain, the sisters became increasingly dependent on Hazzard. Incredibly, she increased their enemas from half an hour a day to two hours, then three hours, expelling every nutrient they needed to stay alive. Dora fainted once as soapy water was being forced through her rectum.

"We must eliminate the poisons," Hazzard would say again and again. "You are not fit to take food yet. We must eliminate the poisons!"

By mid-March, three weeks into their treatment, the sisters could barely walk even with the assistance of a nurse assigned to move their bony bodies about to keep up their circulation and avoid pneumonia. When the sisters were virtually bedridden and unable to think clearly, Hazzard advised them to secure their belongings against thieves who might break into their apartments now that they were in a weakened condition. After several requests, the sisters turned over their family heirlooms and even their deeds to Hazzard. By the end of the month, Dora's mind sometimes wandered and she often became delirious.

Yet the fasting continued. Their nurse, Nellie Sherman, was worried about the sisters. She tried to get them to eat more than the light broth of tomatoes and asparagus tips, but they would not take any more. Nellie took her concerns to a local osteopath, Augusta Brewer, telling him that the sisters "are absolutely under Dr. Hazzard's dominion." Brewer could do nothing but urge Nellie to feed them immediately.

When the sisters could no longer walk and had to be carried, Hazzard admitted them to her newly completed sanatorium. The compound consisted of a two-story main house and a few cabins arranged in a semicircle. The sisters—each weighing no more than seventy or eighty pounds, wrinkled, and unable to concentrate—were placed in a special ambulance and boat launch and transported to the island in the Sound. The nearest telephone was five miles away, and the patients were never visited by outside specialists.

At the main house, Hazzard's husband, Sam, offered to help the sisters with any correspondence. That enabled him to change their wills and leave their property to his wife.

But in time, the sisters must have guessed at least some of what was happening. Claire crawled out of her cabin and offered a small boy money to take a cable message to the mainland. The message reached the Williamson family nurse, Margaret Conway, all the way in Australia. It read only "Come SS Marama May 8 first class. Claire." There was no further explanation, but Conway realized the message was a cry for help. The wording had avoided mention of any trouble because of possible repercussions.

Claire died while Conway was sailing across the Pacific. John Herbert, Claire's uncle from Portland, arrived in Seattle to claim the body. The person he saw looked so different from his niece that he insisted it was not her. Hazzard showed him the shrunken stomach, liver, and intestines. She also produced a typewritten, unsigned letter dated April twenty-third in which Claire supposedly claimed to know that Hazzard's treatment might fail and that she accepted responsibility should she die. Troubled, Herbert returned home.

The Williamson family nurse arrived at the closest port—Vancouver, Canada—on June 1. Sam Hazzard met her at the pier. He expressed his regrets but said that "Miss Claire has died, and Miss Dora is helplessly insane."

Few words were exchanged as Sam took the nurse to Seattle and then to the isolated sanatorium. The nurse was startled to see Hazzard wearing one of Claire's dresses. And there was Dora, standing limply at the door of her cabin by a ravine filled with ferns and brambles. Dora's face was a bluish death mask, her body just bones. As the nurse held Dora close to her, the heiress weakly said, "Help me, help me. Can you take me away?"

The nurse glared at Dr. Hazzard and her husband, knowing that they could invoke signed documents if she attempted to remove the woman. After all, they claimed Dora was hopelessly mad and that Claire had signed over power of attorney to handle the sisters' financial affairs. And there were still unpaid charges on Claire's bill.

Conway stayed at the sanatorium to safeguard the pathetic Dora, who was struggling for her life. After Dora received her daily broth, Conway persuaded her to eat a little extra food that she had brought. Conway began with rice and flour because that was all Dora could eat at her stage of emaciation, and then gradually encouraged her to take solid food. Conway also conducted a small investigation on her own, trying not to draw attention to herself, and learned that several other patients were wasting away as prisoners.

Searching for any proof of fraud, Conway discovered a document Dora was persuaded to sign supposedly turning over $500 to an uncle of hers in Toronto. But the name on the transfer was Samuel Hazzard. Although the Hazzards controlled the mail, Conway slipped in a letter that reached a store on the mainland. The letter asked the shopkeeper to have Dora's uncle return from Portland.

On July 19, 1911, John Herbert sat down with the Hazzards to discuss the release of his niece. Herbert made no threats or allegations. After a long night of negotiations, he paid the $500 the couple insisted was due on the bill, and Dora was finally free—four months after her fasting "cure" began.

As Dora recovered her strength, she and Conway visited the British vice-consul, Lucian Agassiz, in Tacoma, a short, squat man with a handlebar mustache and a proper English sense of bearing. He was furious when he heard of the sisters' deadly ordeal. He hired a private attorney to remove Hazzard's name from Dora's guardianship papers, but that was just the first step.

Vice-consul Agassiz and the attorney took a boat across the Sound and looked over the sanatorium's barn, tent, and five cabins. The vice-consul studied the path where Claire had crawled to deliver her cry for help two weeks before she died. Agassiz felt that it was up to him to save all the others. But Hazzard became suspicious and yelled at the two men, "Get off my place . . . and mind your own business."

The next day, the vice-consul went to see the Kitsap County prosecutor in Bremerton. But the prosecutor said he was helpless; there were not enough public funds to pay for an investigation and a trial. Agassiz sternly warned that this could become an international incident because a British citizen was cheated and murdered, and another would have died without intervention. Prosecutor Thomas Stevenson then made an extraordinary deal: He would bring Dr. Hazzard to trial if Dora would assume some of the costs. Dora's lawyer told Stevenson's attorney Frank Kelley, "If she has to pay to stop her sister's murderer, so be it."

With this strange mix of American and British public and private financing, investigators discovered numerous bank records, letters, wire transfers, and other documents showing how Dr. Hazzard had obtained the assets of her patients after they died in their misery cabins. The charges caused a sensation in the papers: "DR. HAZZARD PICTURED AS FIEND."

Other disclosures were that the Hazzards were not even legally married. Sam already had a wife. He and the doctor had left Minneapolis in a hurry following the 1902 death of patient Gertrude Young on the thirty-ninth day of her fast. An autopsy showed that her body contained virtually no blood. The rings Young's family sought turned up on the fingers of the female Dr. Death.

Hazzard's trial included a roll call of other patients who had died, but in February 1912 the jury came back with a verdict of guilty only of manslaughter. As the sheriff took Hazzard away, she turned and self-righteously stormed, "The high and mighty with diplomas and letters after their names have done this!"

Attorney Kelley told the press that "this case will, I believe, be a death blow to quack medical and healing individuals and institutions throughout the country." It was not quite the death blow, but the crimes of Dr. Hazzard contributed to the growing effort to supervise private sanatoriums.

Perfect Gentlemen

Case No. 1

When police found a middle-aged woman's body on the railroad tracks in Wheaton, Illinois, a little west of Chicago, it appeared that she was shot in the head as she was about to board a train. It was a Friday night in September 1913. Perhaps she was waiting unescorted for a train, yet she looked very much like a proper lady, wearing a long dress and a high-necked blouse. Other clothes were scattered around her as if someone had hastily dumped the contents of a large suitcase or trunk.

The body was soon identified as Allison Rexroat, a dancing teacher in town. She had been dating a young man, Henry Spencer, who worked as a store clerk. Spencer was often seen dressed quite respectably in shirt-sleeves, a vest, and spectacles. Mrs. Rexroat, who had recently divorced her husband, was about ten years older than Spencer. She gave him dancing lessons, and soon invited him to live with her. Rexroat's friends could tell that she was eager to marry again.

Nothing seemed strange until the night of the murder. Someone reported seeing Spencer return to the woman's house with his shoes covered with dust and wearing a diamond ring such as the one Rexroat had worn. A few minutes later, he supposedly threw an empty cartridge from the window. This was an amazingly fortunate lead, and when the police came to question Spencer, they found the victim's blood-stained suitcase.

Spencer then began the first of his long confessions of killing as many as fourteen people. With the dancing teacher, he had asked her to go to his (nonexistent) Michigan farm so they could be married. Instead, he shot her and took the few dollars she had with her. He came home, removed the spent cartridge from his revolver, and waited for the next train to Chicago.

His other victims, he said, included two girls in Paw Paw Lake, Michigan; two girls in Delavan, Wisconsin; and, the previous summer, a woman in Belle Island, Michigan. Then there were two men and two women in Chicago, including one near Cook County Hospital a few days before his arrest. He said he hit the man with a hammer, which he left by some tracks. The recent rash of murders began after he was released from the Illinois state prison in Joliet in 1912.

At first, police were fascinated, but then skeptical. Several of the murders occurred while Spencer was serving time for burglary. Further inquiry to states where Spencer claimed to have left bodies reported back no evidence of such homicides. Spencer, it seemed, took pleasure in identifying with the killers he read about in the newspapers and claimed their crimes as his own. The killer was a known drug user who might have imagined himself a terror in the haze of his opium dreams. He finally committed a real murder and seemed a little glad that he was likely going to the gallows.

When police mentioned that he could not have committed a particular killing he had cited, Spencer replied, in the tough-talk style he used only while in custody, "Oh, the man who did that job was a pal of mine, and I just thought that it wouldn't do any harm for me to take his place. I've got to hang anyway, so what's the difference."

While in the Du Page county jail in Wheaton, Spencer was visited by his sister and an evangelist. He later assured his guards that his soul was "washed of all wickedness," and he was certain he would go to heaven.

One of the reporters assigned to the execution was the best-known of the Chicago breed of news reporters, Ben Hecht. He recalled visiting Spencer in his cell on a hot day and found him the worst murderer he had ever encountered, "a sly, humanless killer."

With Europe on the verge of war, spectators who had received tickets to attend the execution filled picnic benches set up between the gallows and a stockade that kept out the public. Also on the benches, telegraphers were ready to begin clicking as soon as the rope went taut. Dawn came. Spencer appeared in a white shirt with a carnation, as if out on a date. The public executioner fitted him with a long white robe. Spencer smiled as the thick rope was placed awkwardly around his neck.

When asked if he had anything to say, Spencer replied, "Yes I have. This is the happiest day of my life." He then recited the twenty-third Psalm beginning "The Lord is my shepherd," but, according to Hecht, Spencer panicked when death took one step closer, and proclaimed his innocence. Looking at the public executioner, the deputies, and the sheriff, he shouted, "You're all a bunch of bastards!" The inexperienced public executioner bungled the job, and it took Spencer twelve minutes to die.

Case No. 2

The murder of Rexroat brings to mind the case of a ladies' man from Detroit. In early 1918, Herman Neugebauer advertised for a wife in the *New York Herald*. After a polite and then passionate correspondence, Augusta Steinbach agreed to meet him. She arrived by train with all her money, expecting marriage. But no one was at the station to greet her. She supposedly checked into a rooming house and disappeared.

At the start of the Great War, there was considerable pro-German sentiment in the Midwest because of the number of German immigrants who had settled there. But when reports of slaughtered American soldiers began coming in, many German-Americans changed their names or went out of their way to support the Allies. Those who did not could expect trouble. Even the conductor of the esteemed Boston Symphony Orchestra, Karl Muck, was arrested as an enemy alien.

When a friend of Steinbach reported her suspicions about Neugebauer, the police read more into it than just a missing person case. The police could not forget the (false) stories of German atrocities the British had spread to erode American isolationism. They felt Steinbach was murdered for the property she had brought with her from New York, and that her remains were either burned or buried.

A middle-aged woman who answered the door at the house where Neugebauer was supposedly staying said that she knew of no such person. However, the manner of this Mrs. Schmidt was strange. The officers checked with an express agency and learned that Steinbach's trunks were delivered to the Schmidt home. Being confronted with this revelation jolted the memory of Mrs. Schmidt and her husband. The husband said Neugebauer had introduced him to Steinbach and asked him to take care of her locked trunks until she sent for them.

The detectives were beginning to solve a riddle without quite consciously knowing it. Could this forty-one-year-old engineer at Ford Motor Company be posing as the fictional Neugebauer? Police took Schmidt, his wife, and his teenage daughter into custody. That cleared the way for a careful search of the house.

Buried under their cellar floor was a box filled with blood-stained women's clothes.

A neighbor said that in mid-March she saw the Schmidt basement windows covered over with newspapers and heard a woman crying inside. Afterward, Mrs. Schmidt cleaned out the furnace and scoured a box with water at a nearby creek.

The investigators still had no proof of murder, but they discovered that Schmidt was a registered alien. They also learned that Detroit police searching for a woman named Irma Pallatinus had questioned Schmidt. He said she had run away with $700 of his money, was somehow injured, and had died in an unnamed hospital. Without a body, the police dropped the investigation.

Under hard questioning about the Steinbach disappearance, Schmidt finally confessed. He told prosecutors and the sheriff that he had lured Steinbach to his home through a matrimonial ad but that she took poison when he refused to marry her. Then he said he cut up and incinerated her body. Police caught him in so many conflicting details that he finally put his arm around the prosecutor's shoulder and said, "I'll tell you even more. Just let me have some lunch first."

Guards took Schmidt to his cell, where he fell on his knees as if praying. When everyone was gone, he pulled down a heavy iron bed railing from the wall with such force that it crushed his skull and he fell dead on the concrete floor.

But that was not the end of the investigation. Schmidt, indeed, had much more to tell. After his death police found a mummified body under the cellar floor of his home and assumed it was Pallatinus. And more evidence surfaced about Schmidt's past as a confidence man. Before the war Schmidt used bogus names in newspapers in New York, New Jersey, Michigan, and Missouri, appealing to young women who had recently arrived from Europe. Some were merely fleeced, such as a Chicago victim who lost $2,000. Because others vanished, the investigators estimated that Schmidt might have killed as many as three dozen women.

When Schmidt was arrested, his family had recently moved from the murder house to a home near the Detroit suburb of Royal Oak, and investigators were sure that the new home, which was significantly larger than the first, would have one day become the final resting place of numerous other victims if Schmidt had not been caught.

REFERENCES

Fido, Martin. *The Chronicle of Crime*. New York: Carroll & Graf Publishers, 1993.

Hecht, Ben. *Child of the Century*. New York: Signet Books, 1955.

Lane, Roger. *Murder in America*. Columbus, Ohio: Columbus University Press, 1997.

Marriner, Brian. *On Death's Bloody Trail: Murder and the Art of Forensic Science*. New York: St. Martin's Press, 1991.

Nash, Jay Robert. *Crime Chronology: A Worldwide Record: 1900–1983*. New York: Facts on File, 1984.

———. *Bloodletters and Badmen*. New York: M. Evans & Co., 1995.

New York Times, Oct. 6–7, 1913, and Nov. 30, 1913.

———, April 23–24, 1918, and May 3, 1918.

Odell, Robin. *Landmarks in 20th Century Murder*. London: Headline, 1995.

Olson, Gregg. interview. September 1977.

———. *Starvation Heights*. New York: Warner Books, 1997.

Thorwald, Jurgen. *Crime and Science*. New York: Harcourt Brace & World, 1967.

Zierold, Norman. *Three Sisters in Black*. Boston: Little, Brown, 1968.

The 1920s

T he 1919 passage of the Volstead Act, which prohibited
the sale of liquor, turned Chicago from America's second
city in population to its first in crime, with its hodge-
podge bootleg gangs of Germans, Poles, Jews, Irish, and
Italians fighting one another and forming coalitions. The city
was said to have one thousand speakeasies, and a few of the
buildings exist today, with small passages leading to unexpect-
edly large rooms. At first, bootleg gangs engaged in cartage
thefts and competed with one another in a spirit similar to a
college football rivalry, but by the mid-1920s the gangs concentrated on extortion and eliminating their rivals. These
sons of immigrants found ways to realize their father's dreams
in a money-mad world. And they killed only their own. In
1926–1927, there were one hundred-thirty gangland murders

in the city, all unsolved. No one in the business could trust anyone else anymore. Seemingly routine car trips often turned into one-way rides as someone usually hidden in the back seat fatally shot the front passenger during a drive along a country road.

Instead of being dreaded, gangsters were commonly admired for their audacity. Illegal shipments of hooch were part of most coming-out and graduation parties, just as jazz was symbolizing the reckless age. Although business and government were dominated by men born in the 1870s, the young people of the Jazz Age were creating a world of their own. These were the sons and daughters of families with "new money" from the turn of the century, and they were more concerned with spending it than making it. After decades of matronly women with bulges replacing bustles, the women of the 1920s were thin, flat-chested if possible, and wore long strings of fake pearls that flapped as they danced. Marijuana was often passed around for smoking, and cocaine was a hobby of the rich.

When the 1920s arrived, the brash new generation seemed unattached from history. The freedom from Victorian restraints became infectious, and the youth culture spread to the homes of shopkeepers and accountants. The mock childness of Helen Kane's "boop-boop-a-doop" singing inspired Betty Boop cartoons; the song "The Good Ship Lollipop" sold two million copies; and bubblegum was invented in Philadelphia. Amid the frenetic celebration of youth, New York became a kingdom unto itself with its concentration of wealth and its lavish Broadway shows such as the annual Ziegfeld Follies.

Ernest Hemingway and several other famous writers exiled themselves to Paris rather than grapple with a time that had changed faster than they did. They called theirs the "lost generation." Playwright Eugene O'Neill sought universal themes in simple stories, and Sinclair Lewis skewered small-town life, business corruption, and religious hypocrisy in books such as *Main Street, Arrowsmith,* and *Elmer Gantry.* F. Scott Fitzgerald was the chronicler of the age until alcohol and Hollywood destroyed him. But the other arts turned away from human contact; art-deco architecture embraced the machine, and modernism in dance and painting experimented with geometric form and juxtapositions. Such artistic endeavors seemed at odds with what was happening in the streets.

The decade had just begun when, in 1920, a bomb planted by an unknown terrorist killed forty people in Manhattan's Wall Street, overturning a car, spreading blood across the pavement, and drawing hundreds of spectators. Police rounded up all the known radicals, but the killer was never found. The explosion ushered in a period of anonymous hate-induced violence amid raucous frivolity.

The nation had just recovered from a devastating influenza plague, which struck as soldiers returned from The Great War in late 1918 and continued into the first half of 1919. At the height of the epidemic, cities east of the Mississippi counted their daily dead in the hundreds, theaters were closed, and religious services were shortened to reduce contact among parishioners.

During the war, Carl Oscar Wanderer rose to the rank of lieutenant and received both France's *Croix de Guerre* and the Distinguished Service Cross. He returned to America, married his childhood sweetheart, and went to work at his father's butcher shop in Chicago. On June 21, 1920, he took his wife to a movie house to see *The Sea Wolf*. As they were walking home, a ragged gunman tried to hold them up. Wanderer drew a .45 caliber pistol and had a shoot-out with the man, but in the gunfire his wife was killed. Wanderer was still pumping bullets into the stranger when the police arrived. Between tears, the war hero told Chicago reporter Ben Hecht that just that morning his wife had told him she was going to be a mother "and was so happy." It was Hecht's interest in Freudian psychology that helped turn what seemed like an ordinary street crime into a sensational case that was remembered for decades.

A card in the robber's clothes identified the dead man as Edward Masters, a well-known gunman. But the fingerprints did not match any on record. The coroner's jury brought in a murder verdict against a John Doe and commended the grieving widower on his courage. But Hecht had a hunch; Wanderer seemed a phony to him. Although it never made the papers, Hecht thought the decorated soldier might be a closeted homosexual. Hecht assumed Wanderer panicked over his wife's pregnancy.

Hecht discussed his suspicions with fellow reporters, who snickered at his interest in psychology. He then set out to show the police that Wanderer possessed both guns before the killings, hired a tramp to fake a robbery, and killed the stranger as he probably planned all along. As was the custom in the days before criminalistic laboratories, the detectives never thought to test the guns until they were ready to charge Wanderer. Testing showed that all the bullets were fired from the same weapon.

Confronted with the evidence, Wanderer confessed that he had lost his head about approaching domesticity. When the condemned man walked to the gallows, he eased his tension by singing a popular song. Rotund literary critic and playwright Alexander Wolcott commented flippantly that Wanderer should have been hanged for his voice alone.

In the Eastern states, the Great War was regarded as the ultimate folly of nationalism, and a workers' revolution seemed at hand. In 1919, several "foreign-looking" men drove into the path of a payroll car for the White Shoe Company in the Boston suburb of Bridgewater, hoping to use the money to finance a revolt. The would-be robbers opened fire with pistols and a shotgun but retreated when the guards returned fire.

A related robbery with tragic results occurred in the nearby industrial town of South Braintree on April 15, 1920. A guard and a paymaster from the Slater & Morrill shoe factory were carrying $16,000 in a metal box when they were accosted by two men who shot them and drove off in a car containing three others. The guard died on the street. The auto used in both holdups was discovered abandoned. This helped lead to the arrest of Italian immigrants Nicola Sacco and Bartolomeo Vanzetti, who had anarchist literature in their pockets. Sacco, who worked at another shoe factory, had twenty-three bullets in his pocket, and Vanzetti, a fish peddler, was carrying a loaded gun.

The millionaires who influenced American politics at the time attempted to put down anarchism and communism before it could spread. Experts claimed that slugs and a shotgun cartridge definitely linked the defendants to the crime, even though early ballistics tests were not that well advanced. The experts may not have been lying; perhaps they were just satisfied that they had found what they sought. One of the experts did not even use a microscope. Even District Attorney Frederick Katzmann distrusted the evidence. He said, "Heaven speed the day when proof in any important case is dependent upon the magnifying glass and the scientist."

Both men were found guilty and were sent to the electric chair on August 27, 1927. Subsequent opinion supports American anarchist Carlo Tresca's contention that only Sacco was guilty.

The Sacco-Vanzetti case is regarded as one of the most important events in U.S. criminal history because of its repercussions in spreading the socialist movement. But in Chicago, "the crime of the century" was to follow.

The Bird-Watcher

Psychiatric experts estimated Nathan Leopold's IQ at just over 200. At the age of nineteen, Leopold was already a graduate student at the prestigious University of Chicago, set in a sprawling campus near a well-to-do Jewish community on the South Side. Leopold came from a wealthy Orthodox family but renounced his faith early in his teens. He preferred to guide himself solely by reason. Unlike the families around him, he had no interest in the business world and would often go to the fields south of his home to watch birds through binoculars.

Until becoming the companion of Richard "Dickie" Loeb, Leopold had no friends, and he showed no interest in girls. Loeb, an eighteen-year-old graduate student, was a smaller young man from an even more influential family. His father was worth an estimated $4,000,000, and his uncle Jacob was a civic leader who formerly headed the Chicago school board. Loeb had a pretty girlfriend who worked as a model and a secretary, and he bragged to his friends about their sex life. But his close relationship with Leopold soon led to rumors of homosexuality.

After the rumor started spreading, the young men decided never to be seen alone in public. This secretiveness drew them emotionally closer. Perhaps inspired by some Dostoyevskian protagonist, the two concluded that with their intelligence they could commit a perfect crime, and that a crime could be perfect only when it had no motive. We do know that they decided to murder someone just to test their reactions to taking another's life. Some reporters claimed that Loeb devised the murder scheme because he wanted sensual excitement in killing.

Whatever the reason, the outwardly conservative young men decided to abduct a neighborhood boy. Not knowing yet who it would be, they typed a ransom note addressed as "Dear Sir." On the afternoon of May 21, 1924, they used field glasses to watch children playing in a school yard. The boy they first considered was unavailable, but they fixed on fourteen-year-old Bobby Franks. Bobby's father, Jacob Franks, was a vice president of Sears, Roebuck and Company, and the family lived diagonally from the Loebs. Loeb had even played tennis with Jacob several times, but Leopold hardly knew him.

Bobby left the school yard on his way home. Loeb apparently offered the young boy a ride home. One of the men—it was never established which—moments later killed Bobby just a block away by beating him with a cold chisel after the car turned onto 50th Street. They drove with the body to an undeveloped "prairie" and shoved it into a culvert near

126th Street and Hegewisch Avenue, then drove back for the second part of the game.

Jacob became worried when his son did not return from playing ball. He and a friend, who was a former chief city attorney, went directly to the detective bureau downtown. At the same time, Bobby's mother received a kidnapping call from a "George Johnson" saying the boy was safe and that the family would be contacted later.

A railroad worker discovered the child's body the next day, but news was suppressed from the family to make it easier to catch the killers. The family was still hoping for Bobby's safe return when it received a typewritten note demanding $10,000. Jacob withdrew the money from a bank and was on his way to drop it off at a drugstore when detectives intercepted him and informed him that his son was dead. No one showed up at the drugstore to take the money. However, horn-rimmed glasses found ten feet from the body were traced to Leopold, and police eventually traced the typewriter.

The murder of Bobby Franks shocked the country, not only because of the wealthy families involved, but also because there was no logical motive. The families of the accused retained famous attorney Clarence Darrow, usually a fighter for the underdog but also an advocate against the death penalty. Darrow delivered an eloquent plea about furthering civilization, but the judge spared the lives of Leopold and Loeb only because they were under twenty-one. He sentenced each of them to life plus ninety-nine years.

In 1936, Loeb died as he was slashed fifty-two times with a prison-made knife by fellow inmate James Day. Day was acquitted on the grounds that Loeb had made sexual advances to him.

Leopold, the quiet bird-watcher, spent his years in prison improving himself. He blamed his one crime on having been cut off from children his own age in his rapid rise through school, although there were never any children his mental age. He found faith in his cell and learned Hebrew, Japanese, and twenty other languages. In World War II, he volunteered to be a guinea pig for an experimental medicine to fight malaria. Leopold contracted the disease in prison and was cured by the same medicine he was helping to test. For this, his term was later reduced to seventy-five years.

While in prison, he quietly established a fund for emotionally disturbed youths to be supported by royalties from a book he wrote about his prison life, *Life Plus 99 Years*. Leopold remained a model inmate in every way and was released from prison on March 15, 1958. While on parole in 1961, he married a doctor's widow in Puerto Rico, where he became a $10-a-month hospital technician in an impoverished mountain region, sometimes working with lepers. Shortly before his death in 1971, he said, "Nothing gives me more pleasure than to be introduced to someone to whom my name means nothing." Leopold's emotional maturity had come at a terrible cost.

———————

The thrill kill was something new to America, as was the kind of serial killer who evaded detection by moving around the country.

From what we know, Earle Leonard Nelson was orphaned young when his parents died of syphilis in San Francisco. He was reared by a Philadelphia aunt amid an atmosphere of religious fanaticism. Whether relevant or not, he suffered a head injury at the age of ten when he was struck by a trolley or cable car, and afterward his moodiness increased and he complained of intense pain. When he was a teenager, his aunt caught him peeping at her daughter getting undressed. This would have been harmless adolescent curiosity in some boys, but Nelson's voyeurism evolved into pernicious behavior.

The short, blue-eyed man with a dark complexion believed he had a Christlike appearance. Despite a tendency toward giving Bible lectures to others, he developed twin impulses of sexually assaulting teenage girls and killing landladies, sometimes violating their bodies after death.

This divided man of alternating sin and redemption was put in a mental institution for raping a girl, escaped, was sent to prison, and escaped again. He married a young schoolteacher under an assumed name, accused her of consorting with other men, drove her to a mental breakdown, and was arrested for trying to rape her while she recuperated in the hospital. Then he disappeared from the public record for seven years.

When Nelson emerged in February 1926, he was choking sixty-three-year-old landlady Clara Newman to death with her pearl necklace in San Francisco. Over the next year and a half, he rode the rails to rape and strangle half a dozen girls and approximately fourteen women, most of them landladies. The murders occurred in Buffalo, New York, Detroit, Michigan, Council Bluffs, Iowa, and Kansas City, Missouri. He would see a room that was for rent, make inquiries, and grab the landlady in an unguarded moment. Reporters began calling the unknown killer "the gorilla man" for the way he pounced on his helpless victims. Between killings, he worked at odd jobs and sometimes sold jewelry that he had stolen during his attacks.

Nelson tried to escape the law by moving to Winnipeg, Canada, but he could not escape himself. He killed fourteen-year-old blind flower girl Lola Cowan and then middle-aged Emily Peterson. Police obtained a description of the man from a witness, and a posse of townspeople, farmers, and Winnipeg and provincial police officers surrounded him in the woods two miles west of Killarney. Nelson was hanged in Winnipeg in January 1928. The case received little newspaper attention in the United States because Nelson was considered insane. The public was waiting for a crime it considered juicy.

Soon they would have it.

Death on Lover's Lane

Phillips Lane, a few miles from New Brunswick, New Jersey, was a place for couples to go by car and be alone amid the cedars and high grass. On the night of Friday, September 15, 1922, one such couple came pounding on the farmhouse door of Mrs. Grace Edwards, breathlessly telling her of two bodies they'd discovered a mile away.

Lying dead under a crab apple tree were fifty-one-year-old Reverend Edward Hall and a married choir singer from his church, Eleanor Mills. Both were fully dressed, shot in the head at point-blank range, and lying flat on their backs. A long brown scarf covered Mills's face and neck. Most of their blood had seeped into the parched ground. Scattered around the bodies were several love letters, and at Hall's feet was one of his calling cards. The victims could not have been killed as they were positioned; someone had arranged the bodies and placed the calling card as if to dramatize the fact that the minister was having an adulterous affair.

The crime caused a sensation. Hall was the head of the five hundred-member Church of St. John the Evangelist, and his older wife was the richest woman in New Brunswick. Mills's husband, Jim, was a school janitor and part-time church sexton who denied any part in the crime. Jim said that had he known about the affair, he would have "stepped aside and let Hall have her. Then there would have been no murder." That the victims were having an affair came as no surprise to anyone else, because it was rumored that they planned to run away together. In the smaller communities of America in the 1920s, when farms still had no electricity for radios and the newspapers came out every week, gossip was often the main source of entertainment.

The curious piled out of cars or arrived by foot from the nearest streetcar line to hover over the stretch of open land where the crime was committed. Reporters tried to question the large, white-haired Mrs. Hall before the police reached her, but she hung up on them and called a wealthy cousin, Henry de La Bryere Carpender of the New York Stock Exchange, and her family lawyer, New Jersey State Senator William Florence. Both pressed through the crowd to look at the site, then left quickly without talking to the police.

Despite the trampling of perhaps a hundred onlookers, the police picked up a few clues, including the emptied cartridges. The victims were buried quickly as if to put the double scandal of adultery and murder into the past. But two weeks later, under pressure from reporters, the bodies were exhumed for autopsies. The listed cause of death, gunshot wounds to the head, remained the same, but the doctor found some injuries to Mills's throat that were overlooked in the initial examination.

Mills told police that when he saw his wife leaving their home that night, he asked her where she was going and she replied, "Why don't you follow me and find out?" When she did not return by 2 A.M. Friday, he went to the church, found it empty, and looked for her again in the morning. Mills admitted the handwriting in the love letters was his wife's but said that she was a sentimental reader and might have copied them from some books.

Gawkers continued to visit the lovers' lane. Numerous leads surfaced, most of dubious reliability. Colorful pig farmer Jane Gibson said she was standing by her mule near the scene late that Thursday when she saw two or three men and a woman get out of a car and quarrel, but her story kept changing. Assistant Middlesex County Prosecutor John Toolen tried to get more information from Mrs. Hall. He suggested that she must be intensely interested in helping the police bring the killers to justice, but the widow aloofly replied, "I almost feel as if I don't care. They cannot bring him back." Three days after the interview, she dropped State Senator Florence as her lawyer and hired Timothy Pfeiffer, formerly of the homicide bureau of the New York District Attorney's Office, as well as a private detective who was once a top police investigator in New York City.

With nothing else to go on, the police talked to Mrs. Hall's two brothers. Henry Stevens of Levelett, New Jersey, a hunter and sharpshooter, had an ironclad alibi. Willie Stevens, a bachelor and an honorary New Brunswick firefighter, was perceived by most townspeople as a rather slow-witted ne're-do-well, given to spending much of his time lolling about the firehouse.

Willie had wild, uncombed hair, thick glasses, and a bushy mustache. At first he said he never left his house late Thursday and early Friday, then admitted going to the empty church around 2 A.M. on Friday. The grapevine said Willie owned a .32 caliber gun and had sent out a suit to have spots removed on Saturday, the day after the bodies were discovered.

But Willie Stevens was not the only one deceiving the authorities. The man who together with his girlfriend found the victims claimed a friend of his had killed Hall and Mills, but he retracted his story when his friend was arrested. As the investigation stalled, Jim Mills found a cache of his wife's love letters and sold them through an intermediary to a New York newspaper for $500. By then, thousands of people had visited the murder scene. An entrepreneur from New Brunswick leased the property and sold samples from the earth around the tree for twenty-five cents a bag. The same man turned a nearby farmhouse into a museum commemorating the murder.

The grand jury convened but voted not to indict anyone. Mrs. Hall left for a year-long vacation in Italy, Gibson went back to slopping her hogs, and Mills resumed work as a sexton. The calling card left at the scene was locked away in a safe without any attempt to identify a fingerprint lifted from it, and notwithstanding the continuous guessing games carried out in market aisles and bus stops, the community of New Brunswick settled back into its normal routine.

The event that moved the Hall-Mills case toward resolution was a petition filed by piano salesperson Arthur Riehl to annul his marriage to the former Louise Geist. He alleged that before their wedding Louise was employed in Reverend Hall's household, had improper relations with the minister, and was paid $5,000 by the Stevens family to keep quiet about what she claimed to know concerning the murders. The managing editor of the *New York Daily News* pressured the New Jersey governor to reopen the case. He had obtained Hall's calling card and gave it to a fingerprint expert, Jersey City Police Lieutenant Fred Drewen. Drewen concluded that the fingerprint on the back of the card was left by Willie Stevens.

In June 1926, Mrs. Hall was charged with murder, and soon her two brothers were arrested as well. Five hundred spectators jammed the courtroom, including seventy-five reporters, and more than a hundred other newspeople crowded outside. A defense attorney told the jurors in opening arguments that just because Willie Stevens's fingerprint was found on the calling card, it did not mean he had anything to do with the crime; the calling card could have fallen out of the minister's wallet during an ordinary robbery.

The prosecution had the "pig woman," Gibson, who recently had cancer surgery, wheeled into court on a gurney. She testified that among the shouts she heard on the fatal night was a woman saying, "Explain those letters!" She added that there was a brief struggle with two men and a man who may have been Reverend Hall, then a shot, a thud, and two more shots in quick succession. A woman cried out "Oh, Henry!" and another woman screamed. Gibson said that she returned to her farmhouse, but when she started back to retrieve a lost moccasin she noticed a tall white-haired woman leaning over to arrange something on the ground.

The matronly Mrs. Hall, dressed in mourning black, testified that she had never doubted her husband's devotion and never read the love letters until a few weeks before the trial. She said she never left the house except to search the church around 2:30 A.M.—the third person claiming to have gone to the empty church at that hour—because her husband had failed to come home.

The jury returned a verdict of not guilty against Mrs. Hall and her brothers. The elements that had caused a sensation at the time may seem ordinary now, but the case is an example of what can happen when police are careless in gathering and checking evidence, because the clues that could have led to a conviction were all present at one time.

Glamour Capital

There was nothing like Hollywood in the 1920s, not even if Versailles had existed in the hanging gardens of Babylon. Men and women with no training in acting were thrust before the cameras because they had "faces." Often they rehearsed their lines while carpenters sawed plywood and nailed sets together just out of camera range. The lucky actors were nobodies who could relax on folding chairs until they were needed for a scene or two. The unlucky ones were stars, such as pert Mabel Normand, who in her heyday at Keystone was overworked to the tune of fourteen hours a day, six days a week, until she could no longer tell one film from another.

Normand was cute but not pretty, yet she had an affecting liveliness that was perfect for the times. Her steady boyfriend was Mack Sennett, who made her the world's first movie star by using her name in the title of no fewer than twenty-eight of her short films. Between takes, she took young Charlie Chaplin under her wing and showed him how to perform before the camera after his stage success in London. Normand relieved the pressures of stardom with occasional lovers and drugs. Then she became a murder suspect.

It was the most baffling murder that ever occurred exclusively among movie people. Handsome actor and director William Desmond Taylor of the Paramount Famous Players was found shot to death on February 2, 1922, in his two-story home in a bungalow court at Sixth and Alvarado streets. Taylor lived the life of a wealthy bachelor, and he was romantically linked to various starlets after scoring a hit with his 1915 serial *The Diamond from the Sky*. His major films included *Johanna Enlists* and the silent version of *Huckleberry Finn*.

Being a romantic at heart, Taylor had created an adventurous background for himself that made him appear to be a man of the world. But evidence suggested that he was being blackmailed by someone who knew the truth about his past. Taylor claimed to be English but was actually born in Ireland. It was discovered that he abandoned his American wife and daughter one day in 1908 after leaving for the races, taking with him $500 along with some clothes and personal items. In 1912, his younger brother, Denis, disappeared.

On the last day of Taylor's life, he had breakfast while reading the latest news regarding the scandal involving popular comedian Roscoe "Fatty" Arbuckle and actress Virginia Rappe. Rappe had died that September under curious circumstances in a hotel room. Indeed, Hollywood was reeling in the wake of several scandals, and the studios were feeling pressure to use their influence for a show of respectability.

Taylor finished the newspaper, withdrew $2,500 from the First National Bank for unknown reasons, went for a morning swim at the Los Angeles Athletic Club, and stopped at Paramount Studio for a few hours. Somewhere along the way he returned to redeposit all of the money he had just taken out of the bank—again for unknown reasons. He left the bank and bought two copies of Freud's *Inhibition, Symptom, and Desire*. Next, Taylor briefly met with his tax accountant, wrote a few checks, went home, and met with Mabel Normand.

Normand arrived with a bag of peanut shells, which she sometimes used to hide her cocaine. After Taylor escorted the famous actress to her chauffeured car later that evening, leaving the door of his home open behind him, Taylor returned inside and was killed a short time later. No one heard a shot, but a neighbor noticed someone in a mannish coat hurriedly leaving the house.

The next morning, Taylor's valet, Henry Peavey, arrived as usual at 7:30 A.M. to make breakfast and found his employer fully clothed on his back on the living-room floor, his hair still neatly combed, his legs together and his arms at his side. Except for the blood, he seemed to be sleeping. Across the bungalow courtyard, Chaplin's almost matronly leading lady, blonde Edna Purviance, climbed out of bed and rushed to the telephone when she heard Peavey screaming, "Massa Taylor is dead!" Did she call the police? No, Edna notified her friends, Normand and actress Mary Miles Minter, that if there was anything in Taylor's home they did not want the police to find, they should remove it now.

There were a lot of people who could be professionally embarrassed by the secrets in Taylor's house. Before the police could arrive, at least ten of them went through his rooms. They opened drawers, shuffled through closets, and fished through pockets to remove items they knew were there or snooped around for things that might be there. Taylor after all was hated by quite a few people for starting and ending romances, and for reporting drug activities he learned about to the U.S. Attorney's office. He also kept a lot of secrets, including his own.

Among those frantically scouring the house was Paramount executive Charles Eyton, who hoped to get rid of anything that might look bad for the studio. Peavey joined the scavenger hunt, along with Taylor's chauffeur, Henry Flowers. Normand may or may not have been there also, although it is known she returned two days later supposedly looking for love letters to Taylor. According to some accounts, Minter—always in films as a naive ingenue—raced there to get rid of anything hinting at her affair. Some say that while the panicky celebrities removed possible evidence, the studio people might even have planted false evidence, perhaps to incriminate Minter. After all, Minter was still under contract even though her last five pictures had flopped, and the studio could use a moral turpitude clause against her.

Even the fact that there was a murder was nearly covered up. A doctor entered the home, glanced at the body, and attributed death to stomach hemorrhage. But a deputy coroner arrived later, turned over the body, and saw a blood stain on the carpet. There were bullet holes in Taylor's jacket, but the holes did not match the bullet wounds. The motive did not appear to be robbery; the dapper director had $78 in his pocket, a platinum watch on his wrist, and $1,000 in cash remained in clear view upstairs.

Police found a nightgown bearing the initials MMM and possibly obscene photos of sexy starlets. Whether the gown was left by Minter or planted by the studio remains a mystery.

The photos might well have been a rumor spread by the studio to cover up Taylor's alleged fondness for men. His valet was arrested a couple of days before the murder trying to solicit teenage boys, and some have said he was recruiting for his employer. It is not known for sure if Taylor was homosexual.

Normand immediately became a suspect particularly because she was the last person known to have seen Taylor alive. She had always enjoyed the company of the suave Taylor, who was so different from the homely, uncouth Sennett, and Taylor talked of starring her in a film now that her career was rebounding. She told detectives that she got into her chauffeured car and said good-bye to Taylor by kissing a rolled-up window, and the impression of her lips was indeed found on the glass.

Minter seemed overeager to supply police with (false) information by claiming that Normand and Taylor were secretly engaged for about six months. Actually, Taylor was engaged to Minter, whose career was guided every misstep of the way by her movie-struck stage mother, Charlotte Shelby. Everyone was questioned and requestioned, but the case just died away. No one even possibly involved was ever linked to violence or scandal afterward.

The murder haunted Hollywood, and respected director King Vidor could not get it out of his head forty-five years later. Although not a detective or even a writer, Vidor just wanted to know before he died who killed Taylor and why the police claimed they could find no solid evidence. Vidor had made *The Big Parade, The Champ, Northwest Passage, The Fountainhead,* and the Audrey Hepburn version of *War and Peace.* This was 1967, Vidor was seventy-one, and the Hollywood he had known was collapsing. Returning to the secrets of the silent era might somehow renew him, and he might make a film out of it as well.

Working with a retired detective, Vidor went over everything in the police files. He talked to some of the people involved, as well as former silent-film director Allan Dwan, who was a walking encyclopedia of early Hollywood. Vidor came away with a plausible explanation and an unlikely villain.

Most of the unanswered questions revolved around Mary Minter: the appearance of the MMM nightgown, a strand of hair her color on Taylor's jacket, and information that her bossy mother had a gun not unlike the one the killer had used. Vidor's theory was that Minter's mother, Charlotte, overheard a conversation indicating that Mary was about to run away with Taylor, to the ruin of her daughter's career. Charlotte supposedly locked her daughter in a closet to keep her from interfering with whatever she had in mind. Minter escaped and went to Taylor's home to warn him just before Normand's car pulled up a little before 7 P.M. Minter stayed hidden while Taylor talked to Normand for more than an hour. When Normand's car drove off, Minter came downstairs. The time was a little after 8 P.M. Then Charlotte Shelby arrived wearing a heavy coat and carrying her .38 caliber pistol.

From what Vidor could piece together, the young actress watched in horror as her mother shot the director. Minter's sister, Margaret, said Minter rushed home that night and said that something terrible had happened to Taylor. Charlotte gave the gun to her own mother, Julia Miles, who took it back to Louisiana and threw it into a swampy bayou. None of this was a secret. Minter's sister had told this to the police six months after the killing, but officials did nothing. Certain evidence disappeared after that. Everything confirmed Vidor's suspicions that the already corrupt District Attorney Burton Fitts, his successor, an alibi witness, and others were bribed with $750,000 taken from Minter's trust fund, which would explain why the actress sued her own mother for misappropriation. And so the woman who would do anything to further her daughter's career ended it by destroying her.

For confirmation, Vidor went to Minter herself, then in her sixties. She repeated for him not the truth but what she had been told to say long ago, like any good actress; she was at home reading to her family while her secret fiancé was shot to death.

Vidor remained convinced that he had learned the truth, but also that he did not have enough for a film. He filed away his notes and died without returning to the project. A few years after Vidor's investigation, the seventy-eight-year-old Burton Fitts shot himself to death with the Taylor case just one of many on his conscience.

If police had used a lie detector on all the possible suspects in the Taylor murder, all would have likely failed, as would many of the investigators. The polygraph was first used in a crude form in the 1920s to measure two indicators of split-second physical hesitation, delayed heartbeat, and elevated blood circulation. The first component was a copy of a blood-pressure cuff attached by a rubber tube to a stainless steel pen for recording changes in pulse and blood pressure. The second was an expandable device fitted around the subject's chest and connected to a second pen for marking changes in breathing. Simultaneously, a galvo (galvanic response indicator) detected changes in the flow of minute electrical currents in the skin.

Some people can always fool the machine, there are a few ways others can thwart it, and some individuals give guilty responses even when they are innocent. Thus, a polygraph can help an investigation only in conjunction with other evidence. To clinch cases, detectives still had to rely on human intelligence.

Evidence Never Lies

The Southern Pacific "Gold Special" chugged its way through the mountain passes from Seattle toward San Francisco on the bright early afternoon of September 11, 1923. Half an hour after changing the crew at Ashland, Oregon, the passenger train passed the slopes of fir and pine near Mount Shasta and headed for the darkness of Tunnel No. 13 on the California border. This was about to become the last of the Wild West–style train robberies, and one of the bloodiest.

Engineer Sidney Bates glimpsed two men running along the track, and the brakeman cautiously started to slow the train. One man held a shotgun and the other grasped a Colt .45. Because they were wearing baggy, denim "bib" overalls, they did not look like bandits. A third robber in oversized pants holding a box of dynamite with wires hanging underneath it came running toward the mail car.

When mail clerk Elvyn Daugherty refused to open the bolted door, the third man put his box on the sill of the wooden car and dashed to safety. Instead of just blasting through the side, the dynamite turned the mail car into a fireball and sent choking smoke through the tunnel. The robbers had planned to get away in the locomotive, but the coupling gear was impossibly mangled by the detonation. With Daugherty no doubt already dead, the bandits decided to kill the rest of the train crew to make sure there would be no witnesses.

In a few seconds of gunfire flashing through the blackness, the engineer, the firefighter, and the brakeman were shot, and their bodies were left to drape over parts of the train or lie on the tunnel floor. Then the three bandits ran toward the hills. Only after they fled did the passengers venture outside the coaches to stare at the bodies. A conductor who was on the rear coach hurried to an emergency phone at the southern end of the tunnel and called a dispatcher.

The killers expected the tunnel to muffle the explosion, but the roar was heard at the Southern Pacific maintenance camps in Hilt, California, and Siskiyou, Oregon. The workers, thinking the engine had blown up in an accident, climbed into trucks with shovels, picks, spikes, and sledgehammers. At the same time, separate posses from two states rushed to the scene with hunting dogs and whatever they could grab. The dogs bayed and barked and led clusters of gun-toting sheriff's deputies in straw hats and Stetsons over every hill and creek bed as doctors rattled up in dusty black cars.

The telephone lines were buzzing with word that a bunch of killers were on the loose. Even a few biplanes scanned mile after mile of winding road and steep, low mountains, but there was no trace of the men. But civic concern, a love of excitement, and rewards totaling $15,900 in gold led to sightings everywhere. Anyone who did not live in the region was a suspect. Several hunters were stopped for questioning, and two were almost lynched by railroad workers before they were cleared.

Although the police complained of not having any leads, they had all the clues they could possibly want. The police only needed to make deductions from the simplest of traces on what the killers had discarded in their haste: a pair of overalls, a gun with its serial number scratched off, a knapsack, and a battery-powered detonator. Also found were several gunnysack cloths soaked in creosote, which the sheriff's police suspected were dragged across the ground to throw the search dogs off the scent.

The police thought they had found a suspect, a mechanic found working alone in a railyard. The large man was made to climb into the overalls, and they fit perfectly. What more proof was needed?

A railroad detective suggested calling the American Sherlock Holmes, Edward Oscar Heinrich. Of course, Heinrich hated comparisons with the fictional detective, because he made his deductions from painstaking microscopic study rather than instant inferences from glancing at people. Heinrich of California—and pathologist Bernard Spillsbury in England—represented a new breed of criminologist; they adopted strictly scientific procedures regardless of the assumed evidence and instead of common sense. For Spillsbury, dead men told their tales as they lay on the autopsy table. For Heinrich, crime scene evidence was the only infallible witness.

The overalls were sent to Heinrich in Berkeley along with an account of what the swarm of officers had found. Heinrich was sure the rags were just shoe covers such as men working on something messy might wear rather than a device to foil the dogs. Indeed, a man could not avoid leaving a scent by dragging around the rags. Although Heinrich could not yet reconstruct the foiled robbery, he realized that it was well planned except that the men had to guess at how much dynamite to set off. He painstakingly studied the evidence for hours and sent back this report:

> *"You're holding the wrong man. The overalls you sent me were worn by a left-handed lumberjack accustomed to working around fir trees. He is a white man between twenty one and twenty five years of age, not over five feet ten inches tall and he weighs about 165 pounds. He has medium light brown hair, a fair complexion, small hands and feet, and is rather fastidious in his personal habits. Apparently he has lived and worked in the Pacific Northwest."*

The amazed police sent investigators to Heinrich's laboratory, where he explained his conclusions. The supposed oil and grease on the pants, presumably from railroad work, turned out to be pitch, eliminating the mechanic. That the robber was a lumberjack came from creases on the bottom of the pants; woodchoppers keep their trousers tucked into their shoes to avoid filling their cuffs with chips. The grains of "dust" from the pocket, when magnified five hundred times under a microscope, were seen to be Douglas fir needles, peculiar to the Northwest. Fingernail clippings scraped from a pocket showed that the wearer was neat in his personal habits. The hair color and the man's age and race were determined from a single strand of hair carefully removed from a button. That the bandit was left-handed was deduced because the chips were in the right pocket, and a left-handed lumberjack stands with a tree on his right as he chops it down. As for the weight of the robber, lumberjacks wear pants that are a little larger than they are, and the length of the adjustable straps told how tall he was.

Having explained his method, Heinrich handed over a decisive lead. He found a few grains of tobacco spilled when the wearer was rolling a cigarette. Knowing that smokers sometimes jot down things on the cigarette paper they carry, he used a metal probe and gently lifted a sheet of white paper. Instead of what he expected, he found a registered-mail receipt marked 236-L. With this, postal inspectors traced the receipt to $50 a logger named Roy D'Autremont of Eugene, Oregon, had sent to someone in New Mexico.

The case was solved even though it would take four years—and two million "Wanted" posters distributed to every train station in the country—to capture D'Autremont and his brothers, Hugh and Ray. Their trial and conviction in Medford, Oregon, was the city's major social event of the 1920s.

After twenty years in prison, Roy went insane and underwent a lobotomy in the same hospital where Ken Kesey's novel *One Flew over the Cuckoo's Nest* was later filmed. Hugh was paroled in 1958 as he was dying of stomach cancer. Three years later, Ray was released and spent his last years as a custodian at the University of Oregon in Eugene. He contributed to a book about his prison life called *All for Nothing*.

A Climate of Fear

In the 1920s, America was still predominantly rural. Farmers from North Carolina to Washington state were turning more to fundamentalism, radio preachers espoused vaguely paranoid messages, and simple, rural people in small towns became convinced that the biggest problem facing the white race was a threat from blacks who had moved to the North and the West.

The effects of the Scotch-Irish settlement in America to some extent drove this paranoia. These settlers provided much of the pioneer spirit and many of the strengths of the national character, but they were disproportionately represented in scenes of mob actions. They moved to America by the thousands before the Revolution. They had no money for land, and so they worked as common laborers until escaping into the unsettled backlands, and some eventually to the mountains of Appalachia. Whenever new lands were opened up in the United States, the Scotch-Irish were among the first to leave everything behind except for a few clothes and a Bible, and so they fanned out across the nation with no leader but their own rigid sense of right and wrong. They spread their beliefs to other settlers more than being influenced by them, forming an inextricable part of the rural American character.

Evangelism swept across these farming areas, from the Holy Rollers of Tennessee to former baseball player Billy Sunday, who did handstands before his audiences to show how he had to fight the devil. Tent tabernacles were set up for attractive preacher Sister Aimee Semple McPherson, who spoke of healing and being born again in God's grace. While this was happening, several white separatist preachers took to the radio. Blacks found more discrimination in the North and the West than in the previous century. In reaction, black "zionist" Marcus Garvey wrote weekly columns in the early 1920s about how his people should reject America and return to Africa.

In 1921 alone, fifty-nine blacks were lynched in Southern and neighboring states. With the nation on a short fuse, several women found that they could wield enormous power by lying. In 1921, whites in Tulsa, Oklahoma, moved into the black part of town at the urging of the Ku Klux Klan. Old farmers, hardened oil rig workers, and teenage boys with porkpie hats and shotguns slung over their shoulders decided to change America because a white woman claimed she was attacked by a black man in an elevator; all he did was briefly touch her as he lost his footing. The death toll reached one hundred twenty-five or more. Nearly one thousand people were wounded or injured, most of them black.

In Rosewood, Florida, African-Americans lived fairly middle-class lives, which upset some of their white neighbors. To them, it did not seem right that blacks should be their social equals. In 1922, whites, enraged by another woman's lie, moved in with guns and clubs to murder the entire settlement. Anywhere from forty to one-hundred-fifty men, women, and children were killed, some by fire; those who survived fled forever, and officially nothing much happened. The town of Rosewood virtually disappeared overnight.

Someone with enough cunning could take all this hate and fear and harness it into a political force of staggering potential. That someone was David Stephenson of Indiana, and he knew just where to begin.

In 1921, the Chicago Real Estate Board voted to expel any member who sold or leased property to blacks outside the Bronzeville neighborhood. A month later, a Klan recruiter was sent from Indianapolis to turn Chicago into the largest KKK center in America. The friendly, shrewd, cynical Stephenson controlled all the growing chapters from his office in the Kresge Building in downtown Indianapolis. There, he had a bust of Napoleon and a bank of eight telephones, including a fake one he said was a direct line to the White House.

The Klan, which had almost died out by 1914, now numbered 700,000 nationwide and dominated the state politics of Indiana, just across from Chicago. Stephenson was not a racial bigot; he was using the hatred of the times in hopes of becoming a U.S. Senator and then seeking the Republican nomination for President in 1928.

In just two months, the Chicago Klan held a mass rally that drew ten thousand members and two thousand recruits, who received their white robes in a torchlight ceremony on farmland rented for the night.

Overwhelmed by his success, Stephenson could not restrain his lust for power and manipulation. On nothing more than a whim, he devised a plan to rape his secretary, Madge Oberholtzer, a woman of uncommon intelligence. Stephenson thought he would trap her in his private car as the train rolled from Indianapolis to Hammond, just across from the Illinois boundary, and thereby avoid being charged with violating the Mann Act against crossing state lines for sexual purposes.

Oberholtzer thought Stephenson was taking her along on business. But he brutally forced her to keep drinking liquor, and his bodyguards dragged her into the drawing room of his train car.

In a sexual frenzy, Stephenson ravished Oberholtzer and gnawed on her body. When the ordeal was over, and the train pulled into Hammond, Stephenson led her to a hotel and gave her money for a new hat. Instead, she used the money to buy poison and then drank it.

Fearing that the scandal would destroy his political plans, Stephenson had one of his henchmen drive them all the way back to Indianapolis—a journey of about four hours—without taking her to a hospital. After all, he had said, "I am the law in Indiana." Stephenson kept Oberholtzer overnight in a loft above his garage and repeatedly tried to get her to marry him as a cover-up, but she refused. He drove her home, and she died a few weeks later.

Oberholtzer's outraged father insisted that Stephenson be charged with second-degree murder. Authorities agreed because by then the Invisible Empire was becoming visible. Several Catholic attorneys and businessmen in Chicago, responding to the Klan's outlandish papal conspiracy rhetoric, had used spies and trickery to obtain secret membership lists.

Stephenson was sentenced to life in prison. When the Klan-influenced governor refused to grant him a pardon, Stephenson took revenge on him and everyone who had believed in the cause. He opened his own files to newspaper reporters, causing the entire northern Klan organization to implode. Stephenson was released from prison in 1956 and drifted into obscurity.

The decade saw a bizarre example of maternal love when Sarah Louisa Northcott was charged with helping her son abduct, murder, dismember, and bury a number of boys. Gordon Stewart Northcott attacked at least four youths on their chicken ranch near Riverside, California, with instruments of death that included two axes. The case broke when his fifteen-year-old nephew told Los Angeles County police about the murders, and the Northcotts disappeared. In their chicken coop, they left the bodies of two brothers, ages ten and eleven.

In September 1928, the twenty-year-old Northcott and his mother were arrested separately in western Canada, he in Okanagan Landing and she in Calgary. Gordon seemed not to know that he had done anything really bad. He told authorities he wanted to give British Columbia "the most thrilling manhunt in its history." Then he added, "I had to protect my poor little mother from this. I simply could not tell her of what they were accusing me. It would have killed her." Gordon pleaded guilty in California to one of the murders and was sentenced to life. He was later tried for three more killings and hanged in San Quentin. His mother was sentenced to life.

Not even killers such as Northcott could darken the image of the happy flappers in the glittering excesses of the 1920s, when business became the new religion of the middle class. The stock market seemed like one more machine running at peak capacity, and investors everywhere borrowed all they could in hopes of making a fortune.

The mad, drunken times were about to collapse in a single year of gang violence and financial desperation, culminating on Valentine's Day, 1929.

The setup was that "police officers" were to raid a Bugs Moran bootleg liquor loading point in a brick garage at 2122 North Clark Street in Chicago. For weeks, South Side killers watched the place from nearby buildings. To avoid identification, Fred Burke and his friends were brought to Chicago from the violent town of East St. Louis and given an unlimited bank account as well as police uniforms and cars resembling police autos.

One of the spotters called the Al Capone operation just south of the Loop, and the assassins piled into their cars with their pistols and Thompson submachine guns. Six mobsters were in the garage as well as a mob hanger-on. At 10:30 A.M., two "officers" with long blue coats and two "detectives" in civilian clothes concealing their tommy guns announced a raid.

Moran's people willingly lined themselves up against the wall and were cut down with a frightful double rat-a-tat. Moran himself was to have been there but arrived only in time to see the bodies and the blood dripping from the bricks.

The massacre shocked the world. Dr. Calvin Goddard of Baltimore resolved that it was not going to occur ever again in America. Goddard was obsessed with the idea that scientific detection could prevent killing. He took part in the analysis of evidence in the Sacco-Vanzetti case in Boston, and he headed a private lab in New York City.

Now he traveled to Chicago to set up the world's first crime laboratory. He had dreamed for years of a national crime analysis facility, but he needed an event so shocking that the public would support one. Capone supplied him with such an event.

Fearing interference from mobsters, Goddard used donated private funds to set up the Scientific Crime Detection Laboratory at Northwestern University in the Chicago suburb of Evanston. Each day he went to work with a revolver under his belt, and he admitted to often glancing over his shoulder at sudden sounds even though a guard was always stationed at the door. In four years, the lab processed fourteen hundred cases involving firearms before closing in 1934 after the Depression had dried up its funding. Goddard had worked a full year without pay before being forced to abandon his project. But by then, he had achieved his dream. His work inspired new crime labs at Scotland Yard in England and the FBI offices in Washington, D.C. It had taken an act of barbarity, but criminology had finally entered the modern age.

REFERENCES

Bailey, F. Lee. "The 'Torso Murder' Case," *Great Courtroom Battles.* Chicago: Playboy Press, 1973.

Block, Eugene B. *Great Train Robberies of the West.* New York: Coward-McCann, 1980.

———. *The Wizard of Berkeley.* New York: Coward-McCann, 1958.

Blum. *A Pictorial History of the Silent Screen.* New York: Perigee Books, 1953.

Boswell, Charles, and Thompson, Lewis. *The Girl in Lover's Lane.* Greenwich, Conn.: Gold Medal Books, 1962.

Brearly, H.C. *Homicide in the United States.* Chapel Hill, N.C.: University of North Carolina Press, 1932.

Brophy, John. *The Meaning of Murder.* New York: Thomas Y. Crowell, 1966.

Chicago Sun-Times, July 11, 1971.

Chicago Tribune, June 8, 1927.

———, April 11, 1949.

Chowder, Ken. "The ACLU Defends Everybody," *Smithsonian,* January 1998.

Craft, George C. "How I Would Have Handled the Taylor Case," *Celebrity Murders.* New York: Pinnacle Books, 1990.

DeFord, Miriam Allen. *Murderers Sane and Mad.* New York: Abelard-Schuman, 1965.

Fido, Martin. *Murders After Midnight.* London: Weidenfeld and Nicolson, 1990.

———. *The Chronicle of Crime.* New York: Carroll & Graf Publishers, 1993.

Fussell, Betty Harper. *Mabel.* New York: Limelight Editions, 1992.

Halper, Albert, ed. *The Chicago Crime Book.* New York: Pyramid Books, 1969.

Higdon, Hal. *The Crime of the Century: The Leopold and Loeb Case.* New York: G.P. Putnam, 1975.

Kirkpatrick, Sidney D. *A Cast of Killers.* New York: Penguin Books, 1986.

Kohn, George C. "William Desmond Taylor," *American Scandal.* New York: Facts on File, 1989.

Lane, Roger. *Murder in America.* Columbus, Ohio: Columbia University Press, 1997.

Larsen, Jonathan Z. "Tulsa Burning," *Civilization,* February–March 1997.

Leyburn, James G. *The Scotch-Irish: A Social History.* Chapel Hill, N.C.: University of North Carolina Press, 1962.

Mackenzie, F.A. *World Famous Cases.* London: G. Bles, 1927.

Marriner, Brian. *On Death's Bloody Trail: Murder and the Art of Forensic Science.* New York: St. Martin's Press, 1991.

Mowry, George E., ed. *The Twenties: Fords, Flappers & Fanatics,* Englewood Cliffs, N.J.: Prentice Hall, 1963.

Munn, Michael. "William Desmond Taylor: The All-Star Murder Mystery," *The Hollywood Murder Casebook.* New York: Carroll & Graf Publishers, 1990.

Nash, Jay Robert. *Murder, America.* New York: Simon & Schuster, 1980.

———. *The Almanac of World Crime.* New York: Anchor Press, 1981.

———. *Crime Chronology: A Worldwide Record: 1900–1983.* New York: Facts on File, 1984.

———. *Bloodletters and Badmen.* New York: M. Evans & Co., 1995.

New York Times, June 17, 1927.

———, September 22, 1928.

Odell, Robin. *Landmarks in 20th Century Murder.* London: Headline, 1995.

Publications International. *Murder and Mayhem.* Lincolnwood, Ill.: Publications International, 1991.

Schechter, Harold, and Everitt, David. *The A to Z Encyclopedia of Serial Killers.* New York: Pocket Books, 1996.

Snyder, Louis L., and Morris, Richard B. *A Treasury of Great Reporting.* New York: Simon & Schuster, 1962.

Sturholm, Larry, and Howard, John. *All for Nothing: The True Story of the Last Great American Train Robbery.* Portland: BLS Publishing, 1976.

Thorwald, Jurgen. *The Century of the Detective.* New York: Harcourt, Brace & World, 1964.

Tierney, Kevin. *Darrow: A Biography.* New York: Thomas Y. Crowell, 1979.

Wilson, Colin, *The Killers Among Us: Book I. Sex, Madness & Mass Murder.* New York: Warner Books, 1995.

Wolf, Marvin J., and Mader, Katherine. "Enigma: The Unsolved Murder of William Desmond Taylor," *Fallen Angels: Chronicles of L.A. Crime and Mystery.* New York: Ballantine Books, 1986.

The 1930s

For America, the 1930s were a hangover from the exhilaration and excesses of the 1920s. The previous decade ended not on December 31 but with the Wall Street crash in October 1929. One of the greatest countries in the world collapsed in one day of trading and subsequent failed attempts to recover losses. And now the people had to pay whether they understood what was happening to them or not.

The election of Franklin Delano Roosevelt in 1932 led to an alphabet soup of federal programs. The establishment of the Public Works Administration allowed photographer Dorothea Lange to capture the misery on the faces of people who had lost their jobs or their farms. The downbeat mood was reflected in popular songs such as "Brother Can You

Spare a Dime?" "Stormy Weather," "Boulevard of Broken Dreams," and "I Got Plenty O' Nothing."

Aided by an eager press, the people made heroes out of robbers such as John Dillinger, Pretty Boy Floyd, Bonnie and Clyde, and the Ma Barker gang. Police at first went after them not with criminalistics but with the same crude weapons the bandits used: pistols and submachine guns. So many robbers were barreling down roads in the South and the Midwest to escape the law that the government made crossing state lines to elude capture a federal crime. For an increasingly isolationist country, holdups, shoot-outs, kidnappings, and sexual assaults became everyday topics of conversation as one "crime of the century" followed another. The 1920s had its Leopold and Loeb case, and the 1930s had its kidnapping of air hero Charles A. Lindbergh's twenty-month-old son from a window of his home in New Jersey. The boy was later found dead.

In 1930, Congress authorized the FBI to establish a Division of Identification to keep a file of all fingerprints taken by government agencies. In 1932, the FBI in Washington, D.C., opened a laboratory for ballistics testing. Bureau director J. Edgar Hoover offered the lab's assistance to any local police department.

At first, there were few requests and the Bureau technicians were slow in doing the analyses, but soon the lab was testing not only cartridges and slugs but also blood, hair, oil, dust, metallic traces, and other evidence. Sometimes the FBI called on university experts around the country, proving that science was more reliable than Sherlock Holmes.

By the end of 1932, the nearly five thousand law enforcement agencies around the country were using the FBI's one million prints to trace killers and other criminals. In addition, technicians adopted techniques being developed worldwide in response to murders. The victim might be silenced, but blood and contact markings remained.

Although the comparison microscope of the 1920s greatly assisted ballistics tests, the methodology was improved in the 1930s with the periphery camera, which could photograph the whole curved surface of a bullet so that investigators could make a gelatin cast of the slug. This was done by splitting open the cast and spreading it out for comparison.

Still another innovation was the dermal nitrate test, which could detect residue from an exploding cartridge by examining paraffin wax spread over a suspect's hands. Later, the method was abandoned because of many false positives from handling substances containing nitrates, such as fertilizer.

Until early in the century, someone could explain away blood on his hands and clothes by saying he had killed an animal, but new methods were developed to discern human blood specifically. Dr. Leone Lattes of Italy refined this and revealed in his 1922 international textbook *The Individuality of Blood* that human blood types A, B, AB, and O could be discerned even in old stains.

But Berlin serologist Fritz Schiff discovered that the tests became less accurate over time. The groups eventually lose their antibodies and easily could be mistaken for one another. However, Schiff found that fresh serum was attracted to the cells of old stains. In research for a 1931 murder trial, Franz Joseph Holzer of Innsbruck, Austria, developed a test for determining this degree of attraction.

Improvements in blood-testing made it possible to distinguish a killer's blood from his victim's even if they were of the same type. First, scientists learned that type A was made up of two strengths, called A-1 and A-2. Then Viennese professor Karl Landsteiner discovered that by injecting rabbits with human blood it could be further divided by an M factor, an N factor, or a combination of both.

Throughout the 1930s, Landsteiner expanded his work by using rhesus monkeys because their blood was close to that of humans. This led to discovering the rhesus, or Rh, factor in 1940. By then, a drop of blood had become almost as individual as a fingerprint.

Blood tests were used to convict Gerald Thompson, a toolmaker who raped at least sixteen women by attacking them in his car in cemeteries and other lonely areas. Technology also caught up with the "Brick Moron" (maniac) of Chicago when he fled to Los Angeles and changed his name. Confronted with fingerprint matches, he confessed killing several people by smashing their skulls with a brick.

With all this emphasis on scientific examination, police investigations all over the country became more methodical. And killers were caught who had long gone undetected.

"Unspeakable Terror"

Eight-year-old Francis McDonnell, son of a Staten Island police officer, disappeared as he was playing stickball on the street with friends in July 1924. Several of the boys told the police they remembered a thin, older man who seemed to be watching them. Francis's battered body was found the next day after a massive search by friends and neighbors as well as local police officers. Soon, more than two hundred fifty police officers were searching for clues. This was half a century before the term "serial killer" was coined, and academics were only beginning to accept or ridicule the Viennese school of psychiatry. The authorities apparently did not consider the possibility that the abduction might be linked to other disappearances.

Four-year-old Billy Gaffney of Brooklyn vanished in February 1927 as he was playing in a hallway outside his apartment with a younger boy. The three-year-old saw the kidnapper but did not realize the man was real. The child described a gray-haired bogeyman who had come and taken away Billy. The story remained in the papers for weeks, with the *New York Daily News* expressing the growing frustration this way: "Somewhere in New York or nearby is little Billy Gaffney—or his body."

As the search continued, other cases were reported: in Darien, Connecticut, a child's body was found decapitated; in Massapequa, Long Island, fifteen-year-old Mary Ellen O'Connor was discovered murdered. Each new case led to another blind alley. Because science had failed to trace the bogeyman, it took a determined individual to resolve the crimes.

That man was New York City detective William King. A muscular former locomotive firefighter, King joined the police force in 1907 but left to fight on the front lines in World War I. He returned and set up a private detective business but in 1926 rejoined the department. In two years, he was assigned to the Missing Persons Bureau. The chain-smoking detective was not afraid of flames, enemy machine-gun fire, or robbers, and yet the disappearance of a child greatly disturbed him.

In early June 1928, Edward Budd Jr. went to the station house on East 52nd Street, just off Third Avenue, with the drained look of someone who had gone many hours without sleep and was trying to stay hopeful against his innermost fears. He told the desk sergeant that his twelve-year-old sister, Grace, had gone off with a middle-aged man, who gave his name as Frank Howard, to his niece's birthday party. They never returned. The sergeant had him tell his story to Lieutenant Samuel Dribben.

Edward said he wanted to make some money, so he put an ad in the "situations wanted" column of the *New York World* on Sunday, May 27. It stated: "Young man, eighteen years old, wishes position in the country for the summer," followed by his name and address. The next day, the respectable-looking Howard, in clothes just slightly ill-fitting, visited the Budd's modest apartment in the Chelsea district. He was a slender man in his late fifties, dressed conservatively in a dark suit and what must have been a $10 felt hat. Howard said he needed help running a farm near Farmingdale, Long Island. He told the Budds that his six grown-up sons and daughters had moved away, leaving him to milk a half dozen cows and raise three hundred chickens. Howard offered Edward and a friend $15 each a week. "I'll pick up Edward on Saturday and drive him to my farm," he told the young man's parents.

When Saturday came, Howard sent a telegram saying he was buying a cow in New Jersey but would be at the Budd's home on Sunday. When Howard arrived, he brought a jar of pot cheese and strawberries that he said were from his farm. The Budds were taken by his cordiality and thoughtfulness and treated him to a lunch of chicken and apple pie.

That was when the man who called himself Frank Howard saw Grace. She had arrived from church wearing her Sunday best and thought nothing of sitting on his lap as he stroked her brown hair in a grandfatherly way. He gave Edward and his friend $2 to go to the movies and treat themselves to something while he remained with the rest of the family.

Howard mentioned that his sister was having a birthday party for her daughter at Columbus Avenue and 137th Street, and he offered to take Grace with him. Her parents, Edward Sr. and Delia, were hesitant until their guest mentioned all the children who would be there and the fun they would have. "I'll bring her back in a few hours by early evening," he promised, "and then I'll drive Edward to my farm." The pretty child, with a rosary around her wrist, excitedly went with the stranger. That was the last time she was seen.

Hearing the young man's account, Dribben immediately suspected the worst. The supposed address of Howard's sister was fictitious; Columbus ended at 110th Street. Two detectives checked neighborhood rooming houses while a third escorted Edward to the station house so he could look through the "rogues' gallery" of photos of previously arrested suspects.

The next day, a detective checked with the Motor Vehicles Bureau to see if Howard's name was on file, and another went to Western Union's central office in hopes of obtaining the handwritten message Howard had given to a telegrapher. An investigator was sent to where Howard claimed to have a farm. But this and every other channel of investigation turned up nothing. The only course of action was for the police to search for a body. Uniformed officers fanned out to search cellars, rooftops, alleyways, vacant lots, movie theaters, subway stations, and garages.

Even the national papers picked up the story. Reporters linked Grace to other children who had disappeared, even though the police were not yet doing so for the record. This led to sightings in Pennsylvania, Long Island, and upstate New York. Even police in Canada looked into the possibility that Howard had crossed the border. And the Budd family received several disgusting crank letters, each of which had to be checked out.

Although Howard had said that his farm provided the pot cheese he gave the Budds, police were able to trace the forty-cent price written on its wrapping paper to a street vendor. But neither he nor anyone in his East Harlem neighborhood knew the whereabouts of the slender, slightly seedy-looking man.

After two weeks of chasing leads, Lieutenant Dribben called the case "the most baffling" he had ever dealt with.

As part of New York's Missing Persons Bureau, William King was one of several detectives assigned to look for a possible suspect who was going by the name of Dr. Albert Corthall. A Florida prison farm warden thought the man might be Howard, as described in a NYPD flyer. The photo of Corthall—whose real name was Alfred Corchell—was shown to a desperate Mrs. Budd at police headquarters, who said that she was sure he was the man. The search for Corchell lasted for two years, until he was arrested trying to cash someone else's $15,000 check out of state in December 1930. He was extradited to New York and indicted, but the charges were later dismissed.

King by now had traveled fifty thousand miles over the eastern half of the country searching for the wrong people, and he felt no closer to solving the Budd case than when he began. It seemed that every possibility was exhausted. He had no way of knowing that from time to time he had glimpsed the face of Howard while going through the department's thick files of active cases. The man's real name was Hamilton Howard Fish. He came from a dark branch of a distinguished family, and he may have killed more than a dozen children.

The Fish family was honorably represented in American history for more than a century. Nicholas Fish was a close friend of Alexander Hamilton, and Secretary of State Hamilton Fish was called a pillar of the Grant Administration. A member of the family died in Teddy Roosevelt's charge on San Juan Hill, Cuba, in the Spanish-American War, and another was a Congressman who, during the search for Grace's killer, was considered a possible Republican candidate to challenge President Roosevelt.

One would think that carrying the name of Hamilton Fish would be an honor, but the future serial killer hated being called "Ham" and "Ham and Eggs Fish" by grammar school classmates, so he changed his name to Albert. There was an apparent strain of mental disturbance in his family. A younger brother was feeble-minded and died young. An uncle on his father's side had what was regarded as religious psychosis, possibly schizophrenia, and he died in a state hospital. Albert called his uncle's eccentric sister "completely crazy." The boy also had an alcoholic brother, a sister with some sort of mental affliction, and a half-brother who died in a state institution.

Albert's father died when he was young, and his mother placed him in an orphanage. After graduating from its school, he made a living doing odd jobs before drifting into petty larceny and occasionally writing obscene letters to women.

Albert used the "situations wanted" column of the *New York World* to send such a letter to a professional housekeeper, but he was not reprimanded. Fish also experienced occasional religious delusions and had fantasies involving altar boys. Strangest of all was his habit of sticking numerous pins into his body to enjoy the pain, and leaving them there.

Many serial killers have no remorse for what they do, but several have deeply regretted murders outside their repeated fantasies. From family testimony, it seems that Albert showed no conscience over the boys he killed, as if they were never real, but he could not forget the strangling and dismemberment of Grace.

His son, Albert Jr., said in court that his father would scream out in his sleep and wake up sweating. Then, as if in atonement for what he had done, he would strip off his clothes and stick more needles into his body or paddle himself. There was more than just expiation involved, for the man, then in his early sixties, craved a rush of guilt and pain, which was a source of sexual excitement to him.

During the search for Grace's kidnapper, Albert was arrested a few times on minor charges and spent a brief period in the Bellevue Hospital mental ward. The chief psychiatrist found the patient so quiet and cooperative that he released Albert as just a harmless eccentric. Once more Albert slipped away. But three unrelated events led to his downfall: a revived newspaper scare about kidnappings, triggered by the Bruno Hauptmann trial for the abduction of the Lindbergh baby; Albert's penchant for sending obscene letters; and—yes—the ramblings of a cockroach.

"KIDNAPPING: A RISING MENACE TO THE NATION" blared the *New York Times* shortly after the Lindbergh child was stolen from an upstairs bedroom in March 1932. Among the illustrations of four other abduction victims was Grace Budd's first Communion photo.

Usually police found reporters to be a nuisance, but Detective King saw newspapers as a possible catalyst. He kept the Budd case alive in the minds of the public by planting false items, such as one that appeared in the column of influential Broadway commentator Walter Winchell, claiming that the police now had an informant and they expected to break the case in a month.

The kidnapping haunted many New York residents. There was something compelling about Grace's innocence in her white first Communion dress, glimpsed under a winter coat and a rose in her lapel. When Brooklyn housewife Adele Miller saw photographs of a procession of U.S. warships in the harbor she thought a teenage girl pictured with a sailor was the grown-up Grace. Miller went through her clippings on the case, found the address of the Budd family, and sent them the article.

Mrs. Budd immediately called Detective King, convinced that this must be Grace. But once again her hopes were dashed. After the newspaper did a story on the search and reprinted the photo, the girl with the sailor came forward to explain who she was.

A few days later, for whatever reason, Albert sent an unsigned letter to Mrs. Budd, and in horror she turned it over to King. The detective quickly saw that this was not just another piece of crank mail. The letter mentioned the high price of meat in famine-torn China and eventually claimed that the writer choked Grace to death, and then ate her body. The letter included details that were never made public, such as the pot cheese and strawberries "Howard" had brought six years before. The letter also gave Howard's address at that time, 409 East 109th Street, the block the police had searched for the kidnapper.

King found the letter to be a perfect match with the handwritten copy of the Western Union message. Reading over the letter once more, King must have shuddered at the possible truth behind the fantasies. The author—sometimes using "I" but at other times referring to himself as "John"—purported that he was a merchant sailor who was stranded in China in 1894, and that "so great was the suffering among the very poor, that all children under twelve were sent to the butchers to be cut up and sold for food in order to keep others from starving. A boy or girl under fourteen was not safe in the street" and that "John staid [sic] there so long he developed a taste for human flesh." Reverting to first person singular, Albert then mentioned killing several boys as well as Grace. He ended the letter by assuring Mrs. Budd that her daughter had died a virgin.

The envelope flap had a monogram design with the initials PCBA. Albert used the envelope even though he must have been aware that it could become a clue; he even tried to scratch out the emblem with a dark pencil. Detective King pored over lists of groups and found the New York Private Chauffeur's Benevolent Association on Lexington Avenue, but no one there knew anyone named Frank Howard. The detective pressed the members on whether anyone might have removed the stationery from the office.

The next day, Lee Sicowski, a part-time janitor and errand boy, approached King and admitted purloining a few sheets and envelopes six months earlier. Sicowski evidently did not send the letter, and no one in the men's rooming house recognized a description of a thin gray-haired man. But Sicowski also mentioned that six months ago he was living at 200 East 52nd Street.

Bringing a few of the old flyers with him, King spoke to the landlady at the boardinghouse and learned that after Sicowski moved out, a quiet man in his early sixties with a gray mustache lived in the room for a few days. King later discovered that the man who sometimes called himself Frank Howard was trying to kill a scuttering cockroach when he found the envelopes Sicowski had left behind on a shelf. The detective eagerly looked over the register and saw that the handwriting matched the letter and, even more important, there was a fresh name to investigate—Albert H. Fish.

The landlady said that Fish spoke about a son who worked in the Civilian Conservation Corps (*CCC*) in North Carolina, and the young man sent him a check for $25 every month. Fish had even asked her to cash several for him. In fact, she recently cashed the latest check, and Fish was expected to be back for the money in about a week.

Taking no chances, King rented a room there for a twenty-four-hour-a-day stakeout, calling on several detectives to work in relays. He also asked the CCC finance officer to notify him when the next checks were to be mailed, and he told the chief postal inspector in New York to alert him as soon as any letter was sent to Fish. The letter arrived, but Fish did not show up at the rooming house until a week later, December 13, while King happened to be the officer on stakeout duty. The investigator hurried downstairs and found the man who had eluded police in several states for nearly a decade quietly sipping tea.

King walked into the room and said "Mr. Fish . . ." with such authority the killer knew what was about to happen. Fish reached into his vest pocket and pulled out a razor blade. The detective quickly grabbed Fish's wrist and he dropped the blade. King searched him and found other such blades in his pocket.

There was no problem getting Fish to confess. In the detention pen at police headquarters, he readily gave precise accounts to detectives, psychologists, and psychiatrists. "I didn't have any intention of killing the girl," he stated in a written confession. He really intended to attack her brother, but "I was suddenly overcome with a certain bloodthirst." Not all of his accounts were the same. Like most serial killers, he had spent much of his life slipping into and out of fantasies. It seemed clear that he was having fantasies even when he was abducting and killing the children, for he said that as he was strangling Grace he saw her as a boy.

When he abducted the girl, he was carrying what he called his "implements of hell": a cleaver, a small saw, and a butcher knife honed to a razor-sharp edge. He took Grace by subway to the Bronx. From there, they rode the Central Railroad to Westchester County and walked to a vacant two-story ramshackle house the locals called Wisteria Cottage. Hobos sometimes used it for refuge, and children occasionally played "haunted house" in the rooms. There, on the second floor, Fish committed a crime that prosecutors called an "unspeakable evil," strangling Grace and then, by his account, butchering her and eating her over a nine-day period.

The day after his arrest, Fish led King, several other Missing Persons Bureau detectives, and Westchester County officials to the cottage in the Worthington Woods section near

Greenburgh. It was like a macabre real-estate tour as Fish pointed out the various sites where he had committed the crime. After six years, the details were still vivid in his mind because he had relived them so many times. But he told police that five minutes after she was dead, he would have done anything to have her back again.

On an early night in mid-December, officers lit railroad flares outside the house, brought in searchlights, and began digging while surrounded by huddled clusters of more than a hundred people. The officers found no tools, but they unearthed a skull that could have come from a twelve-year-old girl.

Police then learned about other cases, including seven-year-old Francis McDonald, who went off with Fish after playing stickball with friends in Staten Island. Fish said he had cut up the body of four-year-old Billy Gaffney in a public dump in Queens and sank the four potato sacks containing his remains into Bowery Bay.

Fish told authorities that he had felt driven by strong sexual urges ever since he was young. He was especially fascinated by pain. He did everything he could think of, from paddling himself to inserting into his rectum a cloth soaked with gasoline and setting it on fire. X-rays after his arrest showed twenty-nine needles in his body, most of them in his pelvic region. He had even engaged in an act of contrition for Grace's killing by shoving five sewing needles behind his testicles. His son reported finding fresh needles in a collection of stories by Edgar Allan Poe.

The question now was whether Fish was sane.

In Fish's old leather-strapped suitcase police found articles about the notorious German serial killer Fritz Haarmann.

During the starvation period after World War I, Haarmann killed an unknown number of male teenagers and sold their meat at a smuggler's market in Hanover. When Haarman was caught in 1924, a head was found on his stove. He was executed by decapitation. Could fantasies engendered by the articles have been the source of Fish's purported cannibalism of Grace Budd years later?

Whatever monster Fish was with children he didn't know, he was a good father to his own, and they wanted to save his life by having him declared insane. During his trial in White Plains, New York, they testified that their father ate raw meat in the moonlight, built a trap to catch a black cat that did not exist, once declared himself to be Christ, once slept rolled up in a blanket on the orders of John the Baptist, and set fires in the bathroom almost every night. However evil Fish was, though, he was honest. When the prosecutor asked, "Do you still realize that what you did was wrong?" he replied: "Yes, sir. I always watched the papers, and would have come forward if an innocent man was taken." Then, with a meaning not at all clear, he immediately added, "I realize my best days were over."

Fish was convicted of the Budd murder and sentenced to death. The sixty-five-year-old former housepainter said, "Thank you, Judge," and waved to his family in court. There are unconfirmed reports that Fish was so happy to die that he helped adjust the electrodes, but this much seems sure: Death brought relief to one of the strangest pathological killers in American history.

As to how many children Fish killed in his life, reliable sources say from eight to fifteen. Whether any more than one was cannibalized is a secret Fish took to his grave.

"The Most Vicious, Cold-Blooded Killer I Ever Knew"

With the Wall Street collapse, working hard was no longer considered just a way to get to the top—it meant survival. Public attention focused on the American laborer as never before, from Charlie Chaplin's factory in *Modern Times* to the inner struggle of a thug and an artist in the violinist-boxer of Clifford Odets's play *Golden Boy.* The hard times led companies to expect that workers would put up with twelve-hour shifts for eight hours' pay because they were happy just to have jobs. Government statistics showed that a half million U.S. workers were involved in sit-down strikes from September 1936 to May 1937. At the same time, intellectuals reevaluated the American spirit of enterprise with books such as Walter Lippmann's *The Good Society* and Seebohm Rowntree's *The Human Needs of Labor.*

The FBI concentrated its efforts on major crime gangs and then, spurred by the abduction of the Lindbergh baby, cracked down on ransom kidnappings, which had become common at a time when the Depression was turning sentiment against the rich. Wealthy men were abducted in virtually every state in the Union.

When J. Edgar Hoover, the man who was turning the FBI from a restricted agency into a virtual national police force, heard of the disappearance of seventy-two-year-old retired greeting card manufacturer Charles Ross in September 1937, he was determined to find his abductors.

Ross's former secretary, Florence Freihage, told the police that after treating her to dinner, Ross was driving her home on Wolf Road in the Chicago suburb of Franklin Park. Another car was following them, but Ross thought nothing of it. Suddenly "this other car zoomed ahead of us, cut us off, and forced us off the road. Then, these two men got out and approached our car with their guns drawn."

The leader of the two men, John Henry Seadlund, was a small-time crook with a record dating back a decade, from the time he was seventeen. He had drifted around the country taking occasional jobs as a day laborer until the stock market crashed and no one was putting up "help wanted" signs anymore. Seadlund soon turned to crime to get by. In early 1937, he met James Atwood Gray, a petty thief who had come from Kentucky to seek success through bigger crimes. Together, they rolled drunks and robbed a few homes. Stopping an expensive car seemed an easy way to score quick cash.

As the men forced open the driver-side door, they heard Ross mutter, philosophically, "I've often thought about being kidnapped." The two small-time thieves jumped at the suggestion. Seadlund ordered the secretary to remain in her seat and told Ross to get out. As she sat alone in the car, on a dark road fourteen miles west of the Loop, Freihage watched the robbers' car disappear with her boss inside. Hysterical, she drove to the first filling station she could find and called the police.

Ross lived in a luxury North Side apartment. When detectives visited his wife with news of Ross's kidnapping, she became overwrought. "My husband has a slight heart ailment," she said. "If he's kidnapped, he can't live very long. His doctors say he must have constant attention."

But where was Ross? The elderly man was actually being kept chained to an abandoned well in rural Wisconsin, in subfreezing temperatures.

Abductors usually contact the family of their victims right away, but for several days, Mrs. Ross and the police heard nothing. Kidnapping for ransom fell under the FBI's jurisdiction under the 1934 Lindbergh law, and Hoover wanted these men captured quickly as a deterrent to other potential kidnappings. He personally assigned special agent Earl J. Connelly, one of just a handful of men Hoover would send across the country on special cases.

Day after day, Mrs. Ross had no way of knowing whether her husband was alive or dead. But on September 30, a message was delivered to the Wisconsin home of Ross's friend, Harvey Brackett: "I am held for ransom. I have stated I am worth $100,000. Try and raise $50,000."

Brackett forwarded the note to Mrs. Ross in Chicago, and she gave it to Connelly. "It looks genuine," the agent said, because both Brackett and Mrs. Ross recognized the handwriting. Apparently the kidnappers had taken Ross to Wisconsin because he had a friend in Williams Bay who could act as an intermediary for the exchange.

"I'll try to get the money," Mrs. Ross told her husband's friend. "Tell me what to do now."

Within a day, a second note in Ross's handwriting arrived with instructions on how to turn over the $50,000 to the kidnappers through a newspaper ad. Possibly because she could not raise that much cash so quickly, Mrs. Ross offered half that amount, $25,000. Her ad in a Chicago paper ran: "For sale: 1934 Dodge Sedan. $250. William Gegenworth, 5043 South Western Avenue."

The next day, Mrs. Ross received a typed note demanding the full amount and asking her lawyers to "contact a motorcycle shop" the abductors had selected at random. Then she was told to find a messenger and prepare him "for a dangerous mission." Mrs. Ross relented, and her lawyer made the necessary arrangements.

Connelly was concerned about the nature of the note. Why was it typed when the two others were handwritten, unless Ross could no longer write the message himself? But then another note requesting $50,000 arrived at the Ross's house with a photograph of her husband standing in woods and holding a newspaper dated October 2, 1937. The note included additional instructions on how the money should be delivered.

In the Lindbergh case, the money was identified by a list of serial numbers on the ransom bills. But now the Bureau had an additional method—marking the bills with a dye. Mrs. Ross helped put the stacks of marked bills in a zippered pouch for the cyclist, George Kukovac. Although motorcyclists in the 1930s loved speed and independence, they were generally responsible. For the abductors, the advantage of using a motorcyclist to deliver the cash was obvious: unlike a car, there could be no hidden police officers or federal agents aboard a motorcycle.

Kukovac was ordered to paint his machine white and wear white clothes, so the kidnappers would know he was the cyclist delivering the ransom. He headed due west to Rockford, more than eighty miles away. The trip took longer than normal because the young man had to follow a stop-and-start pattern. Were the kidnappers following him to make sure he was abiding by their instructions? Kukovac had no way of knowing. He just knew that someone's life might be depending on him.

When Kukovac emerged from below the wooded hills, he heard a car slowing down behind him. As the auto came closer on the deserted road, its headlights blinked three times. That was the signal. Without looking back, Kukovac unzipped the pouch, dropped it at the side of the road, and kept going.

A day passed. Then two. Mrs. Ross finally received a note stating that the kidnapper would bring her husband back "if I collect and if I have an opportunity to get rid of the bills by that time." When she turned over the note to agent Connelly, he looked glum. The agent knew that the abductors—there is seldom a single kidnapper—were just buying time.

As gently as he could, Connelly let Mrs. Ross know that she would probably never see her husband again. The men apparently had caught on that the bills were marked, and it could take several months or more to carefully spend them in places where they would not be readily checked.

Meanwhile, the crime lab was making progress on the case. A study of the typed note turned up a fingerprint that was traced to Seadlund. The FBI learned that he was twenty-seven, born in a lumberjack community in rural Minnesota, stood about five feet, nine inches tall, and had brown eyes and curly brown hair. All FBI offices in the country were notified, and police in the upper Midwest were sent his description.

The print on the last letter showed that Seadlund had used a new typewriter. More than one hundred fifty federal agents checked on all typewriter stores in the Chicago area to learn whether someone matching his description had recently bought a machine. One clerk remembered such a man, and the agents traced this lead to a "Peter Anders," who had stayed for a few days at a cheap rooming house but left no forwarding address. FBI agents dusted the room for fingerprints and, a few days later, had their match.

Now the question was, where were the abductors? The answer came a few weeks later as Seadlund began leaving a trail of marked bills in Cincinnati, Cleveland, Toledo, Philadelphia, New York, Atlanta, Washington, D.C., Palm Beach, and Miami. Most of the bills showed up at racetracks. Reports followed from Arkansas and Denver. Seadlund was crossing the country to elude capture, but he was making Connelly's job easier.

Because Seadlund was using racetracks to launder his money, Hoover's handpicked investigator reasoned that he might be heading for the widely publicized races at Santa Anita Park near Los Angeles. Naturally, the FBI played their cards close to the vest, refusing to give the suspect's name to the press. The lack of news might have contributed to Sealund's brazen behavior. But Connelly was outsmarting him, assigning an agent with a list of the serial numbers to each betting window.

The investigators were right about Santa Anita Park.

As the thoroughbreds were being brought to the paddock, the agents at the booths, dressed like assistant betting clerks, waited. A curly haired man plunked $10 on the counter and gave the number of a horse. The agent showed no reaction as he took the money, then gestured to agents who were standing around like bettors. Seadlund saw the men encircling him, but by then there was no way out. He quietly surrendered.

One of the agents told Seadlund he was wanted for questioning about a crime near Chicago, to which Seadlund replied, "Yes, I killed Ross," he said—then added—"and I killed my partner, James Gray." Hoover at last had a case to counteract nationwide criticism that his bureau had taken too long in bringing charges in the Lindbergh case.

Seadlund admitted he and Gray took their captive to a cave in northwestern Wisconsin but had a falling out over the expected ransom. The kidnapper said that Ross tried to intervene, and both Ross and Gray were severely wounded as the gun went off. Then Seadlund kept firing. "I killed them to spare them from further suffering," he claimed.

Agents took Seadlund to a fishing area near Spooner, where they dug up both bodies. They also recovered $47,345 of the ransom. "I was lucky at the track," Seadlund explained.

And so ended the career of the man Hoover referred to as "the most vicious cold-blooded killer I ever knew" and "the meanest man who ever lived." Seadlund pleaded guilty, and a judge sentenced him to become the first federal prisoner to die in the electric chair, at Cook County Jail in Chicago.

When other law enforcement agencies witnessed how a killer could be captured even after fleeing across the country, they were no longer reluctant to send copies of fingerprints to the FBI, commencing a new era in American law enforcement.

REFERENCES

Alix, Ernest Kashlar. *Ransom Kidnapping in America: 1874–1974.* Carbondale, Ill.: Southern Illinois University Press, 1978.

Bauman, Ed. *May God Have Mercy on Your Soul.* Chicago: Bonus Books, 1993.

Brody, John. *The Meaning of Murder.* New York: Thomas Y. Crowell, 1966.

DeFord, Miriam Allen, *Murderers Sane and Mad.* New York: Abelard-Schuman, 1964.

Fido, Martin. *The Chronicle of Crime.* New York: Carroll & Graf Publishers, 1993.

Green, Jonathan. *The Greatest Criminals of All Time.* New York: Stein & Day, 1980.

Heimer, Mel. *The Cannibal.* London: Xanadu Publications, 1988.

Lane, Roger. *Murder in America.* Columbus, Ohio: Columbia University Press, 1997.

Marriner, Brian. *Death's Bloody Trail: Murder and the Art of Forensic Science.* New York: St. Martin's Press, 1991.

Messick, Hank, and Goldblatt, Burt. *Kidnapping: The Illustrated History.* New York: Dial Press, 1995.

Nash, Jay Robert. *Crime Chronology: A Worldwide Record: 1900–1983.* New York: Facts on File, 1984.

———. *Bloodletters and Badmen.* New York: M. Evans & Co., 1995.

New York Times, March 15–26, 1935.

Odell, Robin. *Landmarks in 20th Century Murder.* London: Headline, 1995.

Publications International, "Albert Fish," *Murder and Mayhem.* New York: Signet Books, 1991.

Reilly, Helen. "1935: Robert James, the Reluctant Rattlesnakes," in *The Mammoth Book of Murder.* Edited by Richard Glynn Jones. New York: Carroll & Graf Publishers, 1990.

Schecter, Harold. *Deranged.* New York: Pocket Books, 1990.

Thorwald, Jurgen. *The Century of the Detective.* New York: Harcourt, Brace & World, 1964.

———. *Crime and Science.* New York: Harcourt, Brace & World, 1967.

Unger, Sanford J. *FBI.* Boston: Little, Brown, 1976.

Williams, Eugene D. "1936: The Rattlesnake Murder," in *Los Angeles Murders.* Edited by Craig Rice. New York: Duell, Sloan, and Pearce, 1947.

Wilson, Colin. *Written in Blood: Detectives & Detection.* New York: Warner Books, 1989.

———. *Murder in the 1930s.* New York: Carroll & Graf Publishers, 1992.

———. *The Killers Among Us, Book I: Sex, Madness & Mass Murder.* New York: Warner Books, 1995.

The 1940s

Studies show that murders, like suicides, decline during periods of war. The demands on the home front in World War II and the sense that America was helping to save the world from tyranny in Europe and in the Pacific must have galvanized even the unstable, giving them a sense of purpose. The early 1940s actually saw a return to innocence, with novels and films stressing family values. The best-loved books of the time included *A Tree Grows in Brooklyn* and *Mamma's Bank Account*, which was later made into the film *I Remember Mama*. The heartbreaks of the Depression were over. Few demands were made on teenagers, who were encouraged to preserve their innocence. Thousands of ten-cent comic books were sent to service personnel overseas.

Crimes committed in America in the early 1940s were as modern as crimes from today's headlines. The most significant element bringing this about was transportation. A few American soldiers found themselves freed from internal restraints while they served on other continents. It was a freedom that had its downside, too. In 1942, U.S. Army Private Edward Leonski of New York City strangled three older women within two weeks while stationed in Australia.

Back home, gasoline rationing and recruits in transit to military bases jammed trains with passengers. In 1943, an attractive woman awoke on an overnight Pullman train from California to Oregon as a man was slashing her throat. She struggled with her unknown attacker, but he killed her with a deep plunge of his knife. He slipped away before the porter and the conductor could hurry down the narrow aisle. Several people heard Martha James trying to scream, but no one could climb out from behind the flaps over their berths in time to see the culprit. Inquiries led to the train's cook, Robert Lee Folkes, who had a criminal record that included several sexual assaults. Folkes had seen the James woman in the dining car earlier.

Economic, technological, and transportation advances brought more strangers together than at any time in the century. Peace brought emotional release for most people but unease for others. Take Howard Unrah, a mild-mannered veteran who spent his time reading scripture and engaging in target practice, all the while waiting for a word, a signal.

Unrah's inner time bomb exploded in a walkabout of murder in his neighborhood in East Camden, New Jersey, one day in 1949. He believed that people were talking about him, saying cruel things, so he slid a clip into his German Luger automatic pistol and put sixteen extra cartridges in his pocket. His inner rage was about to end. As his mother ironed clothes, Unrah stepped out of his shabby stucco apartment house and fired into a car at two women who had stopped for a traffic signal. When he was out of ammunition, he turned back home, feeling a little better. The other dead included a cobbler in his shoe-repair shop, a tailor, and a six-year-old boy who was killed on the street without any words exchanged.

A newspaper editor heard the police call and, amid the confusion of sending out reporters and directing his writers to pick up side angles on the breaking story, telephoned the Unrah apartment himself on the unlikely possibility that someone would be there, either a relative or a police officer. "Hello," a soft voice answered. The editor was startled to realize he was speaking to the killer himself. By then, the police were firing tear-gas canisters into the house.

"I'm a friend," the editor said, having no idea what else to say. "I want to know what they're doing to you down there."

"They haven't done anything to me yet. I'm doing plenty to them."

When the editor asked how many people he had just killed, Unrah replied, "I don't know. I haven't counted. Looks like a pretty good score."

"Why are you killing people?"

"I don't know. I can't answer that. I'll have to talk to you later. I'm too busy now."

By the time the tear gas had taken effect, Unrah had killed twelve people and wounded four others.

In the wake of World War II, the United States was unequivocally the strongest nation in the world, and soon war heroes such as Generals Patton and Eisenhower were eclipsed by sports stars such as Joe DiMaggio and Rocky Graziano. Bebop and swing filled dance halls with teenagers, Danny Kaye was the rage at the movies, and people walked down the street whistling tunes from *Carousel.* Humorist James Thurber poked gentle fun at the foibles of city dwellers as war brides from three continents arrived by ship to be reunited with the American soldiers with whom they had fallen in love.

New industries sprouted once science returned to peacetime use. Chester Carlson invented xerography in 1946, and the transistor was perfected in 1947. That was the year a plane beat the sound barrier, and Peter Goldmark invented the long-playing record. As companies moved to expand, jobs left the cities and farmland became suburbs.

Yet a dark undercurrent remained. *Carousel* was about the life and death of a wife beater, and the popular 1945 film *Lost Weekend* concerned a man's nightmare of alcohol abuse. Family disruptions during the decade led to an alarming rise in juvenile delinquency, and teenagers no longer committed just petty crimes.

"Catch Me Before I Kill More"

In the early afternoon of June 3, 1945—less than a month after the jubilation that marked the end of World War II—the Chicago police received notice of an extraordinary burglary. A phantom thief had completed his metamorphosis into a killer.

Police Captain Frank Reynolds went to the fifth-floor apartment of attractive widow Josephine Alice Ross on North Kenmore Street, not far from Lake Michigan. Several uniformed officers were waiting for him. Ross's teenage daughter had summoned them. The daughter told the officers that she knew something was wrong when she found their pit bull terrier whimpering under a couch. The girl found her mother stabbed to death in her bedroom, her body fairly clean of stains but lying in blood-soaked bed linen.

Mrs. Ross was stabbed repeatedly in the face and neck, one jab going deep into her jugular vein. Her neck was bound with a nylon stocking as well as her red skirt. The killer also covered up some of the cuts on her nude body with adhesive bandages.

Captain Reynolds went to the bathroom and found what he expected. The tub was partially filled with water and blood. The killer must have crept into the apartment, stabbed Mrs. Ross over and over, bathed her body to cleanse his crime, and then placed her back on the bed. The coroner's physician determined that the bandages were put on about an hour and a half after the killing. There was no indication of sexual assault, and only $12 was taken from Mrs. Ross's purse.

Police expected the killer to be a "fiend" or a "maniac." But the only suspicious person seen around the building was a young man wearing a white sweater, dark trousers, and hair brushed in a pompadour. A janitor said the young man jumped down from the fire escape around noon, which was an hour and a half after the attack. The janitor did not chase him because tenants often used the fire escape as a shortcut to the parking lot. As the janitor spoke to the officers, a train connecting the socially bipolar North and South sides of the city rattled along the nearby elevated tracks.

Police expected a lot of fingerprints from such a messy crime, but even the baseboards were wiped clean.

On October 1, nineteen-year-old Veronica Hudzinski heard a tapping noise on the window of her North Winthrop Avenue apartment, near the El tracks. She opened the window and heard two shots. One of the bullets entered her shoulder. Beneath Hudzinski's window police later found a revolver wrapped in a crude mask that had been made from a shower curtain. Hudzinski had no idea why anyone would want to shoot her.

On October 5, a former Army nurse named Evelyn Peterson was knocked unconscious with a heavy metal bar when a prowler dropped down from a trap door in the ceiling of her sister's apartment on Drexel Avenue—near the South Side campus of the University of Chicago. When she awoke, her arms were bound with a lamp cord. Peterson worked herself loose and looked around to see what the attacker had taken—about $150. Moments later, a young man appeared at her door. He noticed her bloodied face and offered to call a doctor. When he was unable to reach one, he left the apartment and told the manager on the way out that a woman in the penthouse needed medical attention.

Police wondered whether this nice young man was the attacker. They searched the apartment, but everything was wiped clean except for a single partial print. But it would be nearly impossible to manually trace the partial print in the more than one and a quarter million sets of prints on file at Chicago police headquarters. Because each card had ten prints, one for each finger, that made twelve and a half million prints overall.

On December 5, Marian Caldwell was sitting in the kitchen of her North Side home on Sherwin Avenue when a bullet shattered a window, grazing her and lodging in a baseboard. From the angle of the slug, the police assumed the shot was fired from a roof across the street. At the time, no one had even guessed that the recent rash of crimes might be connected.

Then, on December 10, a cleaning woman ran screaming from the sixth-floor studio apartment of Frances Brown, a former member of the women's naval auxiliary who worked as a secretary at a business machine company.

"There's a body in the bathroom!" the cleaning woman gasped as she rushed down the stairs to the lobby of the Pine Crest residential hotel on Pine Grove Avenue, near the North Side El tracks.

When Captain Reynolds arrived, he could not help but notice some similarities to the stabbing of Mrs. Ross. Unlike the Ross home, this apartment was in a shambles, with the contents of drawers scattered everywhere. But bloodstained bedding from the studio couch seemed to point to the bathroom, where the body of the slender brunette was bent over the tub. Loosely placed around her neck was the top of her pajamas. When Reynolds nodded for the officers to remove the pajamas, they saw the handle of a long bread knife protruding from her neck. The point and the curved part of the blade were sticking out from the other side of her throat. She was shot twice: once in the right side of her head and once in her right arm. As with Mrs. Ross, the killer wiped off the blood—this time with the wet and bloody towels that lay on the floor.

Strangest of all was that the killer had used Mrs. Brown's bright red lipstick to leave a message on the beige living room wall:

FOR HEAVENS
SAKE CATCH ME
BEFORE I KILL MORE
I CANNOT CONTROL MYSELF

The top line was slightly over six feet from the floor. Some of the letters were as small as three inches, and some as large as six inches; some of the letters were printed as capitals, and others were in script.

Detectives noticed several faint scratches and smudges on the sill of a living-room window, which was closed but not latched. At around 4 A.M., the agile intruder must have scaled an eight-foot iron fence, climbed onto the fire escape, and then jumped onto the ledge, risking a sixty-foot fall to concrete pavement. Once again, he had remained at the scene for around two hours, but there was no sign of sexual assault. And, according to Brown's sister, Viola Butler, the killer had not taken anything of value although he ransacked the place. What then was his motivation? Once more, police lightly dusted off fingerprint powder throughout the apartment and found but a single print, this one in blood on a door jamb.

The story finally came out during a circulation war among Chicago newspapers. Reporters overlooked all friendships to scoop their rivals, and every graphic detail was carried to provide readers with daily updates.

Although checking the single print against all those on file was nearly impossible, Sergeant Thomas Lafferty was ordered to try. Detective Chief Storms told his men, "We're working against time. He's killed twice, and will keep on killing until we catch him." The investigation seemed stalled, and the police were losing their race against time.

What followed was one of the most notorious crimes in the city's history. On the morning of January 7, 1946, six-year-old Suzanne Degnan was kidnapped from her bed in a North Side apartment building on Kenmore Avenue. Her father went into her room to wake her for school—it was to be Suzanne's first day back at Sacred Heart Convent School after Christmas vacation. James Degnan recently had moved to the cream-colored building to take a management position in the local office of the postwar price control administration.

Degnan found the window open, letting in the cold winter air. The bedcover was neatly folded back, something Suzanne never did, and her slippers were side by side on the rug, which was also unlike her. The apartment was located in the relatively affluent Edgewater neighborhood, where major crimes simply did not happen. In his frantic search to figure out what had occurred, Degnan discovered a piece of oil-stained paper on the floor. On it was a crudely penciled note telling him to prepare $20,000 in $5s and $10s "& waite for word." On the reverse side was scrawled, "Burn this for her safety."

Unbeknownst to Degnan, Storms ordered a body search in garbage cans and sewers across the neighborhood. Almost immediately, the case was taken over by State Attorney William Tuohy and the newly appointed police commissioner, John Prendergast. Recording equipment was set up in the family's home; Degnan begged the kidnapper not to harm Suzanne and said that he was doing everything he could to raise the money. Copies were delivered to the local radio stations with the request that the message be played at intervals throughout the day and evening. But there was no further contact from the kidnapper.

Reconstructing the crime, police found that a ladder near the garage reached about a foot below the sill. Neighbors heard dogs barking around 12:30 A.M. and again at 2:30 A.M. But what kind of kidnapper would spend two hours with his victim?

A break in the case came when Storms noticed that the "e" in the note was written as it is on a typewriter—and as it was in the "Catch Me Before I Kill More" message in the Brown murder. Meanwhile Detective Lafferty was still checking through more than a million sets of fingerprints for a match in the Brown case. When Storms asked him to compare the partial print, he was working with the Degnan ransom note. But Lafferty could not. The print left on the paper had come from another finger.

Two detectives passing by a manhole cover in the Degnan neighborhood noticed that a heavy iron lid was not quite flush with the street, even though police had already checked there on the day of the kidnapping. The officers pulled off the lid and flashed a light down the circular, brick sewer shaft. They saw a small disembodied head floating in the black water.

Police checked other sewer openings and found the rest of Suzanne's body—except for her arms—in sewers within a half mile radius of her home. One part was in a soaked shopping bag the killer apparently had used to carry the remains as he went from manhole to manhole. Only six weeks later did a power company crew find the arms in another open sewer.

A coroner's pathologist concurred from extensive chemical and microscopic testing that the girl died between 12:30 A.M. and 1 A.M., that she might have been strangled with a wire that a detective had found, and that her blonde hair was washed after she was killed. This was a third victim whose body had been cleansed. But despite the washing, there was coal dust in Suzanne's hair and on the soles of her feet, leading detectives to believe Suzanne was cut up in a cellar. A careful examination of basements in the area turned up several faint blood smears in a washtub. Police opened the drain trap and found bits of flesh and yellow hair. Several tenants recalled hearing someone running water between 2:30 A.M. and 3:30 A.M. on the morning the girl was kidnapped. Another resident said the thin door of his basement storage locker had been forced open, but the only thing missing was a shopping bag.

The *Chicago Tribune* offered a $10,000 reward for the killer, but the police had nothing but frustrating dead-ends: talking to janitors, to people who looked like someone, tracking down a laundry mark on a handkerchief found wrapped around the fatal wire, checking out crank letters and calls, and speaking to men who had the same name as the one on the laundry mark, S. Sherman. One crank letter was written in lipstick, like the "Catch Me" message, and another contained a human ear, but the handwriting on the accompanying letter did not match the ransom note Suzanne's killer had written. The police hated to think that the killer was getting away. They were unaware that they could not catch him because he was no longer trying to kill.

Police let *Chicago Daily News* staff artist Frank San Hamel photograph the ransom message as part of a newspaper story. He excitedly told Storms that by carefully examining the paper under a magnifying glass, you could see faint impressions. Police studied the note again by using a bright light held at an angle and could tell that the paper was taken from a pad on which some words had been written on a sheet above it. Hamel helped several detectives decipher the markings. They discovered a few names and parts of phone numbers, leading them to University of Chicago students and a popular restaurant near campus. But four letters that kept turning up together had no evident meaning: eire.

124 · *Homicide: 100 Years of Murder in America*

The University of Chicago was known to draw a percentage of students in the genius category, and the first nuclear reactor—the first solid proof that an atomic bomb could be built—was constructed behind the football stands for the top-secret Manhattan Project. The university's staff included a number of Nobel Prize-winning teachers, and the university itself helped the city shape the surrounding Hyde Park neighborhood. Even so, no one in authority at the university seemed to sense the urgency of the culprit's connection to the school, or, if they did, they were afraid of the bad publicity any connection might bring. After some delay, university officials turned over its complete roster of students and personnel on June 26, more than six months after Suzanne's murder.

On that same day, a young burglar was seen rifling through an empty apartment more than halfway across the city, on the North Side. As the building manager was calling the police, the janitor and a tenant ran toward the teenager. He pulled out a revolver, and they stepped back. The young man cautiously backed out of the building and ran down the street.

The first officer to arrive on the scene, Detective Tiffin Constant, chased the suspect through several backyards and over fences. The young man turned and pulled the trigger twice, but both times his gun misfired. Finally Constant grabbed the strong teenager's gunhand and forced it behind his back. The two then fell to the ground.

An off-duty officer who lived in the area was returning from a swim in the lake when he came upon the struggle. Wearing only his bathing trunks, he grabbed three clay pots containing dead geraniums and crashed them on the burglar's head, knocking him unconscious. Constant kicked away the gun and snapped on the handcuffs.

When the seventeen-year-old student was hauled into the district police station, detectives found the case against him clicking into place. His name was William George Heirens—the source of the mysterious "eire" now made sense—and, although his family lived in the adjacent suburb of Lincolnwood, he had a dormitory room at the University of Chicago. The El tracks did not come near the university, but it was just a short walk to a commuter train that could take him to the Loop stations.

The unusual name of Heirens—both sides of his family came from Luxembourg—sounded vaguely familiar to Captain Michael Ahern. He checked his records and found that the intelligent young man had been arrested for more than a dozen burglaries when he was only thirteen years old.

After some months in a private correctional school in Terre Haute, Indiana, Heirens was transferred to a regular private school near Peoria. While he was home on summer vacation, he was arrested for five more burglaries. There seemed no reason why he had committed the robberies. From all outward appearances, Heirens had a perfectly normal upbringing. His parents were moderately well off. His father, George, was a special investigator for a large steel company. The juvenile court judge set the boy free because he seemed remorseful about his acts.

Ahern and a team of detectives searched Heirens's university dorm room without waiting for a warrant. They found six suitcases full of stolen items including cameras, clothing, jewelry, furs, watches, surgical instruments, and $1,800 in war bonds. Some of the possessions were taken from the Ross and Brown apartments, but Ahern had no idea that his men had just captured the killer. He assumed Heirens was a member of a burglary gang, especially because the teenager had in his pocket a letter that talked about hiding loot, taking the rap, burning plans, and other radio-influenced bad-guy talk. The letter was signed "George M." Also in the room, the officers came across photos of Hitler and other Nazi leaders, and in searching the Heirens's suburban home detectives found several pistols and rifles.

Young Heirens recovered from his head injuries at the infirmary of the city jail, called the Bridewell. When his father went to see him, the boy acted as if he were comatose, gazing at the ceiling with a vacant stare and pretending that he could not hear the nurses and doctors.

Heirens's prints were sent to Sergeant Lafferty, who already had gone through an estimated seven thousand sets of fingerprints in hopes of finding a match for the partial impressions from the Frances Brown and Evelyn Peterson cases. When Lafferty held the cards together, he realized they could be superimposed one upon the other. But police still had no evidence that would tie Heirens to the Ross and Suzanne Degnan murders.

Doctors were sure that Heirens was faking his coma, and investigators decided to use sodium pentathol for the first time in a criminal case. During the war years, Dr. Roy Grinker of Chicago's Michael Reese Hospital had developed narcosynthesis as a way of helping traumatized service personnel recover their memories, often the first step toward physical recovery. But investigators hoped that this so-called "truth serum" would open up a new world of interrogations.

As Prosecutor Tuohy and Detective Chief Storms watched behind a screen, Heirens was wheeled into a small room. Dr. Grinker himself injected a hypodermic needle into one of the young man's veins. In about ten minutes, Heirens fell asleep. When Grinker spoke to him, Heirens replied sometimes in a low, whispery voice and at other times loudly and animated.

After a few preliminary questions, Grinker asked, "Did you kill Suzanne Degnan?" Heirens answered that his other self, "George M," went to the home, saw a ladder leaning against the building, and placed it against a window. Then he explained that "George is a bad boy" and was the one who carried the girl to someplace nearby, cut her up, and cast her body parts into the sewer openings.

After more sessions, Heirens identified his other self as "George *Murman*," which some have taken to be a version of "Murder Man." Heirens said George was five years older than he, and that they had met while he was in an Indiana reform school. They met again in Chicago in 1943 and saw each other frequently after that. Heirens added, while still under the truth serum, that right after the kidnapping he accused George of committing all the burglaries, too, and George went off to Mexico.

The accuracy of the sessions is a matter of speculation, because Heirens had used doses of sodium pentathol at the university to get high. Therefore, his injections did not affect him as fully as someone who had never been exposed to the drug.

Investigators at first assumed the teenager was telling the literal truth and tried to find George Murman. They were unaware that in order to live with the pathological part of himself, Heirens had invented someone similar but more criminal than he, and had even written a bogus letter to himself signed "George M." This was not a "split" personality or a case of multiple personalities. Heirens was never Murman, but Murman was always Heirens. Psychiatrists call the process "splitting off"; it is often seen in serial criminals.

Eventually a handcuffed Heirens led police, along with a swarm of reporters and photographers, on a site-by-site tour of the murder scenes to show how he had entered and fled. But Heirens moved about almost in a daze, as if uncertain exactly what it was he claimed to have done.

Assembling the scattered details of his background showed how such a monster came to be created—not out of evil, but from a desperate attempt to be good.

Heirens's parents, strict Catholics, were emotionally distant. As a young boy, William felt that if he became a good boy, his parents would love him. His mother later told him that all sex "is dirty" and that if he touched anyone he would get a disease. Somewhere in his early adolescence, William apparently resolved never to have sex. His misguided sexual impulses perhaps drove him to rituals paralleling seduction and intercourse, in this case theft and murder.

He was not interested just in stealing, which was why he took possessions only from apartments above the first floor. He would wander around, look over buildings, climb up, and hoist himself through a window. "I get sexual satisfaction out of breaking into a place," he told doctors and prosecutors. "If I got a real thrill, I didn't take anything."

At first he only stole. Later, he would sometimes urinate and defecate at the burglary scene, as if turning upside down his mother's grim warning that "sex is dirty." Finally, although he did not have sexual intercourse with his female victims, he would repeatedly thrust a knife into them. Sometimes he tried resisting his impulses, such as when he clubbed Peterson rather than killing her. After the act, he behaved as a lover, washing the bodies, tending to the wounds, and staying with the body for more than an hour. Although Suzanne was only a first-grade pupil, Heirens said in a confession to the police that even as he was dismembering her he thought she was a woman.

In time, the haze would leave him. He would discover himself with the victim and quickly leave. When the teenager wanted to force himself to stop killing forever, he symbolically sent George to Mexico.

Heirens's crimes did not bring him to a frenzy but rather to a calm that he craved. That allowed him to do well enough in a competitive school and to work as an usher at Orchestra Hall downtown, the home of the Chicago Symphony Orchestra. And to continue being a good boy.

However, prosecutors had a problem with the case. Everyone involved was certain Heirens was rational, but he could easily appear insane to a jury. They agreed to recommend that the teenager spend his life in prison rather than be executed. He pleaded guilty and was sentenced to three consecutive life terms.

His parents changed their name and divorced soon after the trial. Heirens earned a college degree in prison—the first person in the state to do so—and has been a model prisoner. He lives not in a cell but in a dormitorylike room with a television set and art supplies. He remains the longest-held prisoner in Illinois history.

The Black Dahlia

A beautiful woman was stabbed to death in the Los Angeles area; a media circus followed and, officially, the case remains unsolved. No, this was not the Nicole Simpson murder; it was the terrifying and haunting killing of a failed actress who came to be known as "The Black Dahlia."

A housewife and her three-year-old daughter were on their way to a shoe-repair shop on the gray morning of January 15, 1947. The woman saw something in the weeds and discovered the horrible remains in a vacant lot at 39th and Norton.

The corpse was almost paper white. There were numerous slash marks across the victim's face, breasts, and lower torso. Her body was severed at the waist, and both parts were gruesomely aligned about ten inches apart. Her legs were spread wide apart.

Sergeant Harry Hanson was one of the first officers to arrive. Hanson had written a handbook on the necessity of keeping a crime scene intact, so he must have been infuriated when reporters trampled through the lot almost as soon as the police arrived. The weeds were soon dotted with cigarette butts, footprints, and discarded flashbulbs. Hanson called for backup to document and photograph the scene, and two hundred fifty detectives and patrol officers spent the day fanning out through the neighborhood, ringing doorbells, and stopping neighbors.

The victim's face was so severely slashed that it was impossible to photograph her for identification. Medical pathologists studying the body found that a piece of skin cut from her left thigh was stuffed into her rectum. There were some bruises from a beating and rope marks indicating that she might have been hog-tied before her body was cut up.

To learn the name of every sex offender in the city, detectives went to the office of police psychiatrist Paul DeRiver, who had spoken to every offender jailed on sex-related crimes in the past ten years. All of them were still in prison, had died, or had alibis.

Fingerprints showed that the victim had never been arrested in Los Angeles. Investigators wanted to send a copy of the fingerprints to the FBI lab in Washington, D.C., but there was some worry that the mail plane might encounter winter storms to the east, and sending the prints by train would take too long for a quick arrest. Someone suggested using the *Los Angeles Examiner*'s new wirephoto capability. In return for the unprecedented request, the paper could have exclusive details.

As soon as the wirephoto service opened at 4 A.M., a sheet of prints was sent over instantaneously. The FBI reported back that the copy was too blurry to classify. The *Examiner* soon sent an eight-inch by ten-inch enlargement. Within minutes, the police had a name—Elizabeth Short. The victim's prints had been taken during the war when she applied for a civilian job at the Lompoc army base near Santa Barbara, California.

More than just her name came over on the curled paper; police learned that she was born in Hyde Park, Massachusetts, that her family came on hard times after the crash of 1929, when the girl was five. Her father, Cleo Short, gave up his business of constructing miniature golf courses and abandoned the family. Short's mother, Phoebe, worked as a store clerk and held other jobs to feed her five daughters. For a while the family was on welfare.

Short struck out on her own at sixteen, working that winter as a waitress in Florida. She was attracted to service personnel, starting with the pilots at the army air corps base in Miami. She acted older than her age. In 1942, her father sent her bus fare so she could visit him at the Mare Naval Base in Vallejo, California. But after six months, Cleo Short complained about his daughter's laziness, about how she was spending his money to go running around with sailors. She moved from one California city to another. At Camp Cook in Lompoc, soldiers training at a tank division voted her the "Camp Cutie." Short and some other girls were arrested for underage drinking with sailors, and she was sent back to Massachusetts.

It came as no surprise when investigators learned that young, pretty Short then came to California to be in the movies. With her long jet black hair and her fondness for lacy black dresses, she was a striking sight to behold. But Short suffered from asthma, and sometimes thought her condition and the lack of stamina she complained of as a result prevented her from building a career. A pathologist discovered that she had an undeveloped vagina, which would have made it impossible for her to have normal sexual relations.

The more police learned about Short, the more inevitable her murder seemed. One of her USO friends in 1944 was Georgette Bauerdorf. The two would go barhopping along Sunset Strip, often partying with service personnel. But then Bauerdorf was strangled with a towel and her body violated after her death. The killer left her nude from the waist down in a bathtub. Acquaintances told the police that Bauerdorf had become afraid of one of her boyfriends, a tall serviceman, and refused to go out with him again.

In 1945, Short drifted back to Florida, where she fell in love with an airman, Major Matt Gordon, who was later assigned to Long Beach, California. Short stayed in a hotel with him when he was on leave, but he told her that he was not ready for marriage, perhaps because of her flirtations with other men. Not wanting to admit the collapse of her hopes, Short told others that they were engaged or already married.

Soon after the major walked out on her, two soldiers began calling Beth "The Black Dahlia" after a recent Raymond Chandler film, *The Blue Dahlia,* starring Alan Ladd and Veronica Lake. When the papers learned of the casual nickname, Short received in death the fame she had sought in life.

Every attempt to entice public cooperation in the case either led to a dead end or backfired. A police artist created a touched-up picture of how Short might have looked without her facial wounds. Detectives hit the streets with two hundred copies, and the sketch was shown in the newspapers. A barrage of calls came in as fretting husbands and parents reported that the Black Dahlia could be their missing loved one. The number of false leads overwhelmed the department and set back its investigation for weeks without providing a single lead.

By questioning a number of men, investigators put together much of Short's life in Hollywood, except for her final week. That was where the trail ended and remained for decades. Over time, the officers retired one by one, and few people remembered the specifics of the Black Dahlia case.

In the 1980s, a man named Arnold Smith paid someone to deliver to homicide detectives a nine-minute audiotape of what he supposedly knew of the killing, saying that Short was imprisoned and stabbed by someone other than himself in a house at 31st and San Pedro, close to the vacant lot where her body was not so much dumped as put on ghastly display.

Smith's name was in the police files as a sodomite who hung out with female impersonators in skid-row bars. Police became intrigued because some of the details he gave were similar to the Bauerdorf killing. Smith claimed that a casual acquaintance named Morrison had talked to him about picking up young women downtown and choking them, also about the hog-tying and raping of waitresses.

Smith related that Morrison had picked up Short because she had no place to go and let her sleep in his hotel room. She told him he would be disappointed with her. Smith—who insisted he was not Morrison—said Morrison told him a few days later that he had taken Short to the ramshackle house, gave her some beer, hit her, locked her in, and hit her some more. Smith claimed that Morrison did not intend to kill her but things got out of hand, and then he felt he had to kill her. Afterward, Morrison cut her up, cleaned the body in a tub, put the pieces in a trunk, and shoved all of her clothes into the city's storm drain.

The police often heard pathological killers confess by way of telling a story they claimed to have heard from someone else. Why would Smith withhold this information for so long unless he, indeed, was the killer and wanted to talk about it now that he was in his sixties? Investigators set up a meeting with Smith, alias Jack Wilson, in his room at San Francisco's Holland Hotel on 7th Street. But before he could make a statement, Smith dropped his cigarette while drunk and died in the ensuing fire.

In 1992, there was another flurry of interest in the case when a singer and publicist named Jan Knowlton came forward claiming that she had reclaimed memories of her father killing Short and of her helping him. The press and talk shows eagerly picked up the story, and Knowlton helped write a book called *Daddy Was the Black Dahlia Killer,* but the police found too many discrepancies to act on her information. And so the murder remains a fascinating puzzle for Los Angeles police and armchair sleuths the world over.

Lonely Hearts

Before meeting Martha Beck, Raymond Fernandez was a two-bit Romeo in his mid-thirties. He was born in Hawaii to Spanish parents, lived much of his life in the mainland United States, went to Spain as a young man to fight with Franco's right-wing forces in the Civil War, and then switched sides and served with British intelligence on Gibraltar in World War II. He married a Spanish woman, had four children, and left his family to seek work in America. For his passage, he was employed on an oil tanker in December 1945, where he sustained a brain injury when hit by a falling hatch. Whether or not the accident caused his subsequent behavior, he seemed to undergo a severe personality change.

No longer shy around women, Fernandez took up with prostitutes, served time in federal prison for theft, and became a disciple of applied voodoo. He became convinced that he could hypnotize women, even from a distance, and make them fall in love with him. He abandoned plans to bring his family to America and began communicating with women through lonely hearts clubs. These were not organizations but rather letter exchange forums for which men and women paid a nominal fee. When it came time for Fernandez to meet a woman, he wore a slick black toupee to hide the long scar across his forehead.

He treated these lonely widows and spinsters in their fifties and sixties to dinner, charmed them, had sex with them—sometimes seducing two or three women the same week—and found ways to persuade them to hand over their money. He had so much gall that he went on a pretend honeymoon with Jane Thompson to Spain and introduced her to his real wife. The odd triangle stayed together until Fernandez and Thompson had a quarrel in their hotel room. The next morning, a maid found Thompson dead from what authorities attributed to natural causes.

The bereaved "husband" sailed alone to New York with the lease to Thompson's large apartment. But in a magnanimous gesture, he allowed her mother to remain living in the home when he moved in. Despite the new address, he was up to his old tricks.

One of the names received in response to his lonely hearts ads was that of Martha Beck, an obese twenty-seven-year-old nurse who worked at a home for disabled children. Martha had not sent the letter herself, but she had known loneliness all her life. She had always been ridiculed by others in Milton, Florida, about her weight, which doctors attributed to a glandular condition. She was raped repeatedly at thirteen by her own brother. Her mother blamed her, not him, and kept her cloistered away from other males. The girl developed a powerful sex drive, presumably from her glandular condition. Loneliness, sexual cravings, hostility, and a lack of self-worth created teeming impulses she suppressed day after day.

For a while, Martha had a job working with female corpses at a mortician's in Florida. Then she was hired at a hospital on a military base in northern California. She hung out at bus and train stations on her free time to pick up men. She became pregnant, underwent treatment for hysteria, and fled back to Pensacola. She made up a fantasy husband—one supposedly killed in the war—and bought engagement and wedding rings as proof of his existence. After the birth of her first child, she became pregnant again and insisted that the father, a bus driver named Beck, marry her. She had her second child, but Beck spent most of the time away, and they divorced.

As a crude joke, someone apparently sent Martha's name to Mother Diane's Friendly Club for Lonely Hearts. Martha cried when she learned of it, but then paid the $5 fee and wrote that she was "witty, vivacious, and oozed personality." Martha did not mention her weight or her two children.

Fernandez sent Martha letters about how he had been guided to her by a "psychic power" and how their souls "had been in love since the dawn of creation." Then he sent her a telegram announcing he would arrive in Pensacola on December 28, 1947.

This was, for America, perhaps the final months of its sexual innocence. In the next year, the first Kinsey Report would claim that sex—and every kind of sex—was much more prevalent than most people had realized. Whether agreeing or disagreeing with the findings, even newspapers were discussing the subject. But for now, sex was still a forbidden subject.

As much as possible, Fernandez had made himself resemble the current movie heartthrob Charles Boyer. At first he was somewhat taken aback by Martha's size. They made the oddest of odd couples, this charming slender man and the three hundred-pound woman who repulsed most men. She introduced him to her children, served him a fancy meal in her apartment, and the two spent a wildly intimate night together.

When he returned to New York, she wrote him a suicide note and inhaled stove-gas fumes until collapsing. Police arrived in time and revived her. She or a friend of hers forwarded the suicide note to Fernandez, and he panicked at the thought of an inquiry. He wrote back about his sorrow, beseeching forgiveness and inviting Martha to stay a week or two in the New York building he shared with Thompson's mother.

When Martha arrived, Fernandez for once was honest. He told her about his life as a swindler, and he said his schemes would be more convincing if she could pose as his sister. She sent her two children back to her mother in Pensacola.

For the next eleven months, Raymond Fernandez and Martha Beck traveled around the country meeting middle-aged women through lonely hearts ads. Typically, the couple would spend a few days at the woman's home. Fernandez, overcome by love, would suggest marriage, and sometimes he would sleep with the woman as an affirmation of his affection. Once Fernandez and Martha obtained the woman's money or property, they would go on to the next woman.

There was always sexual tension in these hop-and-skip, three-way relationships. Martha would be jealous of the victim being fleeced, but Fernandez usually found time to appease her.

After selling the lease to the Thompson apartment, Fernandez wooed Myrtle Young in Arkansas. This whirlwind romance led to marriage. Fernandez took his bride to

Chicago. For three days, the seething Martha, the dear sister, slept in the same bed as Myrtle to keep Fernandez from enjoying his matrimonial privileges. Eventually one of the two swindlers—it remains a mystery—gave Myrtle a heavy dose of barbiturates that knocked her out for twenty-four hours. When she awoke, still groggy, they put her on a bus back to Arkansas. She was carried off comatose and died in a Little Rock hospital the following day.

It was 1948 when Fernandez and Beck met their next victim, Janet Fay, a sixty-six-year-old widow in Albany, New York. Fay's stepdaughter, Mary, received a note supposedly from Janet saying that she had met the man of her dreams. Fay asked Mary to have American Express send all her boxes and trunks to Florida. But the letter was carefully typewritten, with no mistakes, although Fay had never typed a letter in her life.

Police discovered Fay's body in a shallow grave in the cellar of a Queens house Fernandez had rented. Martha had beaten the woman to death.

The couple moved on to forty-one-year-old Delphine Downing, a Michigan widow with a two-year-old girl. Fernandez, alias Charles Martin, introduced his "sister" as the nurse who had delivered the girl. Then he insinuated himself into Downing's bed while Martha seethed. The little girl, Rainelle, began to cry. Instead of calming her, Martha kept choking the toddler until Fernandez ran across the room and stopped her. The little girl had red marks on her throat that Downing was bound to discover. Then the marriage would be called off, and perhaps she would go to the police.

Fernandez found Downing's late husband's service revolver, returned to the bedroom, and shot Downing as she slept. They decided simply to leave the child somewhere, but when the little girl wouldn't stop crying, Martha took her to a washtub in the basement and held her head under the water. Mother and daughter were buried in graves hammered and dug into the cellar floor, and then covered with cement.

At 4 P.M. the following day, before Fernandez and Beck had a chance to leave the house, some neighbors dropped by to visit Downing. The killers explained their presence by claiming that they were there to buy some household items from the woman. After a little double-talk, the neighbors went away. Fernandez and Martha should have left town, but they decided to relax and see a picture at a nearby movie theater. Neighbors—suspicious about the explanations they were given—contacted the Grand Rapids police. When Fernandez and Martha returned from the show, they saw two officers waiting for them. The couple allowed a search of the house, and the police officers instantly became suspicious of the two patches of fresh cement.

Usually suspects are questioned separately, but speaking to Fernandez and Martha together worked. Fernandez boasted about all the women he had charmed, and Martha agreed with everything he said. Then he reportedly told the officers, "You got me dead to rights." After all, they would rather be charged in Michigan, which had no death penalty.

But the two were extradited to New York to stand trial for murdering Fay. Their defense contended that the two killers were involved in a peculiar sort of sexual-murder ritual the French call *folie à deux,* a criminal madness cultivated and shared by two minds, neither of whom would commit such crimes alone, as in the Leopold and Loeb case. Fernandez and

Martha were examined by so many investigators—from probation officers to psychiatrists—that the court record grew to more than forty-five thousand pages.

The carnival that was played out before the jury had Fernandez irretrievably losing his conscience with the conk on his head from a ship's hatch and Martha becoming a psychopathic personality because of her infatuation with her lover and her belief that she had been hypnotized. As a reporter noted, "Even the defendants at times seemed to be playing for the grandstand instead of fighting for their lives." After forty-four days of trial, both Fernandez and Martha were convicted of first degree murder. They died in the electric chair twelve minutes apart in Sing Sing Prison on March 8, 1951.

REFERENCES

Brophy, John. *The Meaning of Murder.* New York: Thomas Y. Crowell, 1966.

DeFord, Miriam Allen. *Murderers Sane and Mad.* New York: Abelard-Schuman, 1965.

Ellroy, James. *The Black Dahlia.* New York: Mysterious Press, 1989.

Fido, Martin. *The Chronicle of Crime.* New York: Carroll & Graf Publishers, 1993.

Franklin, Charles. *The World's Worst Murderers.* New York: Taplinger Publishing, 1965.

Freeman, Lucy. *Catch Me Before I Kill More.* New York: Crown Publishers, 1955.

Gillmore, John. *Severed: The True Story of the Black Dahlia Murder.* San Francisco: Zanja Press, 1994.

Knowlton, Janice. *Daddy Was the Black Dahlia Killer.* New York: Pocket Books, 1995.

Lane, Roger. *Murder in America.* Columbus, Ohio: Columbia University Press, 1997.

Marriner, Brian. *On Death's Bloody Trail: Murder and the Art of Forensic Science.* New York: St. Martin's Press, 1991.

Nash, Jay Robert. *Crime Chronology: A Worldwide Record: 1900–1983.* New York: Facts on File, 1984.

———. *Bloodletters and Badmen.* New York: M. Evans & Co., 1995.

———. *Encyclopedia of World Crime.* Wilmette, Ill.: Crime Books, 1989–1990.

New York Times, June 5, 1942.

————, September 7, 1949.

Odell, Robin. *Landmarks in 20th Century Murder.* London: Headline, 1995.

Radin, Edward D. "The Other Man," *Crimes of Passion.* New York: G.P. Putnam, 1953.

Wilson, Colin. *Written in Blood: Detectives & Detection.* New York: Warner Books, 1989.

————. *The Killers Among Us: Book I. Sex, Madness & Mass Murder.* New York: Warner Books, 1995.

Wolf, Marvin J., and Mader, Katherine. "Famous in Death: Elizabeth Short," *Fallen Angels: Chronicles of L.A. Crime and Mystery.* New York: Ballantine, 1986.

The 1950s

D wight D. Eisenhower was elected the thirty-fourth President of the United States on the campaign slogan "I Like Ike" simply because no one could possibly dislike this middle-of-the-road, golf-playing chief executive who had once headed the Allied forces in World War II. Complacency reigned. Dreamy ballads had grown stale, and the record-buying public sought out novelty tunes such as "If I Knew You Were Coming I'd Have Baked a Cake" and "How Much Is That Doggie in the Window?" The image of the age was the corporate executive, whether in serious studies such as *The Organization Man* or novels like *Executive Suite* and *The Man in the Grey Flannel Suit*. Most women had their futures handed down to them as housewives and caregivers—and nothing more. Every Monday night on TV, Lucy Ricardo's innocuous duplicity and bungled schemes appealed to millions. Because of erudite presidential hopeful Adlai Stevenson's baldness, intellectuals were flippantly called "eggheads" by their political counterparts.

The Eisenhower years saw the American landscape transformed by highways, allowing people to speed across the country in just a few days. Slums were torn down, leading to slogans such as "Urban renewal is people removal." Life became faster and faster, and distances became shorter and shorter. Regionalism began to fade.

As parents tried to produce children à la cookie-cutter patterns, the seeds of rebellion were planted among the nation's teenagers. Boys who could get away with it slicked back their hair in a D.A. (duck's ass), while their fathers and uncles wore crew cuts. Millions of teenagers left theaters showing James Dean's *Rebel Without a Cause* convinced they had to create their own world because no one else could understand them.

Yet there was a dark side to the 1950s. Officially the war in Korea was just a U.N. peacekeeping action. Many American recruits bristled with leftover fervor from the "Crusade in Europe" their fathers had fought. But they would soon be overwhelmed by China-backed North Korean forces and by the futility of fighting another country's civil war. Prisoners were starved and brainwashed, wounded soldiers came back addicted to drugs, and the narcotics trade gradually took root in America.

U.S. Senator Joe McCarthy of Wisconsin created a Red Scare, and a conservative upsurge found a pretext for persecuting liberals. People who adhered to the principles of the founding fathers were called un-American or worse. Thousands of families built bomb shelters that would have been ineffective in a real attack, and general prosperity lived side by side with a vague tension. The first foothold in the long struggle for civil rights was the U.S. Supreme Court's *Brown v. Board of Education* decision in 1954, ending "separate but equal" schools for blacks and for whites. But the number of memberships in hate groups increased as whites felt threatened by competition for jobs.

A glamorized criminal of the time was the compulsive sexual offender Caryl Chessman, who won one stay of execution after another by finding new reasons for appeal, allowing him to write articles and a best-selling autobiography, *Cell 2455, Death Row*, in which he detailed his innocence. Authorities said Chessman was a lover's lane rapist whose voyeuristic lust had led him to attack young women after seeing them make love with other men. He drew the women to his auto by making it resemble a squad car, complete with a flashing red light and a police band radio. After his arrest under the Lindbergh law, the *Los Angeles Daily News* called Chessman a "criminal genius," and he flashily but unsuccessfully represented himself in his trial. Chessman was convicted and eventually executed.

Beginning in 1957, Los Angeles TV repairman Harvey Murray Glatman posed as a photographer and took at least three beautiful young women to the Mojave Desert, where he tied them up, raped them, strangled them, and hid their bodies in wilderness graves. Glatman was caught when a police officer saw him struggling with a woman who refused to go with him. He died in San Quentin's gas chamber.

In November 1959, prize-winning author Truman Capote was driving through the Midwest when he heard news of robbers who had slaughtered an entire family in Holcomb, Kansas. There was nothing in Capote's background to draw him to the crime. But the author of *Breakfast at Tiffany's* was fascinated at the thought of evil in the heartland, and he spent weeks attempting to speak to everyone in the town.

He learned that drifters Richard Hickock and Perry Smith had gone to the large farmhouse to rob Herbert Clutter. Dick had done prison time, and was full of fun. He falsely boasted that he had beaten a man to death, just to make him seem awesome to his somewhat passive companion. Perry was still injured from an auto accident seven years before, leaving him an aspirin addict and in need of companionship.

Like certain chemicals, two otherwise relatively harmless people can explode when brought together. The two men killed Clutter, his wife, and their two daughters with virtually point-blank shotgun blasts. Then they were tracked down and hanged, providing Capote with the final chapter of *In Cold Blood*. Although he invented dialogue and changed a few details, the book was such a best-seller that it virtually created the true-crime genre.

During this same period, rural police discovered unspeakable horrors in a nine-room farmhouse in Senator McCarthy's own state.

Psycho!

In Plainfield, Wisconsin, roosters crowed just before dawn, cowbells softly clanged twice a day, and dogs barked at passing cars. Summer featured fields of corn and wheat, the late fall was deer hunting season, and winter was characterized by barren ground and short days. The horror began on November 16, 1957, when Frank Worden returned from the first day of the hunting season, and could not find his mother in their Main Street hardware store. What he did find was a pool of blood with drag marks leading toward the door.

Bringing in officers from other counties, police officials laid a map of Plainfield on a desk and divided it into four sections, assigning a team of two officers to each quadrant. Officer Dan Chase and Deputy Waushara County Sheriff Leon Murty drove down a dark lonely road to the home of handyman Ed Gein, nearly five miles from the station house. Forgetting how fast night comes in mid-November, the officers had forgotten their flashlights. They knocked on the door, waited, and knocked again. The door slowly opened by itself. Murty lit a match, saw nothing unusual, and the two left the premises.

Back in town, Officer Chase found Gein sitting in his pickup truck, his outline illuminated by the porch light of a nearby house. When Chase asked Gein what he had been doing since 6 A.M., the small, middle-aged man gave two somewhat conflicting accounts, then blurted out that someone was trying to frame him for Mrs. Worden's murder. But Chase had never mentioned anything about the fifty-eight-year-old woman. Chase radioed the station that he was bringing in Gein for questioning. Word quickly spread of the impending arrest, and Chase had to make Gein lie on the floor of the police car to protect him from violence. Some of the farmers milling around the station house shouted, "Hang him!"

The Waushara County sheriff and Police Captain Lloyd Schoephoerster of Green County decided to see Gein's place after hearing Chase's radio message. They found the doors locked, but the toolshed door was not closed all the way. Schoephoerster flipped on a flashlight, and a shiver ran through him when he saw the nude, beheaded body of Mrs. Worden hoisted to the ceiling by a rope-and-pulley system such as hunters used for eviscerating deer. They passed barrels of junk and piles of discarded clothes. Upstairs, they spied a skull in their shaky flashlight beam. By then, Murty had returned to Gein's home. After discovering a pistol under a pillow, he pushed open the door to Gein's bedroom and found a human head preserved in a plastic bag. Schroephoerster also came across a large piece of skin. The police captain raised the flesh over the flashlight beam. It was a human face with wisps of hair still attached to it. The eye sockets had been cut out. Murty exclaimed, "My God, that's Mary Hogan!" The woman had disappeared three years earlier.

Police officers who went into the farmhouse to search for the murder weapon and other evidence came back with sickly, ghastly expressions. Although police reports tend to be generic and impersonal, Schoephoerster could not help emoting in his account:

> *I had a feeling I never had in my life because I had never seen anything like this. It was so horrible. We found skulls and masks; that is, the skin portion of the head had been stripped from the skull and preserved and put into plastic bags. There were several of those skulls. We found a box that had women's [sexual] organs in it and I noticed one small one was gilded a gold color with a ribbon tied on it; I believe a red ribbon. We found leg bones and discovered the chair seats were made out of human skin . . . There was a knife handle*

made of bone and lamp shades from skin and there was one upper portion of a woman's torso from the shoulders, cut down both sides to the waist, with the breasts and everything completely tanned [processed into human leather].

A cold front passed over Plainfield that night, and the light rain turned into slush and flurries. Because Gein would not confess despite the staggering evidence, he was smuggled out of the police station after midnight, when the crowd had dispersed. Gein finally gave a statement at 2 A.M., but rather than being contrite, he seemed to enjoy all the fuss being made over him.

Gein said that from 1947 to 1954 he dug up nine or ten bodies from three cemeteries in the area, took them home for his own amusement, and returned a few to their graves. The others he cut up for their parts. Gein said he intended to cut up the body of Mrs. Worden and eat it. Investigators suspected that he had cannibalized some of the earlier bodies.

Gein told officer Chase that he would put on a mask of a woman's facial skin and her female organs over his own and parade around in them in his yard in the moonlight. He kept skulls on his bedposts as ornaments and perhaps for company.

Every room was a mess except his mother's, which Gein had nailed shut after her death so that it would never change. Hidden under a mattress in the kitchen was a bag with Mrs. Worden's freshly severed head. Hooks were driven into her ears for some sort of planned display, like a hunting trophy. An X-ray showed that she was shot in the head, but the wound was not fatal. Police supposed that Gein slit her throat.

Although Gein admitted murdering Mary Hogan and Mrs. Worden, he was believed to have been involved in the disappearance of two teenage runaways and a salesman who vanished while driving through town.

Gein's father often drank and was irritable, so as a boy he drew closer to his domineering mother. The woman, a strict German Lutheran, seemed to have disliked males and may have dreaded intercourse. She drilled into the boy that sex was something unpleasant and should be permitted only in marriage. Perhaps as a result, he said, he never had sexual relationships with anyone. As is sometimes the case with pathological killers, Gein's denial of sex appears to be linked to suppressed thoughts of incest. He became withdrawn and had difficulty relating to people. His father died in 1940 of a heart attack. His brother died in a marsh fire in 1944, and there was some suspicion that Gein might have had a hand in it. His bedridden mother died of a stroke the next year, cutting him off from all human contact except his trips to town and a few passing strangers. But he was never fully alone. Sometimes he felt that his dead mother could talk to him while he was falling asleep and that she was sometimes with him.

As to why his life became so bizarre after his mother's death, Gein said he had wished when he was a boy that his penis could have been replaced by female sexual organs. Perhaps his mother had sometimes expressed a wish that he was a girl, and Gein thought she would love him more if he were transformed. Grave robbing allowed him to wear the faces and severed sexual parts of a woman, kept in place by panties, for an hour or so. He admitted that the first woman he killed, Mary Hogan, resembled his mother.

Gein denied that he had sex with the bodies of his victims or the women he had unearthed in the cemeteries. He said he could not even remember killing Mrs. Hogan, but that the time when she vanished "seems like a dream."

Some criminologists have said that serial killers should be confined with video monitoring at all times to study their behavior. But some, including Gein, have been remarkably ordinary and agreeable in prison. The human monster with the sly grin was rather liked by the staff of the Mendota Mental Institute facility in Wisconsin until his death from cancer in 1984.

After Gein's arrest, his "house of horror" was to be auctioned off to someone intending to turn it into a tourist attraction, but one night someone in the town set fire to the home and it burned to the ground. Yet the horror has not died even now. When Gein was arrested, struggling young writer Robert Bloch, who lived about fifty miles from Plainfield, was fascinated by what he was hearing. Unable to afford bus fare to the town, Bloch relied on rumors and imagination to turn the story into the novel *Psycho,* which spawned a 1960 Alfred Hitchcock movie that frightened audiences almost as much as Gein's victims had startled the police. Other elements in Gein's story occasionally appear in other horror films, including the skin masks.

In the period of Gein's crimes, there were two developments in criminalistics that were later to become essential in homicide investigations. One emerged from a laboratory and the other from the deductive mind of a criminal psychiatrist.

In 1953, English physicist M.H.F. Wilkins began working with Cambridge University colleague Francis Crick and an American, John Watson, on the acids comprising the cell nucleus. The result was the discovery of DNA, which by the mid-1990s could be used as well as a fingerprint in tracking rapists and sexual killers.

In 1956, psychiatrist James Brussel sat back in his chair in Manhattan's state office building and provided authorities with a virtual photograph of the "mad bomber" who had terrorized the city with crude explosive devices for sixteen years. At least thirty bombs had exploded, many of them directed at Consolidated Edison property but some in movie theaters and one in a train station. The police thought Brussel might be able to provide a little insight.

"Listen," he said, "I don't know what you expect me to do. If experts haven't cracked the case in more than ten years of trying, what could I hope to contribute?" But he tried anyway.

Brussel stated that the bomber was most likely a man, probably of Eastern European descent, suffering from paranoia, in his forties or fifties, probably Roman Catholic, of an athletic build. He was otherwise law-abiding, had at least two years of high school, and possibly was someone who had worked for Edison until he was discharged for sickness or an accident.

He probably lived with a female relative such as a sister, his mother was dead or had been separated from the family, and his father had been pushy. He had no friends, was single, possibly a virgin, was polite and formal, attended church regularly, wore no jewelry or flashy clothes, and probably lived in Connecticut, possibly Bridgeport, which had a large Polish-American population.

Not all this was said in a flash; the discussion with a police lieutenant lasted three or four hours. Finally, the lieutenant asked, "Is that all?"

"One more thing," the psychiatrist said with his eyes closed. "When you catch him—and I have no doubt that you will—he'll be wearing a double-breasted suit."

"Jesus!" one of the detectives exclaimed.

"And it will be buttoned."

When the police arrested George Metesky, he was living with his sister in Waterbury, Connecticut. And to the surprise of everyone but Brussel, detectives found Metesky wearing a double-breasted suit, buttoned.

Brussel's various assumptions had described Metesky almost as well as if the psychiatrist had actually known the mad bomber. Some of his assumptions were based on logical conclusions from the crimes as well as Metesky's letters denouncing Con Ed. A few were hunches. One was a lucky guess on the basis of faulty research—that paranoids usually had athletic builds. Later research showed that there is no correlation.

Brussel's assessment of the mad bomber set the stage for the development of the field of criminal profiling.

But as early as the 1960s, Brussel was cautioning that such detailed profiling can be effective with only certain types of criminals, generally paranoids. Even so, authorities have found profiling useful in learning where to concentrate resources in serial crimes. Later developments showed that police must keep in mind that a profile based on faulty or insufficient information can actually allow criminals to slip away. For example, a profile assuming there is a single killer is worthless when two people are involved, as it was in the search for the Hillside strangler(s).

Some technological developments in the decade would also aid in crime detection, such as the invention of the ion microscope by F.W. Muller in 1956. The completion of transatlantic cable service the same year improved communication among the police in the United States, Great Britain, and Europe. But it took time for these advancements to be incorporated into day-to-day investigative work. For the most part, police work in the 1950s was confined to the simple question-and-answer method shown on the TV series "Dragnet," although officers also used newspapers and newscasts to turn up evidence, which is exactly what solved the murder of a girl across the bay from San Francisco.

Trace Evidence

Fourteen-year-old Stephanie Bryan disappeared on the warm afternoon of April 28, 1955, in a quiet neighborhood of Berkeley, California. She was such a shy, well-behaved, and studious girl—the daughter of a radiologist—that the community was shocked. Bryan was last seen saying good-bye to a friend near the Claremont Hotel in the foothills above Tilden Park. Possible leads poured in when the search was featured in the *San Francisco Chronicle*. Several people reported seeing a girl who looked like Bryan getting into a car near the hotel or on Highway 24 heading for Contra Costa County.

Police chief August Vollmer was known for advocating scientific investigation over the less effective method of knocking on hundreds of doors. But first his men needed something to go on. The police offered a $2,500 reward for information solving the girl's disappearance. This led to more calls, one from a recently released mental patient who erroneously claimed he had taken the girl.

The first real lead came on the eleventh day. An electrician named David Tyree said he discovered a French textbook in a field in Franklin Canyon, in Contra Costa County. Unaware that the book may have belonged to the missing girl, Tyree threw away the soiled paper cover and gave the book to his teenage son. The boy turned over the volume to the police, but it did not have any useful fingerprints, and not a single clue turned up in an inch-by-inch search of the canyon.

An Alameda woman named Georgia Abbott called to say that she had been looking in a box for materials to use in a costume for an amateur theatrical production when she noticed a leather handbag she had never seen before. Inside was a wallet containing Bryan's student ID card and an unfinished letter. While her twenty-seven-year-old husband, Burton, was talking to a chessmate, she brought up the card and asked, "Isn't this the girl who disappeared?"

"I can't figure out how it got there," her husband said. "I'm positive I didn't put it there."

Burton's chessmate suggested they call the police.

When the officers rushed to the home, Burton suggested that someone might have left the bag when their garage was used as a polling place in May. Police were skeptical, and Burton Abbott allowed them to search the basement and the garden.

The next day, officers with picks and shovels found nothing in the garden but in the basement uncovered schoolbooks, notebooks, and two library books Bryan had borrowed—and a brassiere belonging to the girl. Under grilling at the station, Burton steadfastly kept to his theory that the killer must have planted the evidence on election day. He explained over and over to them that on the afternoon the girl disappeared, he was driving to his family's cabin three hundred miles away for the opening of the fishing season. He even provided a list of his stops for gasoline and coffee. Burton also voluntarily took a lie-detector test, but the results came back inconclusive.

Police thought they had enough circumstantial evidence to consider him a good suspect, but the U.C. Berkeley accounting student seemed too ordinary to be their man. Burton was a war veteran studying under the G.I. Bill. While stationed in Kentucky years earlier, he developed double pneumonia, which brought out his latent tuberculosis. One lung and five of his ribs had to be removed. At the time of his questioning in the Bryan case, he weighed only one hundred thirty pounds. He had trouble breathing and lifting heavy objects, although his condition was improving. His only recreation was fishing in the mountains, and he spent most of his leisure time reading or visiting friends at a coffee shop near his home.

Trinity County Deputy Sheriff Harold Jackson and two half-bloodhound, bear-hunting dogs searched the area around Burton's ramshackle cabin two and a half miles north of a town called Wildwood. Jackson had the dogs sniff Bryan's brassiere for her lingering scent and set them loose. The hounds ranged for awhile, then headed up a steep hillside to a thicket of manzanita bushes, where they started stomping and baying impatiently. Jackson and the Berkeley officers noticed a loose pile of dirt. They carefully removed the earth and saw a badly decomposed female body, which had been attacked by wildlife. Her panties were around her throat, and her skull had been bashed. The search for Stephanie Bryan was over.

Police roped off the area as the coroner and every available officer headed for the scene. Abbott seemed dazed when police came to arrest him a short time later.

Abbott's trial drew together half a century of advances in science and criminal psychology. The early part of the lengthy proceedings was filled with conflicting testimony about whether Abbott could lift an adolescent girl and where he was at the time Bryan disappeared. There were also gaps in the circumstantial case, such as why anyone would bury the belongings of the girl so far from her body.

Prosecutors called to the stand Dr. Paul Kirk, a criminologist from the University of California. He mesmerized the spectators with trace evidence he had found during hours of study through a high-powered microscope. The mat in the defendant's car still had tiny specks of human blood. Woolen fibers carefully lifted from the auto matched fibers in the sweater the girl was wearing, and a few strands of hairs left behind were identical to sample hairs removed from her body. In addition, clay from Burton's boots matched the earth at the *bottom* of Stephanie's shallow grave.

In closing arguments, prosecutors used Abbott's ordinariness against him. They told the jury that he was a sexual psychopath, and that his pose of deliberate politeness "was a symptom of the disordered personality," a mark of some pathological killers.

After six days of deliberations, the jurors found Abbott guilty of both kidnapping and murder. Burton still professed his innocence as he was led to the gas chamber at San Quentin. He took a breath while strapped to the chair and held it for as long as he could.

The Exterminating Angels

The late 1950s were the age of the rebel, even for those who were never aware of what they were rebelling against. Nineteen-year-old Charles Starkweather was a good-looking young man who thought he resembled James Dean—in looks. Inside, Starkweather was cold and unfeeling.

Starkweather came from the poor branch of a family that traced its roots hundreds of years back to Britain's Isle of Man. His people were good and law-abiding but never rose from the working class.

Starkweather's job was to haul away trash from behind the homes of the wealthy in Lincoln, Nebraska. Often, while driving his garbage truck, he would stick out his head and shout to strangers, "Go to hell!" As he later told people, he felt everything was closing in on him. He claimed he knew the reason: It was all those rich people who, he supposed, were looking down on him. "The more I looked at people the more I hated them, because I knew they wasn't any place for me with the kind of people I knowed."

He went around with fourteen-year-old Caril Ann Fugate, an average-looking student who had come to hate her mother, Velda, and her stepfather, Marion Bartlett. Fugate was an injustice collector, too, telling herself over and over that her parents favored their cute blonde little girl over her. Fugate also hated her parents because they did not like her new boyfriend.

Psychiatrists maintain there are some disturbed people who need a partner to validate their fantasies. In effect, the acts of the accomplice make the fantasy element real. Usually such people are said to have "borderline personalities," but the label does not matter. Starkweather and Fugate should never have met, but they did, and their murder spree began on December 1, 1957.

That was when the bandy-legged, red-haired Starkweather walked into a Crest service station in Lincoln with a bandanna over his face and a gun in his hand. He went through the cash register, then drove the frightened attendant to the edge of town. Starkweather shot the handsome young man in the head in a struggle for the gun. Police could not figure out who did it.

Starkweather spent the next six weeks with Fugate, practicing knife-throwing and shooting, and probably thinking about killing. On January 21, 1958, when Fugate's parents accused him of making their daughter pregnant, Starkweather shot them both and stabbed the stepfather. Then he clubbed their three-year-old daughter with the butt of his cheap rifle and threw a knife into her throat. With blood and bodies all around him, he sat down and watched television because he needed a distraction. Later, Starkweather and Fugate dragged the bodies of her family to outbuildings, then returned to the house for a long orgy of fun. It was, Starkweather was to say, the finest time of his life.

Starkweather then drove Fugate in an old Ford to the farm of August Meyer and shot him to death for no reason other than that he was there. By then, it was time to purchase more ammunition, because they had no idea how long fate would let Starkweather keep killing.

They were heading for a storm cellar when Robert Jensen and his sixteen-year-old daughter stopped their car and asked if there was anything they could do. The Jensens should have kept driving. Starkweather drew a gun and ordered them to walk into the dark, damp cellar. Then he shot the father, and sodomized and shot the daughter.

Starkweather and Fugate drove off in Jensen's car for a hundred miles, changed their mind, and headed back to Lincoln, as if to make their capture easier. Starkweather knocked on the door of C. Lauer Ward's French provincial home, killed the maid and Ward's wife with a knife and a gun, and shot their dog. When Mr. Ward returned home, Starkweather shot him in the back. He finally had his revenge on the rich.

When Starkweather later shot a sleeping salesperson, Fugate, pretending to be a kidnap victim, ran screaming from her lover's car. Starkweather sped off without her and roared through a roadblock. He slammed on the brakes when a bullet crashed through his windshield and nicked his ear. The man who had killed eleven people without batting an eye thought he was bleeding to death from a slight wound to his ear.

Brought into custody, Starkweather said, "Shooting people was, I guess, a kind of thrill. It brought out something." Charles Starkweather thought that one way of outdoing the rich was to become a celebrity. He became livid when his lawyer chose the insanity defense. As Starkweather said, "Nobody remembers a crazy man." He was electrocuted, and his story was fictionalized in the film *Badlands*, starring Martin Sheen and Sissy Spacek.

The Piano Seller

Police officers on patrol outside Annapolis, Maryland, on a lazy June night in 1957, slowed when a terrified army sergeant ran up to their car, breathing heavily. "He just stopped our car and shot her," the sergeant gasped between huffs. The officers told the sergeant to calm down and tell them what had happened as calmly as he could.

The sergeant said he was driving with his girlfriend, Margaret Harold, when they stopped to admire the roadside wildflowers. As they drove on, a blue or green auto swerved into their path and stopped them. A tall, thin-faced man with long hair jumped out and ran over to them. The stranger leered at Harold as she sat in the front seat, then pulled out a revolver and climbed into the backseat. Keeping the gun at the sergeant's head, the man ran the fingers of his other hand through Harold's hair and along her neck. When she shuddered and tried to get away, the gunman shot her in the head. The sergeant said he pushed open the door and ran for a mile, most of the while expecting to be shot in the back.

The officers drove to the sergeant's car and examined Harold's body, slumped over on the passenger's side, a bullet hole covered with blood on the side of her head and her dark hair hanging limply. A team of fingerprint specialists could find the impressions only of Margaret and the sergeant.

In their search of the area, detectives came upon a small, vacant cinder-block building. Through the basement window they could see pornographic photographs hanging from floor to ceiling. The police entered and found that one photo was different. It was a black-and-white picture of a pretty, fully dressed, young woman. The photo was printed on heavy glass paper. Technicians at the FBI lab in Washington, just twenty miles away, could find no prints on the photograph. Because the paper was the kind used in college yearbooks, agents checked with a number of institutions. They learned that the woman was Wanda Tipson, a 1955 graduate of the University of Maryland in Baltimore. But Tipson could not provide any clues as to who took the photograph. The investigation was at a standstill.

In January 1959, an entire family disappeared while driving near the low hills around historic Fredericksburg, Virginia, about forty miles south of Washington and sixty miles from Annapolis. A truck found abandoned had belonged to burly feed deliveryman Carroll Vernon Jackson and his wife, Mildred, both twenty-eight. They and their two young daughters vanished while returning from a visit with relatives. The truck still had the key in the ignition. Skid marks showed that Carroll may have been forced into a sudden stop. Again, no prints were found other than those of the victims.

Two months later, a neighbor of the Jacksons was walking along a shallow depression near an abandoned sawmill, intending to gather sawdust to protect his roses from an approaching frost, when he found Carroll's body face down in some brush, his hands bound with a necktie, a bullet hole through his head. Under him lay the body of his eighteen-month-old daughter, Janet, who probably suffocated from the weight of her father's body.

A little more than two weeks later, a pair of thirteen-year-old boys were climbing a roof to look for a kite near the scene of Margaret Harold's murder when they noticed what seemed like a gopher hole, but with some human hair sticking out of it. The frightened boys ran off to bring the police. Chief William Wade and his lieutenant, both of whom had worked on Harold's murder, dug away at the shallow grave and found the body of Mildred Jackson, a silk stocking tied around her neck. On top of her body was the remains of her five-year-old girl, Susan, her skull fractured.

The coroner determined that Mildred was subjected to a beating and one of the most brutal rapes he had ever seen, and then she was strangled. Thinking that the rape might have been committed in the pornography-filled basement, the police returned and found a red button matching the ones on Mildred's dress.

Without any supporting evidence, police thought once again of the lanky man described by the Army sergeant, and suspected that he must have some connection to the University of Maryland. The FBI encouraged newspapers to do stories about the bistate search for a tall, thin man driving a blue or green Ford. One response came from the killer himself. It included a newspaper photo of Mildred and her five-year-old girl, with a drawing of a smothering hand across the mother's mouth. The letter detailed how the sender had captured the family, then killed the husband and the baby first. "Now the mother and daughter were mine," the letter went on. He called the murder of Mildred, an ordeal of several hours, an "execution." The tone was boastful and mocking.

A Norfolk, Virginia, man wrote to authorities that the killer might be his friend Melvin David Rees, a rather bright jazz guitarist. The friend said he had been with Rees the night that Harold was killed and that the musician was "hopped up" on Benzedrine and acting wildly. The friend said that later, when he uneasily tried to ask Rees whether he had killed the Jackson family, the musician suspiciously evaded the question.

Melvin Reese's father worked for the Potomac Telephone Company in Hyattsville, Maryland, and his mother was employed by the Department of the Interior. The parents were active in civic affairs, and their two married daughters— both older than Rees—were esteemed in the community. Rees was well-behaved and considered an upstanding young man. But something always held him back. He attended the University of Maryland for awhile, but was arrested for assaulting a woman in his car. Despite the woman's refusal to press charges, Reese left school and began selling pianos at a music store in West Memphis, Arkansas. In the back of the store, he kept some books on Freudian psychology along with comics and dirty magazines.

The federal agents returned Rees to Maryland, where the Army sergeant identified him as the killer. "But I'm innocent," Rees insisted, "Innocent!" The federal agents obtained a warrant to search his parents' home near Washington. The couple was sure the investigators were making a mistake. But in the attic, the agents discovered a nickel-plated .38 pistol hidden in a saxophone case. Along with it were numerous notes Rees had written to himself about his various crimes against women, including a copy of the letter he sent to the newspaper about how he had killed the Jacksons. An examination of the pistol showed that it was used to kill both Margaret Harold and Carroll Jackson.

Neighbors recalled Rees as a nice young man, "cold and reserved . . . but a gentleman." He was so controlled that after killing the Jackson family he went to the music studio and taught seven students and two band groups.

In a study called *The Psychology of Strange Killers*, James Reinardt said Rees could keep the surface polished, but "then there came a time when imaginary acts could no longer be contained within the bounds of fantasy. Alone, he became restless and his imagination took him along 'car parked' lanes that he had traveled before." In Maryland, Rees was sentenced to life for the Harold killing, but he was executed in Virginia for the Jackson murders.

A Trail of Bullets

The times, they were a-changing. This was 1959, but part of the 1960s culture had already entered into the mainstream. The Kingston Trio was singing "The Ballad of Tom Dooley," and disc jockeys were playing Bobby Darin's unlikely smash-hit "Mack the Knife." James Bond burst from the pages of *Casino Royale,* and the Italian film *La Dolce Vita* titillated American audiences with Federico Fellini's vision of glamour, amorality, and emptiness. The Beatnik culture of New York and San Francisco merged with the rebel strain in the suburbs and rural areas. And the escalation of a police action in Vietnam led thousands of college students to heed Henry David Thoreau's cry for simplicity, inner honesty, and civil disobedience.

On February 2, 1959 the body of twenty-seven-year-old August Norry lay with eighteen bullet wounds on the Daly City hills just south of San Francisco. After conducting a preliminary search, the police found a truck with a bloodstained interior near a lovers' lane. Either the killer had used the truck to get away, or someone stole the truck but soon decided to abandon it. Either way, it did not make sense.

Norry was a landscape gardener, and his wife was expecting their first child. Family and friends called Norry "a man without an enemy." But he was a womanizer who, before he was married, boasted to friends at local bars about his prodigious sexual conquests.

A boy who lived in the area called the police and said he had seen a "freckle-faced blonde" on Sunday afternoon, the day of the murder, "driving like mad" in a truck such as the one described in the papers. But the Bay Area was filled with freckle-faced blondes. The *San Francisco Chronicle* received an anonymous letter from the boyfriend of a possible suspect that gave the registration number of the truck—something that had not been made public. The writer was interested if any reward was being offered. There was not, and he never wrote again.

There was still one lead open to the San Mateo County sheriff's office—a trail of the bullets. Norry was killed with a special kind of .38 caliber bullet called a "wadcutter," which is used in target practice. A small box of such bullets was found near the body. Target shooters like to buy their gunpowder separately, then put it into molds to suit their tastes. To help recover their costs, target shooters often sell the bullets to someone else. That at least gave the police a starting point.

These cartridges had three grooves around the base to hold lubricating oil. The only manufacturer of molds for such three-cannelure bullets was in Connecticut. The firm supplied the police with the names and addresses of its four distributors in the Bay Area, but the distributors reported selling dozens of molds. Inspector Eugene Stewart thought of a way to reduce the search. The unfired cartridges held more than the usual amount of gunpowder, a practice called "hot loading" for firing especially fast. Stewart and several other officers visited every store selling guns in San Francisco and northern San Mateo County to learn the names of customers known for buying molds and then hot loading.

This led them to five men. One of them, Lawrence Schultze, lived near Daly City in a town most known for its graveyards. Schultze at first was reluctant to talk, because he had already been charged with being part of an auto theft ring. But he agreed to cooperate when detectives assured him they were interested only in solving a murder. He said two boxes of his hot loads were stolen from his car a few months before. The police sent a sample of the lead he had used to a spectrograph laboratory in San Francisco.

An examination showed that the lead was the same as that in the slugs removed from Norry's body. By then, detectives were wondering about the patness of Schultze's account. Schultze spoke to his lawyer and came up with the truth. He said that around the beginning of the year, he had sold a box of fifty cartridges for $3 to a casual friend, Penny Bjorkland. She brought him a .38 revolver and said that she wanted some ammunition to use for target practice. A few evenings afterward, he loaded the bullets for her, took her to the hills, and they fired off a few rounds to be sure the bullets were all right.

While Bjorkland was at work as a mail clerk in a San Francisco business office, police went to the Daly City home she shared with her parents and three younger brothers. She arrived, did not seem surprised to find the officers waiting for her, and admitted buying the bullets. But she would say nothing about the murder. As her shocked parents watched, the officers led her away.

Bjorkland was kept overnight in a cell at the county jail in Redwood City, about twenty miles away. When she began talking to the jail matron, Esther Brown, the older woman turned on the intercom so that officers in the booking section could listen and take notes.

"For about a year or a year and a half I've had the urge to kill someone," Bjorkland told Brown. "I'll admit the motive sounds crazy. But I wanted to know if a person could commit a crime like this and not worry about the police looking for her or have it on her conscience." She added, "I've felt better ever since I killed him."

Over the next few hours, she poured out her story, and police were able to corroborate everything. Two weeks before the murder, Bjorkland took the gun from the bedroom of a friend, William Freeman. "I've wanted to kill somebody ever since I started target shooting," she said. "I used to go up in the hills and point my pistol at a target and pretend it was a human." Almost by chance, she met Norry and thought she might make him her surrogate victim. He was in the hills dumping lawn clippings from his truck. She flirted a little and he took her to a drive-in for some food. He lied and said he was twenty-three and unmarried, but "he never did anything improper or out of the way." But thinking he was single made it easier for her.

They met again in the hills the next day. This time she was concealing a revolver behind the elastic of her pedal pushers, and the small box of ammunition was in her purse. She invited Norry to join her for target practice. After she fired a single test shot, Bjorkland turned and pointed the gun at him.

As she demonstrated for the detectives and the jail matron, she fired all five remaining bullets into Norry. He slumped forward and she reloaded, walked around the rear of the truck, fired at him from outside the driver's window, then went back to the passenger side and fired again. Finally she dragged the body across the grass and drove off with his blood soaking the seat and spilling across the floorboard.

Investigators stared at Bjorkland, looking for a motive and wondering how someone could speak of murder with such indifference. "Had he mistreated you, or kissed you, or made any improper suggestions?" one of them asked, as if he had not been listening. Bjorkland shook her head no. She had simply killed out of curiosity. She dumped the empty cartridges in a street drain outside her home and threw the gun away in a drain in San Francisco. At last she said, "I don't want to talk about it. It makes me sick."

The "urge slaying" created a sensation in the press. When reporters were allowed to speak to her the next day, one asked whether she considered herself mentally ill. "No!" she insisted, and added that she was completely free of alcohol and drugs. "I figured if I got caught, I got caught."

Although Bjorkland seemed strangely disconnected from her parents, she told reporters that her home life had nothing to do with the killings. Maybe, maybe not. Bjorkland admitted that she deliberately picked fights with her mother, and she realized that her parents would suffer forever from the knowledge that she had killed someone. In fact, psychiatrists concluded in their pretrial evaluation that Bjorkland hated her family so much that she was glad to be in jail. One of the experts found that the killing was to "wreak vengeance on her mother." Bjorkland pleaded guilty and was sentenced to life in prison, although she had hoped for a second-degree verdict that would have meant only a five-year term.

REFERENCES

Allen, William. *Starkweather.* Boston: Houghton Mifflin, 1976.

Block, Eugene B. "A Tangle of Inconsistencies," *The Fabric of Guilt.* Garden City, N.Y.: Doubleday, 1968.

Boucher, Anthony, ed. *Quality of Mercy.* New York: E.P. Dutton, 1962.

Brophy, John. *The Meaning of Murder.* New York: Thomas Y. Crowell, 1966.

Brussel, James A. *Casebook of a Crime Psychiatrist.* New York: Dell Publishing, 1968.

Capote, Truman. *In Cold Blood.* New York: Random House, 1965.

Chessman, Caryl. *Cell 2455, Death Row.* New York: Permabook, 1957.

Colby, Robert. "Stephanie Bryan Is Missing," *The California Crime Book.* New York: Pyramid Books, 1971.

DeFord, Miriam Allen. *Murderers Sane and Mad.* New York: Abelard-Schuman, 1965.

Fido, Martin. *The Chronicle of Crime.* New York: Carroll & Graf Publishers, 1993.

Franklin, Charles. *The World's Worst Murderers.* New York: Taplinger Publishing, 1965.

Gollmar, Robert H. *Edward Gein.* New York: Pinnacle Books, 1984.

Green, Jonathon. *The Greatest Criminals of All Time.* New York: Stein & Day, 1980.

Lane, Roger. *Murder in America.* Columbus, Ohio: Columbia University Press, 1997.

Leyton, Elliott. *Hunting Humans* (original title, *Compulsive Killers*). New York: Pocket Books, 1988.

Marriner, Brian. *On Death's Bloody Trail: Murder and the Art of Forensic Science.* New York: Facts on File, 1991.

New York Times, September 29, 1961.

———, June 26, 1990.

Nash, Jay Robert. *Crime Chronology: A Worldwide Record: 1900–1983.* New York: Facts on File, 1984.

———. *Bloodletters and Badmen.* New York: M. Evans & Co., 1995.

Odell, Rodin. *Landmarks in 20th Century Murder.* London: Headline, 1995.

Reinardt, James Melvin. *The Psychology of Strange Killers.* Springfield, Ill.: Charles C. Thomas, 1962.

San Francisco Chronicle, January 26, January 28, July 1, and July 21, 1956.

———, March 16, 1957.

———, April 16, April 17, and July 21, 1959.

———, July 21, 1991.

Sifakis, Carl. *Encyclopedia of Crime.* New York: Facts on File, 1982.

Wilson, Colin. *Written in Blood: Detectives & Detection.* New York: Warner Books, 1989.

————. *The Killers Among Us: Book I. Sex, Madness & Mass Murder.* New York: Warner Books, 1995.

The 1960s

What most people think of as the tumultuous 1960s really didn't begin until 1963. In August of that year, Dr. Martin Luther King Jr. declared, "I have a dream. I have a dream today that the rough places will be made plain and the crooked place will be made straight." There was hope for a troubled time, and for people of all races.

But in November 1963 the assassination of President John F. Kennedy in Dallas ended the much-fabled era of Camelot and an angry cynicism swept through the country like a chill wind. Race riots broke out in the cities, and when black activist Medgar Evers was shot to death in Mississippi, the police did little to find the killer. Civil rights activists James Cheney, Michey Schwerner, and Andrew Goodman were murdered by Mississippi Ku Klux Klansmen and others in the summer of 1964. In February of the following year, Black Muslim leader Malcolm X was killed by black assassins as he addressed an audience at a Harlem theater in New York.

In the early morning of March 13, 1964, a cry was heard that was not soon forgotten. Twenty-eight-year-old Kitty Genovese was being stalked in a residential street of Queens, New York. A knife was thrust into her. "Oh my God, he stabbed me," she screamed. "Please help me, please help me!" The lights went on in several apartments, but no one came out or threatened to call the police. The attacker, Winston Moseley, continued stabbing her. "I'm dying," Genovese cried out with draining strength, "I'm dying."

The attacker drove off. Genovese staggered into a vestibule. Moseley, evidently seeing that no one would come to her aid, and possibly wanting to make sure she did not live to identify him, returned to the scene of the crime, searched for her, and finished her off.

A study showed that thirty-two law-abiding citizens had heard Genovese's cry for help. Some were afraid, but most said they did not want to get involved. It was an attitude that would have been incomprehensible fifty years earlier. Such apathy was a product of the turbulent times.

Dr. King was shot to death on the balcony of the Lorraine Motel in Memphis on April 4, 1968. When riots broke out in several cities the next day, no one echoed King's call to resist violence.

Just two months after Dr. King was murdered, the late President Kennedy's brother Robert, who had just begun a bid for the presidency, entered the kitchen of the Ambassador Hotel in Los Angeles and was killed by Sirhan Sirhan. When asked his motive, Sirhan said he wanted to call attention to the needs of Palestinians under Israeli domination. He later repudiated his confession in prison.

Between June 14, 1962 and January 4, 1964 an intruder called the "Boston Strangler" killed and in some cases mutilated thirteen women.

His approach was to pose as a handyman to gain access to the victim's home and then choke her from behind. As was the case with the legendary Jack the Ripper, he killed victims he considered disposable. These victims lived alone, were financially comfortable although not rich, and several had foreign accents.

The strangler's last victim was nineteen-year-old Mary Sullivan. A card reading "Happy New Year" was left between her toes. Some observers thought the elaborate nature of Sullivan's murder—as with Jack the Ripper's final victim—suggested that the killer was saying farewell to his attacks.

After a hunt that involved every conceivable kind of suspect, the police arrested a rapist and petty burglar named Albert DeSalvo, who gave a detailed confession that clarified everything except why he killed. DeSalvo grew up in near poverty, and his father was often violent toward his mother. That violence was sometimes said to be the cause of the stranglings, yet DeSalvo's brother was perfectly normal and law-abiding.

Under an arrangement with his attorney, DeSalvo was sentenced to life for the previous rapes but was never tried for the murders. He escaped with three other inmates, gave himself up, and eventually was stabbed to death in a prison brawl.

As the events chronicled in the DeSalvo case were unfolding, criminal science was keeping pace with criminal behavior. Herbert Leon MacDonnell was working for Corning Glass Works in upstate New York as an expert in porous glass technology, but his hobby was forensic medicine. In April 1966, a Corning employee shot a man in a deer hunt. By closely studying the fatal shotgun pellet, MacDonnell determined that, among other things, the pellet had lost fourteen percent of its force before it struck the victim. That meant it had hit a tree first and then ricocheted into him. The jury found that the shooting was a tragic accident and acquitted the employee.

Techniques of "blood fingerprinting" were also developed in the mid-1960s. This included raising latent fingerprints on a porous surface, such as clothing or unpainted wood, by using iodine fumes and spraying the surface with a chemical called ninhydrine. Investigators could now even find fingerprints left on flesh by using a special X-ray technique.

Unfortunately, the police still needed a record of potential suspects' fingerprints on file somewhere. It was as if the Zodiac killer, knowing that, flaunted his anonymity.

Zodiac—the only name by which we know him—cannot be classified because his crimes fit no pattern except to kill, get away with it, and baffle the authorities. His series began just before Christmas 1968 in the hills outside Vallejo, just northeast of San Francisco. A teenage couple was on their first date. The boy was shot to death in his car, and the girl was brought down by a bullet as she ran. On July 4, 1969, a Vallejo waitress and her boyfriend were killed. A month later, the killer sent a cryptic message to Vallejo and San Francisco newspapers. Inspiring the future movie *Dirty Harry,* the sender threatened to keep on killing unless the press published his letter. The letter was signed with his symbol, a circle divided by a cross, or the crosshairs of a gun sight.

Later, he sent a letter stating, "This is Zodiac speaking." Navy experts gave up deciphering the first message with a computer. But two people who had never cracked a code in their lives—a high school teacher in Salinas, California, and his wife—excitedly discovered that the first message stated, with some possibly intentional misspellings: "I like killing people because it is such fun. It is more fun than killing wild game in the forrest because man is the most dangerous anamal of all . . . The best part of it ia thae when I die, I will be reborn in paradice and all the I have killed will become my slaves."

Having established a pattern of killing couples in parked cars, Zodiac went on to break the pattern. He killed two college students as the couple picnicked. Because he was no longer striking at night, he was wearing an executioner's hood. Instead of using a gun, he sliced the young man and woman to death. Cecelia Shepard was stabbed two dozen times in the form of a cross, and the killer wrote the dates of all his murders on the couple's white car.

Thirteen days after the picnic murders, Zodiac killed college student Paul Stine, who was driving him in a cab around the trendy Presidio Heights area of San Francisco, not far from the Golden Gate Bridge. He then sent the newspapers a letter saying a school bus might be his next target. Police Chief Thomas Cahill published a sketch showing an ordinary, clean-cut man with short brown or slightly reddish hair. He was thought to be about five feet, eight inches tall, around thirty-five to forty-five years old, of average build for someone that age, and made to look even more ordinary by squarish glasses.

But there were no further crimes claimed by the Zodiac. He could be dead, in an institution, or mingling with the crowd today along Fisherman's Wharf.

Midnight to Dawn

A nursing exchange student from the Philippines lay in terror under a bunk bed in Chicago on July 14, 1966, as she saw an intruder's legs returning to the room where earlier he had tied up Curazon Amurao and her eight roommates. One by one, the tall, slender man with a bony face and a vacant stare took away her roommates. And they never came back. Sometimes Amurao heard what sounded like a sigh but never a real scream. Her only hope was that in his craze, the methodical prowler had not counted the women he had tied up in the second-floor bedroom.

The man was Richard Speck, who was rather passive and not particularly bright. He was raised Baptist but seemed disinterested in religion or anything else for that matter. His five sisters felt he could not get on by himself, so he was sent from one to another and took a few laborer jobs in between. Speck had never been violent, but he broke up with his good-looking wife, and part of his mind wished he could have killed her. When he broke into the town house near South Chicago Hospital, one of the young women he saw resembled his wife. He wanted to kill her and the others because—who knows? The psychiatrist who studied Speck at length did not even try to guess except to diagnose Speck as suffering from a head injury sustained long ago.

Although several studies have attempted to link brain injury with pathological murders, no direct cause and effect has yet been convincingly established.

At fifteen, Speck had the words "Born to Raise Hell" tattooed on his arm to impress other boys. Drinking helped him overcome his fears, and sometimes he would commit petty burglaries under the influence.

Since arriving in Chicago, he sometimes lived in flophouses along skid row. On summer afternoons he could see hoboes and winos sitting virtually shoulder to shoulder along West Madison Street in their dark jackets and pants, and usually wearing threadbare white shirts with stains rather than ties. Speck moved among them as an outsider among outsiders.

Yet Speck had a sense of humor, and he was loyal to his friends. But his thinking was disorganized, giving him a slow, distant appearance. He was always looking for ways to express masculinity, such as talking about pinups he had seen, but many noticed a feminine quality in Speck's mien. He was all right when he was with one of his sisters, but his life had a tendency to disintegrate when he was on his own. As psychiatrist Marvin Ziporyn observed, Speck was a "boy who never came close to being a man."

Speck had been drinking excessively on the night he broke into the town house. A few recent experiences had brought him into a depression. The night before, he had had a bad experience with a prostitute. And he was unable to get a job on an oil tanker plying the Great Lakes, even though this was the height of the shipping season. In his depression, Speck thought everything would be better if he could get some money to catch a train for New Orleans. There would be plenty of work at that port, he thought. He could have borrowed the money from his sisters, but he wanted to show them and everybody else that he could fend for himself.

For the first and only time in his life, Speck was drinking and using drugs at the same time. The combination might have pushed him over the edge, drawing out his smoldering hostility against his former wife and perhaps other women he believed had dominated his life.

Most of the student nurses who lived in the town house were getting ready for bed as Speck approached the building. Gloria Davy, the student who resembled Speck's wife, was still out on a date.

Speck forced open the back door, possibly not knowing anyone was inside. One of the four women he encountered initially may have mentioned that the student nurses in the other bedroom could hear them. For whatever reason, Speck knocked on their door. Curazon Amurao opened it and saw the six-foot, fair-haired Speck with his disturbingly sleepy eyes. He smelled of alcohol. She glanced down and saw that he was holding a knife and a small black gun. He quietly told her and her roommate to join the others in the larger bedroom.

Instead, Amurao and two other Philippine exchange students rushed to a small closet, and the three of them held shut the door. They heard Speck say, "I'm not going to hurt you. I'm only going to tie you up. I need your money to go to New Orleans."

They believed him because they had no other choice; he had a gun and they could not hold the door closed forever. Besides, he had not once even touched any of the women. The exchange students let go of the door and joined the others, having no idea what was about to happen.

Even with two weapons, there were too many students for Speck to handle. He had them all lie on the floor and tied them up with strips he had torn from a sheet with his large hands. So far, he had kept his word; none of the girls was harmed. But at 11:30 P.M., Davy came home.

Speck threatened her and tied her up, and next he waited for another student nurse to return, who brought a friend to stay the night. It was around this time that Speck lost all control. With all nine young women bound helpless and lined up single file, he forced one after the other into another room and strangled them. Only Davy was sexually assaulted—in a brutal way that came from anger rather than lust. Her body was savaged with the knife. The others were killed quietly.

Amurao was one of several women who had rolled unseen under a bunk bed after Speck's slaughter got under way. But Speck had found the other girls, and Amurao was sure her time was near.

Twice as Amurao lay trembling under the bunk bed, she heard water running as Speck evidently washed his hands to be fresh for another murder.

Lying alone in the dark room, Amurao was in such terror that she no longer knew whether the man was still in the town house or not. She must have been startled when an alarm clock went off at 5:30 A.M. She stayed frozen, listening for sounds of movement or footsteps that never came. Then another alarm clock buzzed. Nobody moved to shut them off. Twenty minutes passed, then half an hour. Finally she forced herself to climb out from under the bunk. She found the eight bodies. Too horrified to think of going down the stairs to escape, she pushed her way through the screen and jumped to the ground.

Speck had left the town house long before and returned to skid row. Police used fingerprints found all over the rooms to identify the culprit and then showed his photo on television. There was no place to hide. Two weeks later, Speck slashed his wrist in the sleazy Star Hotel and was rushed to Cook County

Hospital, where a doctor noticed his "Born to Raise Hell" tattoo and called the police.

Speck was sentenced to death, but in 1972 the Supreme Court ruled against the death penalty. His sentence was commuted to eight consecutive terms of fifty to one hundred and fifty years. He was denied parole seven times.

Speck became a nonentity in prison. He was smuggled in drugs and had a sexual relationship with another male inmate, although whether he had homosexual tendencies before being jailed is unknown. A crude videotape of the men seemingly doped out together caused a scandal when it was made public in 1997, six years after Speck's death in prison of natural causes.

The Watch Tower

On Sunday evening, July 31, 1966, while the temperature lingered in the nineties, Charles Joseph Whitman, a former Eagle Scout, sat down at his desk and wrote a message to the world: "To whom it may concern. I do not understand what is compelling me to type this note. I've been having fears and violent impulses. I've had some tremendous headaches."

Whitman, reared in Florida, had conflicts with his aggressive father and told himself as a boy that he would never be like his dad. But some of his father's traits showed up anyway. Whitman fought off his aggressive moments by trying to make himself gentle and mild-mannered.

The young man had planned to rise through the military ranks during his grade-school years, but he was forced to quit the University of Texas because of unsatisfactory—and

unworthy—grades. He married, but his only source of pleasure was his love of guns. In 1964, the Marines court-martialed
Whitman for carrying a pistol to camp and aboard a ship,
lending money at interest, and threatening another Marine.
He received a sentence of thirty days hard labor and was honorably discharged. His wife was teaching science in Austin,
and Whitman moved there. He took one course after another
at the university, but his mind was drifting. He kept in shape
doing exercises he'd learned in the service. With the Vietnam
war escalating, Whitman apparently brooded over how he
should be there.

He went to a university staff psychiatrist for a consulta-
tion, and the doctor found the large young man seething with
hostility toward his overbearing father. Whitman repeatedly
mentioned that he was having thoughts of going up the university's bell tower with a deer rifle and shooting people.

At the time, the former altar boy was distressed that his
mother was leaving her abusive husband.

He talked about leaving the wife he loved and becoming "a
bum." Twice that summer he struck his wife, only to realize he
was acting as his father had done. Whitman knew he could no
longer change his life by sheer willpower. He seemed to enter a
suicidal depression that would initially take the form of killing
those dear to him, then strangers, and finally himself.

Whitman picked up his wife at her summer job, dropped
her off at the house, then drove across the river to his
mother's home. He stabbed her in the back, shot her, and left
a note saying that he loved her and had put her out of her
misery. He returned home and stabbed his wife to death as
she slept. Whitman then went on a shopping spree, buying a
Bowie knife, a machete, a shotgun, two rifles, three pistols,

and plenty of ammunition. He also purchased supplies for a long siege and put everything in his marine footlocker. He drove to the three hundred and seven-foot granite-faced tower rising from the main building of the university. That was his hill. He was going to defend it with his life.

When a woman at the observation level asked him what he wanted, he struck her with his rifle butt and fatally shot her in the head. Twelve feet below the clanging bell of the watchtower, Whitman waited. No one heard the first shot, but a teenager fell dead from his bicycle. Suddenly people began scattering amid the steady crackling of sniper shots.

One shot wounded a pregnant young woman and killed her fetus. A man who knelt in horror by his wounded girlfriend was shot dead. For twenty minutes, Whitman fired at everyone at whom he could get a steady aim within his wide radius. They included a professor, a police officer, a Peace Corps trainee, and a number of students. The sidewalks and landscaping had become a no-man's-land of the dead and the dying.

One hundred officers converged around the tower, many of them off duty. Half a dozen officers and a newly deputized university employee who had been an Air Force gunner broke through the barricade Whitman had put up on the observation deck and fanned out in three directions, keeping in whispered radio contact with officers at better vantage points. Whitman saw or heard something and moved toward the approaching officers. They simultaneously fired dozens of bullets into him, just to make sure he was dead.

The university employee then took a towel from Whitman's supplies and waved it as a signal that the tower had been taken back. Whitman killed thirteen people on the ground, totaling sixteen deaths that day, and he wounded more than thirty.

A small brain tumor was found in the autopsy, making headlines around the country. But further study showed that the almond-sized growth could not have been a direct cause of Whitman's Day of Death.

Blackouts

In January 1968, nineteen-year-old Linda Slawson disappeared one afternoon while out selling encyclopedias. Slawson was pretty with short hair in contrast to the times, and she was wearing high-heeled shoes. A harmless-looking man let her into his home in a suburb of Portland, Oregon struck her with a two-by-four board, and strangled her while his wife and mother-in-law were upstairs. His actions were done entirely on impulse, but he was so sexually and emotionally aroused that he began to think of killing more.

In July of that year, sixteen-year-old Stephanie Vilcko left her home to go swimming with friends and never came home. In November, twenty-three-year-old Jan Whitney of the University of Oregon vanished while driving north between the home of friends in Eugene and her apartment in McMinnville. Her Nash Rambler was found empty near the small campus city of Corvallis. No one thought of connecting Whitney's disappearance with the Slawson case because they occurred fifty miles apart.

In March 1969, a teacher found Vilcko's skeletal remains along the banks of Gales Creek near Forest Grove, about twenty-five miles from Portland. Nine days later, nineteen-year-old

186 • *Homicide: 100 Years of Murder in America*

premed student Karen Sprinker of Oregon State University in Corvallis disappeared while staying at her parents' home in Salem. The beautiful woman with long black hair was to have met her mother in a restaurant but never arrived.

When people who had been in the restaurant parking lot were asked if they saw anything unusual, they said they noticed someone who was dressed as a woman but might have been a man. Police conducted an intense but standard investigation. One of those questioned, Sprinker's boyfriend, was unable to offer the police any relevant information.

On April 21, twenty-four-year-old Sharon Wood left her job as a secretary at the Portland state historical department and entered the basement parking garage to go home. A heavy door closed, and she felt the presence of someone behind her. She turned and saw a man with a gun. "If you don't scream, I won't shoot you," he said. She fought back, kicking him and biting his hand. She collapsed just as a Volkswagen bus approached. When she came to, the man was gone.

The next day, a fifteen-year-old girl told police that a man matching the description of the person who attacked Wood tried to grab her near Salem, but she screamed and ran away. The following day, Linda Dawn Schlee failed to meet her boyfriend at a YMCA. The twenty-two-year-old was just over five feet tall and exceptionally pretty. The day after Schlee disappeared, the body of Janet Shanahan, also twenty-two, was discovered strangled in the trunk of a car in Eugene.

A year and a half after Schlee disappeared, a fisherman came across her body, anchored by an engine block, in the Long Tom River twelve miles from Corvallis. The brassiere she wore was not her own. Scuba divers searching the river for clues found Sprinker's body. Both her breasts were cut off.

Authorities developed a profile of the victims: They were teenagers or women in their early twenties, very good looking, usually long-haired, intelligent, outgoing, and most often abducted at the end of the month. Although police were not even close to working out an informal profile of the killer, they made a few inferences. If he was the person who was seen dressed as a woman in a parking lot, he was probably a little heavy. He must have been strong to lift and drop bodies attached to auto parts into the river, and he might be an auto mechanic or an electrician. He also was choosing victims at different locations in hopes police would not connect them. The officers put out what they knew on a teletype network to other police departments in the area.

Extra patrols were set up at campuses and near bridges. Officers driving by parking lots instinctively went slowly and scanned everyone. Then a call came in from a female student who said a stranger had phoned her, using her first name, and tried to impress her about being a Vietnam war veteran, presumably to ask for a date. So what, the police thought. Then came another such call. And another. Someone was looking up women in a campus phone book and trying to set up meetings. One woman actually met the man.

The student, who happened to be majoring in psychology, described him as somewhat overweight, freckled, and in his thirties. He was driving an old junker. In what must have sent shivers through the investigators, the girl said that during their conversation he put his hand on her shoulder and said, "Be sad. Think of those two girls who were found in the river." When she declined to go for a drive, he added, "How do you know I wouldn't take you to the river and strangle you?" The serial killer was entering his burnout phase; he was getting careless.

On Sunday, May 25, a student called the Corvallis police to say that a supposed Vietnam veteran had tried to make a date with her over the phone, and she agreed just to stall for time. When the man pulled up in his old but well-repaired car, the police were waiting for him. When they asked the driver, Jerry Brudos, what he was doing, he told them he was an electrician working in the area, and that he had a wife and two children. He was a little overweight, freckled, and strong.

The officers sounded casual, almost friendly, and Brudos let them look around his home. There was a hook on the ceiling in his garage, and several ropes lying around. One of them had a distinctive knot such as the one used to bind the victims to automobile parts before they were dumped in the river. The detectives asked Brudos about his part-time work as an auto mechanic and discovered he was doing a job near where Whitney's car was found on the highway. The detectives sensed that this unassuming man was the killer, as unlikely as he seemed.

The fifteen-year-old who was accosted immediately picked out Brudos from a collection of photos. As the officers arrived at his home to arrest him, they saw his wife, Darcie, driving out. Under a blanket in the backseat was their man. He didn't get away. When Brudos was ordered to change into a uniform at the police station, the lockup keepers saw that he was wearing women's underwear.

Over the next few days, Brudos talked to the officers about his interest in women's underwear and shoes, and eventually about the murders. All of the victims conformed to a general type, a pretty teacher he once had. He would stare at her, and once he stole her shoes.

Brudos was born in South Dakota. His older brother, Larry, was considered the bright one in the family. Their mother was disappointed when Jerry was born—or so Brudos thought—because she had wanted a girl. It is possible that the boy became fixed on the idea that if he had been born a girl he would never be in competition with his brother, and he would therefore win his mother's undivided affection.

The family moved a dozen times, making it difficult for the boy to make friends. Brudos amused himself instead by playing in junkyards and, he said, became fascinated by women's shoes. His mother had such a cold, distant personality that he would go to a pretty neighbor for warmth and affection.

When sex is a forbidden subject, forbidden sex sometimes becomes exciting, as it was for the sixteen-year-old Brudos. He stole the underwear of a pretty eighteen-year-old neighbor and told her he could help her get them back because he was working undercover for the police. One evening while his family was away, Brudos invited her to his home. When she arrived, he called her to the second floor. There, a tall figure with a mask jumped in front of her with a gun and told her to take off all her clothes. He then took photos of her with his flash camera but did not touch her. The masked man left, and moments later Brudos came running in, claiming the masked man had locked him in the barn. The girl knew the masked man was Brudos, but she was too frightened to tell anyone.

Brudos—then and later—was too shy around women for even a casual conversation. He needed to feel in control. Once he could not get an erection with a girl he was dating, the seventeen-year-old Brudos beat her in frustration, and she called the police. That led to his confinement at the State

Hospital in Salem, Oregon. He entered the Army, was discharged, and lived with his parents—until his brother came
home, and he was asked to move into a shed. Brudos's resentment of his parents for still seeming to favor Larry added to
his brutal fantasies.

Still a virgin, Brudos imagined himself capturing young
women and setting up a butcher shop in his home, complete with a freezer. As he would tell psychiatrists, he
thought of this home as a torture complex where he would
beat his captives, sexually play with them, and keep their
bodies forever.

When he was twenty-three and still fairly slender, someone he knew at a radio station where he worked introduced
him to seventeen-year-old Darcie Metzler. Partly because
Darcie wanted to move away from her family, she later agreed
to marry Brudos.

Darcie was too inexperienced to know that her husband
was using her to live out elements of his deadly daydreams.
He took photos of her as she slept, as if imagining a dead
woman. And, as he would say later, he would have sex with
her only after imagining ghastly scenes of mutilation.
Although his behavior became increasingly odd, he never
harmed her. He put on weight, sometimes appeared before
Darcie in women's underwear, and padlocked the door to the
garage, where the freezer was. He kept Darcie out of the attic
by claiming he had seen mice and rats there.

Darcie discovered her husband developing photos of nude
women who seemed to be sleeping, and Brudos claimed he was
doing this for a friend. He kept boxes of women's underclothing
and shoes, but Darcie had no idea they came from women her
husband had murdered. His wife also found a full-sized plastic

woman's breast, and police later discovered that a real breast had been made into a paperweight that was kept on a shelf.

All of Brudos's victims were killed in a period of blackout, allowing Brudos to remain a normal family man except for a few hours in his life.

The evidence was overwhelming, and Brudos pleaded guilty to four counts of murder. He was sentenced to life in prison.

The Coed Murders

Although the multiple killers of the 1960s were mostly outcasts or people who could no longer function in life, John Norman Collins had numerous male and female friends at Eastern Michigan University in Ypsilanti, which is near the larger university town of Ann Arbor. In high school, Collins was both an athlete and an honor student, but his grades as an education major slid as he began to entertain dark thoughts. There was some confusion in his mind about sex, and so he would fluctuate between acting prudish to being fashionably open during these years of the Sexual Revolution.

As a child he fancied the idea of becoming a state police officer. Now he was thinking of ways to kill.

Collins loved motorcycles. At one time he had four of them. He loved the speed and enjoyed giving rides to teenage girls. After all, the six-foot student had the size, looks, and sense of humor that made him immediately attractive.

Like Brudos, Collins had a young and pretty aunt, and in his early adolescence he may have been horrified at having sexual

192 • *Homicide: 100 Years of Murder in America*

thoughts about her. This overreaction could have opened the way for his intense fantasy life. Collins was raised Catholic, which might have added to his struggle with forbidden impulses.

It seems as if Collins did not have direct sexual thoughts about his Canadian-born mother, who was married three times and had a number of boyfriends. But when his pretty blonde sister started going out on dates, he abandoned his generally affable character and often kicked the floor while calling her a tramp.

The first victim was a nineteen-year-old woman with a guitar across her shoulder who had gone to find solace in the pines and wooded slopes of Half Moon Lake. She found that visitors were being turned away because of an abundance of picnickers, so she accepted a ride from a stranger. She was found dead in a shabby lovers' lane area two months later. Her body appeared to have been moved at least once, suggesting the killer may have lived in the area.

The next victim was a twenty-year-old art student who accepted a ride from a tall, good-looking young man wearing a university T-shirt. She was later found dead in Ann Arbor by construction workers. The upper part of her body was badly decayed, but the lower half somehow was preserved, as if covered for weeks by a tarpaulin that was then removed.

The third victim was a female law student who was shot in the head and then garroted. A pathologist found no signs of sexual assault.

Victim number four was a sixteen-year-old drug pusher who was beaten to death. Her nude body was violated with a tree branch.

Police insisted that the three killings were unrelated, but reporters knew better. Ann Arbor detective chief Harold

Olson finally established a task force of officers and a young secretary from the university. Collins, the police buff, knew what was happening. Victim five was killed outside the university area, in Benton Harbor.

Besides the obvious similarities in the women chosen for murder, authorities discovered a strange link: Most of them were killed at the time of their menstrual period.

Collins and a Philippine-born friend worked the night shift at Motor Wheel Corp., the brake drum division of Goodyear. During summer vacation, they apparently stole a trailer and drove to the beautiful Monterey peninsula of California, where the Pacific swirls in white foam against outcroppings and low bluffs. The two men went on a chain of burglaries in the general area, possibly just for kicks. While they were there, a seventeen-year-old girl was abducted in the valley town of Salinas, and her nude body was discovered in a ravine that cut through the hills around upscale Carmel. Some people living near the scene of the abduction remembered seeing a handsome young man who said he was an education major. He was driving a car with Michigan plates.

After Collins returned to Michigan, a thirteen-year-old girl—who looked several years older—was strangled with electrical cord and slashed repeatedly across the torso. She may have been raped. Once again, police thought the killer had come back to move the body.

While the girl was still missing, police searched an abandoned barn nearby and found nothing. They examined the barn again when the body was discovered, and came across one of the girl's earrings. Was the killer planting clues? Young Sheriff Doug Harvey said, "He's laughing at us."

Michigan victim number six was a little older than the others, in her early twenties, and slightly taller and heavier. She was stabbed again and again in a frenzy, and her throat was slashed. She was also the second to be shot.

The murder sparked a disturbance of more than a thousand people from the Ann Arbor area because of a fantastic rumor that someone at one of the two colleges was killing women for scientific experiments. Sheriff Harvey had to quell the outburst with tear gas and two hundred officers drawn from across the area. Later, famed psychic Peter Herkos waived his fee to see if he could help. He provided authorities with interesting possibilities, but nothing led to an arrest.

By then, Collins had developed the China Syndrome of serial killers; his line between fantasy and reality had become so blurred that he became bolder and less cautious. He abducted a cute, petite student from her room. She was choked, beaten, rolled down an embankment, and violated after her death.

Witnesses to the abduction provided a police artist with enough information to make a sketch. And because the killer sometimes returned to the body, Sheriff Harvey kept a twenty-four-hour stakeout near a mannequin about the latest victim's size. Nothing came of the stakeout, but the sketch led to several female students who reported that a strange man had given them a ride.

One said he told her he did not like earrings because they defiled the body, and another said the man put his large, powerful hands on her throat to demonstrate how he had strangled a cat, but he let her alone when she told him to stop. Several women who spoke to the man said they found it odd that he asked them if they were having their period.

Collins was just one of several young men questioned. He looked and acted nothing like a multiple killer. But under the strain of questioning, he sometimes dropped his congeniality and let his anger show. With nothing to go on, detectives moved on to another possible suspect but kept Collins in mind—and under watch. But no one could have guessed where the long-awaited break would come from.

When Collins's thirty-two-year-old aunt and her police-officer husband returned from a twelve-day vacation, their son noticed some dried paint on the floor of the laundry room. A bottle of ammonia was gone as well. Crime lab technicians conducted a Benzedrine test, but the chemical did not turn blue-green, meaning that no blood had been spilled there. But police did find small, cut hairs. Suddenly, there was a connection.

The aunt had cut her son's hair in the basement some time before. Small hairs, perhaps from her son—all less than an inch long—were found in the panties of one of the victims. The killer must have dragged his prey into the basement while the family was away, removed her underpants, put them on the floor, then later picked them up and slid them back onto her, unaware he was giving authorities one of the smallest solid leads that ever clinched a multiple murder case, apart from future cases involving DNA testing.

Searching further, technicians found blood on the concrete in front of the washtubs. And there was something else: The trailer stolen in Michigan was found abandoned in a run-down part of Salinas, more than two thousand miles away.

Collins's friend pleaded guilty to the California burglaries but denied having anything to do with the Salinas murder. Collins was indicted for the murder, but Michigan Governor William Milliken refused Governor Ronald Reagan's request for extradition. It did not matter. Collins was convicted of the Michigan murders and was sentenced to hard labor for life.

"The Devil's Business"

Charles Manson had been in one correctional center or another for most of his life since he was thirteen. His mother was a runaway pregnant teenager in the midst of the Depression. That was how he came to be born illegitimately in Cincinnati in November 1934, although all his relatives were in Kentucky and West Virginia. When he was four, his mother was arrested for assaulting a man she had hustled along the riverfront, and Manson was sent to his strict grandparents in West Virginia. The religious couple let him know that they rejected him as the result of sin by their rebellious daughter.

When his grandfather became ill, Manson was sent to an aunt and uncle in Illinois. Although he had no idea who his father was, he would play "father" with neighborhood children, especially the girls, and it made him feel good.

He was caught stealing at thirteen and was sent to the Gibault School for Boys in Terre Haute—the same disciplinary school where serial killer William Heirens spent part of his childhood.

When Manson was released, his mother wanted to rid herself of him and sought a court declaration that called the boy "errant." She then fled the county. Once again, Manson was sent to reform school. A kindly priest gathered donations to send him to Boys Town in Nebraska, which might have turned him around, but he escaped after just three days, stole a car, and robbed a store of $2,000. He was sent to another reform school.

Released at twenty-one, Manson married a waitress he had gotten pregnant, but she left him. He took up with another woman and went to California, but there he was arrested for car theft. For some time he went around with a leather jacket and an Elvis hairdo committing small-time crimes until he was arrested on federal charges of check forgery. He was released and took a bus to Berkeley. There, he mingled among the flower children, those waiflike men and women who greeted strangers gently and often offered them flowers. Whether consciously or not, he was recruiting a handpicked family that would listen only to him.

In time, Manson recruited several women and a teenage boy. He bound them to him in a kind of shared paranoia, prescribing freedom from the law. "You are free. Free to live, free to die, free to kill," he told them. One of the songs he wrote and strummed on his guitar stated, "There is no crime, there is no sin."

Manson was an engine of diffuse hate, and his hypnotic eyes compelled his followers to do what he said. He had told them, in effect, that the world hated them as much as they hated the world, and this was the only family there was.

Sixteen-year-old Charles "Tex" Watson, who was often strung out on drugs, felt important when Manson talked about their mission. The narcissistic Susan Atkins once faked a suicide attempt for the thrill of it. Investigators were to find that Patricia Krenwinkel, also known as Kate, was trying to protect herself by holding onto her childhood behavior well past adolescence. She considered herself plain, and felt unloved until Manson made love to her. Lynette Fromme lived in a kind of drug nirvana since she was fourteen and seemed to share a secret private world with another woman in the Manson family.

An acquaintance of Manson's, Gary Hinman, threatened to expose the members for something. But whatever those crimes, they were never made public because Hinman was stabbed to death. Two of the Manson women took part in getting rid of fingerprints and other evidence.

Manson became apocalyptic and spoke of Exterminans, the angel of the bottomless pit, who he claimed was to be the fifth member of the Beatles. As proof, he interpreted the lyrics of "Helter Skelter" and other songs on the band's "White Album" as personal messages to his disciples. As for what they were summoned to do, Manson was still thinking about it. One scheme was to end lawlessness in Los Angeles by pouring LSD into the drinking supply. Another was to commit a monstrous crime against fellow whites to set off a race war of annihilation that they could watch with satisfaction.

Polish-born filmmaker Roman Polanski had a huge success with his Satanic film *Rosemary's Baby*. Polanski had a gift for portraying tension; few viewers could forget the hands coming out of walls in *Repulsion*. He married beautiful actress Sharon Tate and lived behind iron gates in an exclusive part of Los Angeles. Drifting toward their home, one aimless day at a time, Charles Manson and his "family" were approaching.

In her home on Cielo Drive, Sharon Tate was excited about the impending birth of her child. Roman Polanski was away in London, but she kept the house alive with guests. She had no idea the Manson family had chosen her neighborhood to ignite the war against the world.

Early on August 9, 1969, at Spahn Ranch, Manson told Atkins, also known as Sadie Glutz, to get a knife and dark clothes. Glutz called another family member by phone and told her to bring three sets of dark clothes. Manson stayed behind while Linda Kasabian, Watson, Krenwinkel, and Glutz—shorn of nearly all her hair for some symbolic reason—drove up to the gates to Tate's home. Watson deactivated the controls, and they started up the hill with several coils of white nylon rope, along with some guns and knives.

They shot a young neighbor, Steven Parent, when he stopped their car and asked what they were doing. No one in the house heard anything. Tate was resting, and one of her guests, Voytek Frykowski, lay on a couch in another room, high on a drug called MDA and unaware of the intruder until it was too late. Watson put a revolver to the man's head but Frykowski, not understanding, asked, "What time is it?"

"Don't move or you're dead," Watson said. "I'm the Devil. I'm here to do the Devil's business."

Frykowski was tied up with a towel as Tate sat talking to guest Jay Sebring, a Hollywood hairstylist, at opposite ends of a bed. Sebring was shot through the chest to the screams of another guest, Abigail Folger. The intruders then tied up Folger and Tate with a rope thrown over a beam to keep them standing. The unconscious Sebring was attached to the other end as a weight.

Watson told the women, "You are all going to die." The plan was to draw and quarter them. Watson shot Frykowski in the back when the inebriated man broke free and tried to escape. Folger freed herself and ran, only to have her throat slit. Sebring recovered consciousness, but Watson soon hacked him to death.

Tate had seen only some of the attacks. She desperately told the intruders, "All I want to do is have my baby." Glutz held back the actress's arms as Watson stabbed her through her brassiere. When Tate was dead, Watson, Glutz, and at least one of the other women took turns stabbing her for a total of sixteen times. They butchered their other victims more and left cryptic messages written in blood on the walls.

Two nights after the murders, the family drove to the home of wealthy grocery chain owner Leno LaBianca. Manson, Watson, Leslie Van Houten, and Krenwinkel tied him and his wife back to back. Then, by common account, Manson left. The LaBiancas were separated, and Watson stabbed Mr. LaBianca a dozen times. As Van Houten held the wife, Krenwinkel severed her spine with a hateful thrust of the knife. In all, her body bore more than forty wounds. On the refrigerator, Katie scrawled "Healter [sic] Skelter," the race war that never happened.

Perhaps no other event of the 1960s made the world seem so upside-down as these two nights of senseless slaughter. What was most shocking was that the victims were chosen virtually at random—there was no rational motive—which created a sense that no one was safe. The roundup of Manson and his followers began when Atkins (aka Glutz), in custody on an unrelated charge, told a cellmate about the Manson family. The arrests added to the mystery in that no motive could be found for the crimes.

The family turned their trial into a circus of shouting and acting out their contempt for everyone. Manson, Atkins, and Krenwinkel were convicted on seven counts of first degree murder for the Tate-LaBianca killings, and Van Houten was convicted on two counts.

REFERENCES

Altman, Jack, and Ziporyn, Marvin. *Born to Raise Hell.* New York: Grove Press, 1968.

Block, Eugene B. "Trials in Contrast," *The Fabric of Guilt.* Garden City, N.Y.: Doubleday, 1968.

Brophy, John. *The Meaning of Murder.* New York: Thomas Y. Crowell, 1966.

Brussel, James A. *Casebook of a Crime Psychiatrist.* New York: Dell Publishing, 1970.

Chester, Graham. *Berserk!.* New York: St. Martin's Press, 1993.

Cleckley, Hervey. *The Mask of Sanity.* New York: New American Library, 1982.

Cooper, David, ed. *The Manson Murders.* Cambridge, Mass.: Schenkman Publishing, 1974.

Damore, Leo. *In His Garden.* New York: Arbor House, 1981.

DeFord, Miriam Allen. *Murderers Sane and Mad.* New York: Abelard-Schuman, 1965.

Gilmore, John, and Kenner, Ron. *The Garbage People.* Los Angeles: Omega Press, 1971.

———. *Cold-Blooded,* Portland: Feral House, 1996.

Helpern, Milton, with Knight, Bernard. *Autopsy.* New York: New American Library, 1979.

Holmes, Ronald M. and Holmes, Stephen T. *Murder in America.* Thousand Oaks, Calif.: Sage Publications, 1994.

Jenkins, Philip. *Using Murder: The Social Construction of Serial Homicide.* New York: Aldine de Gruyter, 1994.

Katz, Leonard. *The Coppolino Trial.* New York: Bee-Line Books, 1967.

Keyes, Edward *The Michigan Murders.* New York: Reader's Digest Books, 1976.

Knappman, Edward W., ed. "Carl Anthony Coppolino Trials: 1966 & 1967," *Great American Trials.* Detroit: Gale Research, 1994.

Lane, Roger. *Murder in America.* Columbus, Ohio: Columbia University Press, 1997.

Lefkowitz, Bernard, and Gross, Kenneth G. *The Victims.* New York: G.P. Putnam, 1967.

Life, March 4, 1966.

Livsey, Clara. *The Manson Women.* New York: Richard Marek, 1980.

Lyton, Elliott. *Hunting Humans.* New York: Pocket Books, 1988.

McDonald, John D. *No Deadly Drug.* Garden City, N.Y.: Doubleday, 1968.

Marriner, Brian. *On Death's Bloody Trail: Murder and the Art of Forensic Science.* New York: St. Martin's Press, 1991.

Moser, Don, and Cohen, Jerry. *The Pied Piper of Tucson.* New York: New American Library, 1967.

Nash, Jay Robert. *Crime Chronology: A Worldwide Record: 1900–1983.* New York: Facts on File, 1984.

———. *Bloodletters and Badmen.* New York: M. Evans & Co., 1995.

Newsweek, March 14, 1966.

New York Times, November 22, 1965.

———, March 26 and July 23, 1966.

———, April 29 and May 21, 1967.

Odell, Robin. *Landmarks in 20th Century Murder.* London: Headline, 1995.

Purvis, James. *Great Unsolved Mysteries.* New York: Gosset & Dunlap, 1978.

Rule, Ann (writing as "Andy Stack"). *Lust Killer.* New York: Signet Books, 1983.

Time, November 26, 1965.

Sanders, Ed. *The Family.* New York: Avon Books, 1972.

Sifankis, Carl. *Encyclopedia of American Crime.* New York: Facts on File, 1982.

Watson, Tex (as told to "Chaplin Ray" Hoestra). *"Will You Die for Me?."* Old Tappan, N.J.: Fleming H. Revell, 1978.

Wecht, Cyril. *Grave Secrets* rev. ed. New York: Onyx Books, 1998.

Wilson, Colin. *Written in Blood: Detectives & Detection.* New York: Warner Books, 1989.

———. *The Killers Among Us: Book II. Motives Behind Their Madness.* New York: Warner Books, 1995.

The 1970s

Part I:
Murders from Florida to Alaska

The beginning of the 1970s was marked by political instability and a widening division between generations. As the war in Vietnam escalated, the intensity with which students at campuses across the nation protested our involvement in southeast Asia grew as well. The 1972 arrest of G. Gordon Liddy and others attempting to break into Democratic National Headquarters at the Watergate hotel eventually led to President Nixon's resignation and a burgeoning sense of cynicism throughout the country.

The first sensational crime of the new decade centered on Dr. Jeffrey MacDonald, the handsome, Princeton-educated physician accused of fatally slashing his wife and two young children at their home in Fort Bragg, North Carolina, on February 17, 1970. MacDonald said his family was massacred by terrorists who had broken into the home. The former Green Beret, whose claim of innocence was supported by his wife's parents, was acquitted at a court martial. MacDonald was later convicted of the murders in a civil court in 1979. His guilt was never solidly established, but no trace of the Mansonlike terrorists has ever been found either.

The nervousness of the times brought a frenetic quality to lifestyles in the new generation. Women cut their hair shorter and men let their hair grow longer. Bell-bottomed pants, miniskirts, and leisure suits hustled into discotheques across the country. And the sexual revolution was in full swing. On the evening of New Year's Day, 1973, attractive twenty-eight-year-old Katherine Cleary went to Tweed's bar on Manhattan's Upper West Side hoping to find a man for casual sex.

The handsome drifter she took up with, Joe Willie Sampson, felt ashamed of his homosexual orientation and was trying to live straight. When Cleary ridiculed him about his problems satisfying her, Sampson lost control, beat her, jabbed her with a carving knife until it broke, and shoved a candle into her vagina. Sampson hanged himself while in custody in May 1973. The story of his single act of violence served as a warning of the times in the novel *Looking for Mr. Goodbar*.

While his wife was away, John Wayne Gacy would cruise hustler pickup locations in Chicago and bring young men back to his suburban home. Most of his victims were strangled from behind in what Gacy referred to as "the rope trick." The small-time contractor hid most of the bodies in a crawl space beneath his home; the others were buried around his garage or thrown in a nearby river. He was convicted of thirty-three individual killings—more than anyone else in American history—and was executed in 1994.

Later that same year Patty Hearst of the Hearst newspaper dynasty was kidnapped by African-American terrorists calling themselves the Symbionese Liberation Army. She was later caught on tape taking part in a robbery with her abductors. Hearst was captured in 1979 and released from prison four years later.

For two years beginning in 1976, residents of New York City lived in fear of a sniper who came to be known as Son of Sam. Police eventually traced the six murders to twenty-five-year-old David Berkowitz. Sam, as it turned out, was the name of a neighborhood dog that had irritated Berkowitz.

In 1978, the Unabomber struck for the first time, sending an explosive device to Northwestern University in Evanston, adjacent to Chicago. Over the years, his attacks would kill four and injure twenty-nine.

Two sensational crimes occurred at the end of the decade. In 1978, Dan White assassinated San Francisco Mayor George Moscone and city supervisor Harvey Milk, an open homosexual. In a defense that drew scornful amazement across the country, White's lawyer said his handsome young client suffered from the effects of eating too much junk food. The defense came to be known as the "Twinkie defense." White was convicted of a reduced charge of manslaughter and served less than five years in prison.

Again in 1978, charismatic cult leader Jim Jones took members of his People's Temple to Guyana, where about nine hundred of them died next to one another in murders and suicides—a Masada without a cause.

There was a sense of unreality about this troubling chain of events. In several major cities, the homicide rate peaked around 1974, although the national peak occurred in 1980, at 10.2 murders per one hundred thousand people.

A Marriage Made in Hell

At forty-five, John Emil List was a slender, still good-looking man behind his glasses. Formerly an accounting supervisor for Xerox Corporation, the mild-mannered List had begun selling insurance from his home with little success. He and his lean blonde wife lived with their three children in Westfield, New Jersey. Neighbors always saw List in a suit, white shirt, and tie—the perfect image of respectability.

John Emil List was a descendant of a Bavarian Lutheran family. Someone who knew him as a child called him the neatest and quietest little boy she had ever seen. But inside, List was seething.

He was a bookish boy with few friends. He grew up thinking Halloween was an evil celebration of paganism. He preferred going to serious plays and listening to classical music. In the Army during World War II, he saw little action but earned a sharpshooter's badge. He came back from Europe with an antique Austrian Steyr pistol he had bought, but he put it away unused.

List's Army reserve unit was called up in the Korean War, and he was stationed at Fort Ellis, near the forested tidewater area of Newport News, Virginia. There he met willowy Helen Taylor, a recent war widow. Helen, distraught over the loss of her husband, needed someone emotionally stable to help her pull through, and she married List in 1951. List inherited a family: Helen had a nine-year-old daughter, Brenda, and was close to her own mother, Eva.

List lived comfortably for awhile following his father's sale of the large family farm. The couple moved to a suburb of

Detroit and had Patty in 1955 and John Frederick in 1956. The Lists seemed genuinely happy living the American dream.

Helen had a mind of her own. She liked the attention she received at social gatherings tied to her husband's accounting jobs. She flirted harmlessly while List sulked. List, it seemed, could sulk like no one else.

When Helen became pregnant again in early 1958, she became depressed and confined herself to bed, and List had to look for a larger home.

In 1965, Helen began suffering from cerebral atrophy, possibly from a viral infection. List often had to cook dinner and take care of the house. He was also teaching Sunday school. Yet no unimaginable pressures were ever placed on List: His tension came from trying to live up to his unrealistic image of himself. He became uptight about Democrats and the Communist threat, and what he considered the increasing immorality of the 1960s and early 1970s. The family moved from Michigan to New Jersey, and his mortgage payments began piling up now that he was in business for himself. Seeking a cause for his anxiety, he must have told himself that his children were drifting away from religion, and that they could be saved only if he sent them to God.

His teenage daughter, Patty, was not quite pretty but was tall and shapely enough to play "Stupifyin' Jones" in her high school production of the musical comedy *L'il Abner*. As List sat in the audience watching Patty in a scanty outfit being ogled by teenagers dressed as hillbillies, he decided that she was bound for damnation.

On Halloween—a holiday List detested—his teenage daughter imitated actress Elizabeth Montgomery and dressed as a witch as she went trick-or-treating in Westfield. Less than a week later—November 5, 1971—List gathered his children in one room and told them they would all die soon. They did not know what to make of what he said and did nothing. Four days later, while his children were at school, List took out a .22 caliber automatic and the 1912 automatic pistol he had brought back from World War II. He put out a note for the milkman to stop deliveries. Then he shot his wife from behind and dragged her bleeding body forty feet. He arranged her bathrobe to cover her legs and put a kitchen towel over her face. He sat down and wrote notes to the school, saying the children would be spending a few days with their grandmother in North Carolina. When Patty arrived home, he shot her, too.

List washed, changed clothes, and went to a bank to cash a check so he could pay a former employer a modest amount of money he had embezzled. He picked up his thirteen-year-old son, Fred, from his after-school job. He let the boy go inside their home and then shot him in the head. Fifteen-year-old John Frederick came home early from soccer practice, only to be shot several times with both guns.

List did not want anyone to think he had killed his family out of anger, so he arranged the bodies—his wife in her robe, their three children in winter clothes—in the form of a cross, with Helen's arms reaching across the children's bodies. The murders took him twelve hours to complete. When he was done, he drove to his mother's home in another part of town and killed her, too.

The List case drew national concern because of its unspeakable nature and because years went by before anyone saw John List again. There was speculation that he might have married into another family and could be planning to slaughter them as well, which was the basis for the three *Stepfather* films inspired by the case.

Amid such speculation, the bald, aging List was living quietly as Bob Clark in Denver. His private demons had apparently left him. In 1985, he married again. In time, he and his wife, Delores, moved to Virginia. The case was revived again following an episode of "America's Most Wanted" in which an artist sculpted a bust of what List might look like eighteen years after the murders. Tips poured in, and FBI agents arrested List in his Richmond-area home in 1988. In August 1990, he was convicted and sentenced to five terms of natural life in prison.

The Candy Man

There still might be bodies of teenage boys lying under a beach outside Houston, but the bulldozers stopped after twenty-seven were found because that is how many were said to be there. Houston at the time of the killings was the fastest growing city in the country owing to the booming aerospace industry. Droves of people arrived every day, which might explain why the modest police department had little time to track down at least thirty missing boys assumed to be runaways. Most had come from broken homes or virtually no home to speak of.

Many of the boys reported missing were lured by a young man named Dean Corll, who then tortured and murdered them. But no one connected these disappearances to "the candy man," the nickname Corll had acquired while managing his mother's small candy factory. He was known for offering children leftover pecans and caramel. Corll worked hard—over two shifts a day—but liked to have his fun. Friends said there was a teddy-bear quality about him.

Corll's mother, Mary West, would stroll into the factory from time to time, flashing her diamonds and fluffing her minks. She was an attractive woman in her early fifties. West, a Methodist from Colorado, had married and divorced five times, twice with Arnold Corll. She drifted into the Church of Religious Science and, to keep her son pure, never discussed sex with him.

West's confrontational, attention-seeking, and overdramatic relationships with men were all played out in front of her children. Because West made such a strong impression, it was little wonder that Corll identified with some of her traits, even though part of him wanted to be masculine.

Corll apparently did not realize his homosexuality until he was in the Army, and then he panicked. The overprotective West defended him against her husband to the ruin of her marriage. She insisted that Corll was uninterested in sex in any way, shape, or form because that was how he was brought up.

Even so, Corll was far from coddled. West continually pushed her son to increase production to surpass that of a rival candy factory owned by a former husband.

A lifelong friend of one of the boys who disappeared was fifteen-year-old Elmer Wayne Henley, who played poker with Corll and also became his drinking and drug-taking partner. Corll cruised the streets in a car with Henley and an older teen, David Brooks, who apparently recruited boys for Corll. In appreciation of Brooks's friendship and services in finding boys, Corll bought him a late-model Corvette. Brooks got married and drifted away from Corll's circle, but the school-boys kept disappearing.

Then in August, a quivery voice called the police department and said, "Y'all better come right now, I killed a man." Officers who responded to the call at 2020 Lorimar saw Henley, another stuporous young man, and a teenage girl sitting on the stoop. Henley gestured to the front door and said, "In there."

The tall, naked body of thirty-three-year-old Dean Corll lay motionless, with multiple bullet wounds. Nearby was a seven-foot by three-foot torture board made of plywood with handcuffs secured near wrist holes. Nylon ropes were threaded through other openings of the board, and each rope was attached to another set of handcuffs. In the backyard was a plywood shed with airholes in the side. Police found a few hairs on the hasp of the door.

Gradually, the incredulous police were told that Corll regularly had Henley and Brooks bring boys to him. During parties, Corll would sometimes force the boys into anal or oral sex on the torture board, and then he would shoot or choke them to death.

There was to be a 3 A.M. party the night of Corll's death, but Corll was angry because one of the teenage boys brought a girl. "God damn you," Corll roared, "you ruined everything!" But the fifteen-year-old girl had nowhere else to go. What Henley said happened next is an account that the police and prosecutors used because they had no other explanation.

Henley said he had passed out after "huffing" acrylic paint fumes. He awoke to find his ankles tied together and Corll snapping on the handcuffs. "Man, you blew it, bringing that girl," Corll supposedly said, "but I'm going to fix you now!" The other young man and the girl were already bound together while still unconscious from the acrylic paint fumes. Corll turned up the radio and pointed a pistol at Henley, who begged for his life.

When Henley said he would do anything, Corll let him loose and ordered him to cut off the clothes of the limp girl. Corll then spread-eagled the second young man on the torture board. Henley told authorities that he grabbed the gun from Corll and shot him.

Following up on Henley's statement, officers began digging up the ground around an old boat shed Corll had rented southwest of Houston. Before long, their shovels struck a layer of lime. Digging with their hands, they found their first skull. Next, they located the body of a boy who had been strangled with a cord.

By midnight of the first day, the officers had unearthed an additional seven bodies. Brooks was contacted and he admitted to helping bury most of the victims there and also on High Island.

After the bulldozers stopped their final digging, the father of one of the boys still missing went out to the wasteland around the shed and dug for hours every weekend in hopes of finding his son. He never did.

In 1974, Elmer Wayne Henley was sentenced to six terms of ninety-nine years in prison for taking part in some of the murders. Prosecutors called him "a monster who should be removed from society."

A Journey Through
Love and Death

Sandy Fawkes was a young English journalist who was in America on an assignment to interview a few celebrities, including Vice-President Spiro Agnew. She knew so little about the United States that she expected most of it to look like the Grand Canyon. The single mother met twenty-eight-year-old Daryl Knowles at a restaurant in downtown Atlanta in November 1974. Daryl had rugged good looks, perfect manners, a light Southern or Western accent, and flashy clothes in keeping with the disco crowd.

Fawkes later said Knowles was a strange man—an awkward lover who sometimes spoke like a child. He was intrigued by her being a writer and suggested that some day she write about him, because he was going to die soon. "It might be in two days or two months, I don't know when. But within a year, I'll be dead." To explain his strange remark, Daryl told her he was being hunted by the mob.

Skeptical, Fawkes asked, "Are you sure it isn't a morbid obsession? Have you seen a psychiatrist?"

"I saw one once. He told me I have a perfect criminal mind."

Most of their days were spent driving in Knowles's sleek, white Chevrolet Impala. Knowles paid for everything, their food, gasoline, and lodging. Fawkes characterized the affair as a pleasant holiday together. "It was like playing a game of being lovers, of being a partner in another's dreams." They separated in West Palm Beach, and Fawkes assumed that was the end of the affair.

But soon she received a call from the police, who wanted to talk with her about Knowles. Fawkes soon discovered the truth behind Daryl Knowles.

As a teenager and as a young man, Knowles committed so many car thefts and burglaries that he was outside of institutions only a few months at a time. He was paroled in May 1974 and flew to San Francisco to marry a woman who had written to him in prison, but she turned him away because she found him frighteningly intense in person. In a mindless rage over the rejection, Knowles killed three people at random while walking the streets of San Francisco.

Knowles flew to Jacksonville, where he smothered a woman with a pillow, beginning a four-month rape and murder rampage that claimed eighteen more lives. In one of his last attacks, he met Carswell Carr in a Georgia gay bar, went home with him, tied him up, and jabbed him twenty-two times with a pair of scissors. He also killed Carr's fifteen-year-old daughter because she was a witness. Knowles stole Carr's bright yellow, double-breasted blazer—the same one Daryl was wearing the night he met Fawkes. The white Chevrolet Impala Knowles had chauffeured Fawkes around in actually belonged to murder victim William Bates of Lima, Ohio. The watch Daryl later gave her came from another victim. Knowles, who had grown up in the backstreets of Jacksonville, was a rare breed of serial killer. Although he usually killed in simple robberies, he preferred to murder in order to assume his victim's persona for a few hours.

Police had contacted Fawkes after Knowles was seen trying to rape a woman at gunpoint, and then he abducted her sister as a hostage. To the surprise of the police, Knowles let his kidnap victim live and tried to hide out in the swampy woods he knew so well. But a young farmer saw Knowles and held him at gunpoint until the police arrived.

Fawkes spoke to Knowles briefly in the station lockup and returned to England. But Knowles had decided never to face prison again. While being transferred to a high-security facility on December 18, 1974, near Douglasville, Georgia, Knowles picked the lock of his handcuffs with a straightened paper clip and made a grab for an officer's gun. Knowles was shot and killed instantly by Georgia Bureau of Investigation agent Ron Angel.

A Deadly Charm

Deviant crimes beg the question of whether some people are born without a conscience. That is, does compassion for others come from our genes? Or do these criminals learn early in life how to manipulate people and situations to their advantage? For centuries, there was no word for such people. Then they were called psychopaths. Once newspapers began misusing *psychopath* to mean anyone acting insanely, psychiatrists led by Hervey Cleckley began using the term *sociopath*. Cleckley concluded that such criminals are sane and that some are even brilliant. On occasion, a sociopath shares traits with what psychiatrists call the "narcissistic personality." The result is someone bright, attractive, and cunning—someone like Ted Bundy.

On the last day of January 1974, psychology major Lynda Healy disappeared from her dormitory at the University of Washington. Central Washington State College cheerleader Susan Rancourt vanished in April on her way to see a counselor.

Sixty miles away, Donna Gail Manson of Evergreen State College in Olympia was last seen leaving for a jazz concert. In Corvallis, not far from Seattle, a search began for Oregon State University student Roberta Parks. She left her dorm for an ice cream sundae and never returned.

The only connection between the disappearances seemed to be that each was a college-age white female with long, straight hair parted in the middle. While no bodies had yet been found, police feared the worst: They had a killer on their hands.

Terrified female college students had their boyfriends escort them to and from their campus homes. But being with someone was no guarantee of safety. On Sunday, July 14, small, bouncy Janice Ott disappeared amid a crowd estimated at forty thousand people cramming Lake Sammamish State Park outside Seattle. Just forty-five minutes later, nineteen-year-old Denise Naslund disappeared from the same state park.

One witness, pretty, long-haired Janice Graham reported that a polite young man with an English accent and his arm in a sling had asked her for help in getting a sailboat out of his car. He said his name was Ted. She grew suspicious when she approached his car and there was no sign of the sailboat he had mentioned. He asked her to get into the car, and Graham declined. Minutes later, she spotted the man walking to his car with another young woman—possibly Janice Ott.

In September, grouse hunters found the remains of Janice and Denise in the foothills near the state park. Later, the bodies of Lynda, Susan, and two other women were found on fog-shrouded Taylor Mountain in the Cascade range.

Tourists found one of the missing women in a canyon outside Grand Junction, Colorado, in early 1974. The unidentified woman had been beaten and strangled. Twenty-six-year-old Julie Cunningham disappeared in the ski resort of Vail, Colorado, in March, and the next month twenty-five-year-old Denise Oliverson vanished in Grand Junction, leaving her bicycle under a bridge. The city, which was built only in the 1950s, looked like a tidy suburb under the shadow of a mesa in the middle of nowhere.

A task force was formed that autumn in a town near the Nevada-Utah border to discuss the disappearance or murder of approximately ninety teenage girls and young women in the Western states in just five years. Some of the women were runaways and some died in accidents. Among the others, a few conformed to what might be called the "Ted pattern": pretty, outgoing, long-haired, and last seen talking to a man in his mid-twenties.

Utah had at least three of the victims: Nancy Wilcox, Debby Kent, and Melissa Smith, daughter of the Midvale police chief. Seventeen-year-old Melissa was beaten, raped, and strangled. Not all the victims had been sexually assaulted, but some had been both raped and sodomized.

The same day Debby Kent disappeared in the town of Bountiful, a young man attempted to persuade beautiful Carol DaRanch to get into his car by posing as a police officer. He slapped handcuffs on her, but the nineteen-year-old woman broke free. When the man tried to club her with a crowbar, DaRanch kicked him and ran to the safety of a shopping mall. Police had discovered a handcuff key on the ground at Debby Kent's high school, and the key fit the handcuffs that were on Carol. The description of the would-be abductor Carol and witnesses gave the police matched earlier descriptions of the man who had called himself Ted.

The task force stepped up its efforts, feeding thousands of names into its computer—men who fit witnesses' descriptions and who went by the name Ted. One of the names that was a match, but was quickly discounted, was Theodore Robert Bundy.

Meanwhile, four more young women had disappeared.

In July of 1975, Utah Highway Patrol Sergeant Bob Haywood arrested Ted Bundy on suspicion of burglary. In Bundy's car were plastic bags, handcuffs, rope, gloves, and pantyhose with holes cut out for the eyes, nose, and mouth. Gas receipts and maps placed Bundy at the scene of at least two of the disappearances. Carol DaRanch was called in to identify Bundy, which she did. He was arrested for attempted kidnapping.

On June 30, 1976, a judge in Salt Lake City sentenced Bundy to serve one to fifteen years for the thwarted kidnapping attempt of Carol DaRanch. He was put in the same prison as Gary Gilmore, who was awaiting a place in history as the first person to be executed in the United States since the Supreme Court reinstated the death penalty that year. Gilmore chose death by firing squad following his arrest for killing a motel desk clerk in a robbery. He was executed on January 17, 1977.

Bundy was extradited to Aspen, Colorado, to stand trial for the murder of Caryn Campbell. He escaped the courthouse by pushing out a window in the library on the second floor and jumping to the ground, running to the icy waters of the Roaring Fork River to hide his trail. He was caught eight days later, only to escape again. This time under tight security, Bundy carved a small hole out of the ceiling of his cell and crawled into a guard's apartment. He stole a car, abandoned it in a blizzard, and walked to an interstate bus station. He arrived in Denver on New Year's Eve and took a plane to Chicago. From there, he took an Amtrak train to Ann Arbor, Michigan.

Always drawn to large congregations of young women, Ted went to Florida State University in Tallahassee less than a month later. After months of incarceration, Bundy was ready to explode. While his earlier murders revealed a desire to control and torture his victims, his style now degenerated into a need to simply kill women, seemingly as many as possible. On January 18, 1978, he committed his most careless crime— invading the Chi Omega sorority house as if he were immune from capture. In just seconds, he fatally shot Lisa Levy and bit off her nipple, strangled Margaret Bowman, and wielded a heavy oak limb as he severely bashed Karen Chandler and Kathy Kleiner. Four blocks away, he attacked Cheryl Thomas—who would survive but lose hearing in one ear—in her room and fled.

In one final, desperate act, on February 9, 1978, Bundy fatally beat twelve-year-old honor student Kimberly Leach in Lake City, Florida. Her body was found eight weeks later in a hog shed, and even then it was clear that there had been massive trauma to her pelvic area. Her neck had been sliced through.

The day after the Leach murder, Ted Bundy made the FBI's Ten Most Wanted List.

Bundy stole a car, which was spotted by Pensacola police officer David Lee. After a short car chase, Bundy tried to escape on foot and was quickly caught. He scuffled with the officers but was quickly subdued. "I wish you had just killed me there on the street," he told his captors.

Theodore Robert Bundy, America's most notorious serial killer, was in custody.

There was nothing in Bundy's background to explain why he had become the most hunted killer of the decade. In fact, his arrest was shrouded in controversy, as swarms of friends and acquaintances came forward in Ted's defense, unable to accept that someone as charming, as All-American as Ted could be a brutal murderer. By all accounts, Bundy was always the perfect gentleman.

But beneath the veneer, a monster had taken shape.

Bundy was born at a Vermont home for unwed mothers. Afterward, his young mother returned to her parents in northwestern Philadelphia. She claimed to be the baby's sister, but her neighbors knew better and considered her sinful.

Bundy's mother married an Army cook she had met at her Methodist church, John Culpepper Bundy, a short and bashful man who gave Ted his last name. Together they had two daughters. Ted became attached to his stepsisters and did well in school. In adolescence he turned to politics. He decided to study law as the surest way to run for office, possibly the U.S. Senate.

Working as a busboy at the Olympic Hotel, Bundy became love-struck with a woman, whose name has never been publicly revealed. She was youthful yet mature, friendly but serious. The woman had luxurious long hair, like most of his future victims, loved skiing, and came from a well-off Los Angeles family. Bundy arranged a date with her, and tried to impress her by assuming a Cary Grant-style British accent, and maintaining that he came from a prominent Philadelphia family. But she soon saw through Ted's story, and the two parted ways. Ted fell into a depression and eventually dropped out of college.

He threw himself into politics, determined to become the type of man he had pretended to be—a man of influence and power. He worked for the Washington State Republican Party. But for all his gifts, he could not concentrate for any length of time. He returned to college and worked at a suicide hotline in an old mansion on Seattle's Capitol Hill. There, he worked with Ann Rule, a former police officer who would later become a famous true-crime writer. She would later base the book *Stranger Beside Me* on Ted.

Some have said that Bundy's illegitimacy deeply troubled him, but he used it to gain sympathy with practically every woman he ever met, including Rule. Despite her investigative instincts, Ann found nothing strange about this likable, vulnerable young man. He seemed to be a model citizen.

But by then, even Bundy's girlfriend, who goes by the name Elizabeth Kendall, had become suspicious of his activities. It occurred to her that the disappearances took place when Ted was gone. But she was too in love to think clearly. It was easy to see what Kendall saw in the twenty-eight-year-old law student. Bundy had wavy brown hair, soft blue eyes, and a strong jawline. He was such a wonderful substitute father to Kendall's daughter that on her fifth birthday, Bundy made her a cake himself.

And yet there was a strangeness to him. Kendall sometimes found him examining her body under the covers with a flashlight, and his moods changed quickly. Sometimes he snapped at her, but other times broke down crying for no apparent reason.

She found unexplained things in their apartment and car. Things Bundy obviously stole—a pair of crutches (Bundy had not been injured while with Kendall), plaster of paris, and a lug wrench taped at one end. Kendall once saw him with a fake mustache and another time noticed that he had surgical gloves in his pocket. But Bundy was charming, and a good liar. Kendall believed even his flimsiest explanations.

It was not until Bundy persuaded her to be tied to the bedposts during sex that Kendall became afraid. The third time he did so, Bundy seemed to lose himself and tried to choke her. She panicked, and started screaming. Ted seemed to wake up as if from a trance, and broke down in tears. Earlier, on July 4, 1974, they spent the holiday on the Yakima River in an inflatable yellow raft she had given him. She fell into the river, perhaps nudged, and as she struggled she could see that Ted was making no effort to save her. When she pulled herself back into the raft, Bundy said, "Can't you take a joke?"

As Kendall recalled these frightening incidents, she began to fear that her beloved Ted might be *the* Ted everyone was looking for. She went to the police.

During questioning, Bundy crumpled a pack of cigarettes and told detectives, "I'm the most cold-hearted son of a bitch you'll ever meet." Another time he said that he had tried to stop himself from killing after his first escape, but that after his second "it wasn't controllable."

After his final arrest, he told Kendall that he never had blackouts; he remembered everything he had done. "Pretty scary, isn't it?" he added. Bundy's only remorse was for the fact that he had been caught. Bundy received the death penalty for Kimberly Leach's murder.

While in prison, dozens of experts interviewed Bundy in an attempt to understand how such a handsome, popular type could become such a depraved killer. Bundy said that "the fantasies were taking over my life . . . The act itself was a downer," a sentiment shared by many serial killers. He admitted that the thrill of the hunt and the control over his victims' life and death was his driving force. The sex and the actual murder were secondary. In an attempt to explain why he needed to kill young women, Bundy offered only the simple answer that he wanted to. He did it because he enjoyed it.

Always self-serving, Bundy tried to barter information about unsolved cases for more time, but eventually, his time ran out. On January 23, 1989, the ashen and shaking Bundy was strapped into the electric chair of Starke prison in Florida where he received 2,000 volts. He is said to have spent the previous night weeping and praying.

No one is sure how many women Bundy killed. As his execution approached, he confessed to at least nine, including two in Idaho for which he had not been a suspect. But he denied the Florida attacks and several others. The FBI estimated that Bundy had killed thirty-six women, and prosecutors said "at least" fifty.

Part II:
Murders in the Golden State

There occurred in California in the 1970s such a rash of pathological killings by men sane and mad that they sometimes occurred simultaneously in the same area. Authorities used the differences and similarities in each pattern to put such crimes in perspective. The FBI established its Behavioral Science Unit largely to offer profiles and help track pattern killers, and in 1976 Dr. Donald Lunde of Stanford University in northern California coined the term "serial killer" in his book *Murder and Madness.*

In the 1970s and early 1980s, hitchhiking was still a popular mode of transportation for many Californians. But the jeopardy facing hitchhikers was epitomized by an event in September 1978; a fifty-year-old man picked up fifteen-year-old Mary Vincent, hacked off both her hands in a sadistic frenzy, and left the girl to stumble in traffic for help.

In the Sonoma County area, north of San Francisco, six women were found murdered from February 1972 to December 1973, but the crimes were never solved. Four more nude bodies of women were discovered around San Francisco from May through July 1973, and those killings were also never cleared.

Buried Secrets

On a May morning in 1971, Goro Kagehiro noticed a shallow trench in his peach orchard in Sutter County—a part of northern California once trod by thousands of gold miners. The depression was at least six feet long, two and a half feet wide, and 3.5 feet deep. But Kagehiro had a busy day ahead of him, with workers arriving to thin trees, and he did not get back to the trench until that evening. By then, the trench was all covered over. Kagehiro noticed heavy tire tracks in the loose dirt and called the police.

Deputy Sheriff Steve Sizelove and Kagehiro started digging, only to uncover the largest mass murder case in U.S. history up to that time. First, they found just a piece of a blue denim pants leg, then a shoe, and a foot. Sizelove sent out a radio call that brought a half dozen uniformed officers and detectives to the site.

In half an hour, they dug up a migrant worker Sizelove had seen walking along Colusa Highway near Yuba City. The man had been stabbed in the chest, his left cheek slashed, and his skull smashed open like a melon, possibly with a machete.

Who would do such a thing to a harmless seasonal worker? The man did not have enough money to be robbed. He probably did not stay in any one place long enough to make enemies. The case was headed by Sheriff Roy Whiteaker, who at thirty-one was the youngest sheriff/coroner in California.

An officer in nearby Marysville recalled that a similar migrant was severely beaten and cut by an unknown assailant some time back at the Guadalajara Cafe, a restaurant owned by Natividad Corona, whose brother, Juan, was in charge of hiring migrant workers for Kagehiro and others. Juan, a short, stocky man in his late thirties, was known to have fits of temper so violent that his family sometimes had to tie him down. The night of the migrant's beating, Juan was seen in town carrying a short-handled hoe such as that used in weeding beans. The victim of the cafe attack was too terrified to identify his attacker, however. He sued and won a judgment against Natividad Corona, who sold the Guadalajara in 1970 and returned to Mexico. But Juan stayed behind.

This admittedly loose connection was just one of several leads pursued in tracking the murderer of the migrant at the Kagehiro farm. But new evidence strengthened the connection. The tracks at the first gravesite came from a new Chevrolet van, just like the one Juan owned.

An additional gravesite was discovered the following day as Ernesto Garcia was riding his tractor on the J.L. Sullivan ranch. The body was that of another drifter, whose clothing was mismatched as if he had been carelessly dressed in someone else's clothing. Sheriff Whiteaker, using officers on loan from neighboring departments, ordered his men to do a foot-by-foot search. The police made a plaster cast of a possible footprint found near one of the graves, and collected several items including a cigarette stub and a meat market receipt.

Investigators looking into Juan's history learned that he had spent some time in a state mental hospital around 1956. He was committed for three months at his brother's request. When Juan was released, he went back to Mexico for awhile but returned to the United States to run his own business. The two brothers drifted apart, especially after Juan married Gloria Morena, a cook at a labor camp.

Before detectives could serve a search warrant for Juan's employment records, other officers found a fourth grave. This victim was naked from the waist down. Several additional bodies unearthed nearby suggested that they too had been killed as part of some sexual act.

In all, twenty-five bodies were found. The final victim discovered had two crumpled bank slips in his pocket with Juan Corona's name and address stamped on them.

In searching Juan's home—and the barracks and cookhouse of the Sullivan ranch, where he worked—officers found an ax, a bolo machete, a meat cleaver, a broad knife with a possible blood stain, and a pistol that seemed to have a similar stain under its barrel. Plenty of evidence to arrest the hiring contractor and take him to jail.

Corona's San Francisco attorney, Richard Hawk, found weaknesses in the case, including some mix-ups at the overwhelmed crime laboratory. To make his client appear innocent, Hawk affected outrage at the allegations and threatened to file a $350 million libel and slander suit against law enforcement officials. He told reporters that this was a case of persecution in a county that did not want to see Mexicans rise above the level of migratory workers.

Because the public needed a suspect, Hawk suggested that Natividad, Juan's brother, returned from Mexico, killed all those men, and then went back to his homeland. The suggestion was impossible to immediately disprove. And Natividad's name was on the registries from when he took men to several run-down Marysville hotels in the late 1960s. Hawk hinted that because Natividad was gay, sleeping with the men he allegedly killed made him hate them for stripping him of his manhood in a culture that values *machismo*. But the Natividad Corona detectives interviewed in Mexico was a frail, aging man with diabetes, and there were no records to show that he had ever returned to California after selling his restaurant a few years earlier.

The prosecution's case was built on tenuous circumstances, but when laid side by side before the jurors the evidence was formidable. When the jurors felt they were hopelessly deadlocked at eight-to-four, Hawk—perhaps ill-advisedly—asked the judge to urge them to continue deliberations. The last holdouts succumbed, and Corona was convicted. In prison, he was attacked by fellow inmates, receiving thirty wounds to his face alone, and continued to talk of an appeal. Questions remain as to who might have helped Corona get rid of much of the bloody evidence.

Partners in Murder

Multiple killings by two or more people traveling in cars and vans were a new phenomenon, and nowhere were such murders more prevalent than in California in the 1970s.

Case No. 1

At least ten times in the mid-1970s, trucks and cars passed along a busy highway in southern California without anyone noticing two men hauling large garbage bags of dismembered bodies. The bald, older man was Patrick Kearney, a tall, slender computer genius for Hughes Aircraft. Kearney's companion was a trim, muscular young man with a dark mustache and a Texas accent.

The two buried their first victim under the floor of their garage in Culver City and then moved. Anywhere from ten to twenty-seven teenage boys and young men were shot and dismembered, their remains left in bags and dumped from Los Angeles all the way to the Mexican border. The pair picked up their victims cruising areas including the Sunset Strip, the red light district of Selma Avenue, and McArthur Park, not far from downtown Los Angeles. The victims would be assured of a good time, only to be killed in remote areas. Then Kearney and his good-looking lover would return to their home in Redondo Beach as if nothing had happened.

Not one decisive lead led to an arrest in the "trashbag murders." Police learned just enough to identify Kearney and his lover as suspects and issued a wanted poster. On Friday, July 1, 1977, Kearney and the other man walked into the Riverside police station, forty-five miles from Los Angeles, and pointed to the poster. The younger suspect uttered, "We're them."

Kearney agreed to plead guilty to three of the murders with the informal understanding that the Texas man would be set free. Authorities were so glad to close the case, that the second indictment was dropped. The younger man was released.

Case No. 2

While the murder team of Kearney and his Texas lover was living in Redondo Beach, Roy Lewis Norris and Lawrence Sigmund Bittaker were abducting girls for rides of torture nearby. Norris had just been released from the Atascadero state hospital following a rape conviction, and his partner was still on parole for a weapons charge. These ex-convicts went to high school campuses and photographed pretty students, possibly with the goal of capturing them later. In all, five hundred photographs were found, and the number of girls who disappeared ranged from thirty to forty, although conclusive evidence tied Norris and Bittaker to only five deaths. Some of the bodies were found in the San Gabriel Mountains. One skull still had an ice pick imbedded in the ear.

Norris's stay at the mental hospital seems to have taught him only cunning, and Bittaker was said to have a near-genius IQ of 138. They would pick up hitchhikers in their new silver GMC van, which they facetiously called "Murder Mack," but sometimes they abducted their victims by force. One girl was sprayed with a disabling chemical, another was literally lifted out of her shoes. The men would record the screams of the girls being raped. The use of pliers, wires, and sledgehammers as instruments of torture and death led the crimes to be called the "toolbox murders."

230 · *Homicide: 100 Years of Murder in America*

One girl escaped from the van in terror. Bittaker ran after her and forced her back into the van, but not before the fight was noticed by people at a tennis court. The incident led to their arrest. Norris pleaded guilty and agreed to testify against his friend in return for a sentence of forty-five years to life. The *Los Angeles Times* indicated that the jury heard some of the most shocking testimony in American court history. The jurors also had to sit uneasily through one of the scream tapes. After three days of deliberations, Bittaker was convicted of five murders and sentenced to die by electrocution.

Case No. 3

Police said they had never seen anything like it. Gerald Gallego of Sacramento had such overwhelming sexual fantasies, that his attractive wife agreed in 1978 to help him abduct women to carry them out.

When Gerald was ten, his father died in the new Mississippi gas chamber for murdering two police officers. The boy may have given in to his darker impulses on the presumption that his father's traits were bound to come out sooner or later. As he told a court psychologist after his arrest, "I have the feeling that my father is inside me." Several close male relatives had also been convicted of first- or second-degree murder.

After being in and out of jails for a variety of petty crimes, Gerald held several jobs as a driver and supposedly had an incestuous relationship with his daughter from a failed marriage. He met his future wife, Charlene, in Reno, and fascinated her with his show of outward masculinity. Gallego was sexually aggressive in bed, but whenever he met with personal problems, such as losing a job, he became impotent. The only way to continue satisfying his girlfriend—later his wife—was by refueling his fantasies. Charlene is said to have watched and possibly taken part in a sex party Gallego had with his fourteen-year-old daughter and a female friend of the girl.

Charlene came from an affluent family but she shunned her background. Writer Eric van Hoffman reports that she had an IQ of 160. She had used narcotics since she was twelve and was almost an alcoholic at fourteen, yet she played classical violin well. For awhile she had a black boyfriend, and then she took up with Gallego.

On September 12, 1978, Gallego told Charlene he wanted a pair of teenage girls he was watching from inside his van. Charlene offered to sell the girls some marijuana if they would accompany her to the vehicle. The girls followed Charlene to the van. Gallego then appeared with a gun and tied them up.

The couple drove around with their captives along the seemingly endless slopes of pine in the mountains outside Sacramento. Charlene thought Gallego was just having a little fun when he unbound the girls, told them to get out, and walk ahead of the van. Then he shot them both. A few days later, Gallego and Charlene were married in Reno.

Sometimes while driving around, Gallego would see a pretty teenager and say to his bride, "Baby, I want to take her." Then he would prepare his gun and ropes while she slid into the driver's seat. Charlene insisted that she never witnessed any of the killings, but investigators believe she may have taken part in the rapes.

After eight murders, Gallego got drunk one night and was so taken by college student Mary Beth Sowers that he was determined not to let her boyfriend, Craig Miller, get in the way. Gallego abducted the pair at gunpoint in front of a friend of theirs. Gallego and Charlene drove the handsome young couple for awhile, then Gallego had Miller get out of the van and make a run for his life. Gallego brought him down with a shot in the head. Then he and Charlene took Sowers to their apartment. Afterward, he and Charlene drove her to a shallow gully, where Gallego killed her.

With the police connecting all the crimes in California and Nevada, Gallego and his wife took a bus to Salt Lake City to hide out. Then they went to Denver. They were in Omaha when Charlene wired her mother for money, and her mother contacted the FBI. The couple was arrested when they went to pick up the cash.

Gallego arrogantly acted as his own attorney and put his wife on the stand. Badgered about whether she loved him, Charlene replied, "No. It was more of a protection. You kept telling me over and over how much you loved me and how much . . . you would take care of me and never let anybody hurt me, which was just another lie."

But his defense was just a charade. After Gallego was sentenced to die in the electric chair in California, he was transferred to Nevada and tried on murder and kidnapping charges there. In an unusual procedure, the prosecution was financed through public contributions. Gallego was executed by lethal injection, and Charlene was sentenced to nearly seventeen years in prison.

Case No. 4

Bodies of young women kept turning up in remote areas near Los Angeles. At first the victims were primarily prostitutes. Then they were attractive young women who were stopped on the street by two dark-haired men claiming to be police officers. One of the women who refused to get into their car was the adopted daughter of actor Peter Lorre.

The more disturbed member of the "Hillside Strangler" team was Kenneth Bianchi, a good-looking young man who called his lifelong loneliness "a lingering beast." His mother had been a promiscuous teenager who handed her son from one person to another until he was finally adopted at four months old. Growing up in Rochester, New York, the boy was ashamed of his bed-wetting, and he resented the officials at his Catholic school for doing nothing to stop the ridicule by his fifth grade classmates. There were also daily problems in the home.

Bianchi's adoptive mother became paranoid. Her hypochondria spread to concern for her son, and she took him to a doctor eight times in five months. A social worker later recommended that both mother and son receive psychiatric treatment. When Bianchi's adoptive father died when Bianchi was thirteen, his mother stopped doting on him. She seemed to be manipulating her son into remaining dependent on her while at the same time distancing herself from him by demanding that he act mature. It is little wonder that a doctor found Bianchi a deeply hostile boy.

Bianchi wanted to be a police officer and spent two years saving lives as an ambulance technician in Rochester. During that time, three girls were murdered around Rochester by someone deemed a "sex maniac." There were some who believed in retrospect that Bianchi might have been the killer. The murders were more than likely committed by someone else, but his proximity to the crimes might have stirred his own homicidal fantasies.

Probably due to his confusing relationship with his mother, Bianchi developed a love-hate relationship with women. "I hate women," he said. When asked why, he replied, "They hurt."

Despite his precarious emotional state, Bianchi was no criminal. That is, until he took up with his short, wiry, cousin Angelo Buono. Buono, who was in his early forties, had already spent time in prison. Once again, two people who might not have been killers on their own became a runaway machine of murder together. The cousins might have begun their reign of terror by discussing the availability of women around the Strip and how easy it would be to have their way with them. Eventually, it was not just talk. While Buono's fantasies were of rape, Bianchi's were of murder.

Bianchi's girlfriend, Kelli, was pregnant when the attacks began in 1977. Bianchi was attached to Kelli more in a child's way than as a man: He sought friendship and mothering from her, and her pregnancy was unsettling to him. This seemed to trigger Bianchi's violent feelings toward women. He and Buono picked up someone they considered disposable—a black prostitute named Yolanda Washington. She was raped, strangled, and her body thrown from their car on a hillside near Forest Lawn Cemetery.

Next was fifteen-year-old Judith Ann Miller, who lived on the streets to make money rather than staying with her family and in school. Miller disappeared from Hollywood Boulevard and Wilcox Avenue, and her body was posed on another hillside with her legs spread.

The third victim, Lissa Teresa Kasten, was a waitress and dancer who was never involved in prostitution. Her body was found on a hillside cul-de-sac in Glendale, and her car was missing. Bianchi and Buono next kidnapped twenty-year-old art student Kristina Weckler in Glendale and tortured her. They kept her alive for hours to add more excitement to their "game."

Two girls, twelve and fourteen years old, were abducted near the Eagle Rock shopping center. Another victim was again a prostitute, seventeen-year-old Kimberly Martin—who accepted clients by appointment only because of her fears of the man the press was calling "The Hillside Strangler."

Kenneth Bianchi was growing cocky, becoming careless. He and Buono began trying to abduct women off the street in broad daylight, and many witnesses were able to describe them. Bianchi felt invincible, and wanted to step up the pace. Buono, on the other hand, believed Bianchi was becoming a liability, possibly bragging about the crimes and even chatting with police officers about the case. Buono had a girlfriend of his own whom he wanted to marry and start a life with. He persuaded Bianchi to leave town alone. Bianchi headed for Bellingham, Washington.

Though the team of Buono and Bianchi had fallen apart, Bianchi was not ready to stop killing.

On January 12, 1979, he separately abducted and murdered two young women by himself—twenty-seven-year-old Diane Wolder and twenty-two-year-old Karen Mandic. But this was not Los Angeles, where people paid little attention to their neighbors. The disappearances made the radio newscast, and a woman reported seeing a missing Mercury Bobcat suspiciously parked on a dead-end street by a wooded area. Inside the car, police found both victims strangled. When officers questioned Bianchi, they found evidence that he had heavily masturbated in his home after the murders. He was arrested.

Bianchi admitted to five of the California murders but denied the two in Washington, and received five life sentences. Before the penalty was imposed, he was examined by some of the best-known criminal psychiatrists in the country, including Dr. Donald Lunde, creator of the term "serial killer," and Dr. Cornelia Wilbur, who had treated the woman called "Sybil" for multiple personalities.

The contradictory findings of the experts proved that serial killers show more similarities among themselves than do psychiatrists. Bianchi was diagnosed as a multiple personality, a dissociate personality, a sociopath, a schizophrenic, and a manic depressive. Bianchi indeed made a show of insanity, bringing out "Steve," who he claimed was responsible for the killings, under the appearance of hypnotism in a videotaped session with a psychiatrist. The psychiatrist told Bianchi that another doctor was sitting across the table, and would like to meet him (there was no one there). The "hypnotized" Bianchi stood up and pretended to shake hands and hold a conversation with the man. A truly hypnotized subject will not interact in this manner. Bianchi was faking.

One factor that disproved the multiple personality evaluation was that for awhile in California Bianchi had passed himself off as a psychiatrist, using carefully stolen and faked documents. Bianchi—despite whatever problems he may have had as a child—was far too clever to be ruled insane.

As soon as Bianchi learned that he would not be allowed to plead insanity, he panicked and offered to testify against his cousin in return for no death penalty.

Buono was tried separately, and it took three months to find twelve jurors who said they had not formed an opinion on the case after years of news stories about the crimes.

Bianchi was the state's star witness against him. After a trial that lasted longer than Manson's, Buono was convicted of killing the two schoolgirls and Kimberly Martin, but he was acquitted of killing the first victim, Yolanda Washington.

Life's Blood

Three days after Christmas 1977, Ambrose Griffin was driving his wife from a supermarket north of Sacramento when a truck came by. Shots were fired, and Griffin was killed without any reason.

On Monday, January 23, 1978, a laundry truck driver returned to his home not far away from the scene of the Griffin murder and discovered the slashed body of his twenty-three-year-old wife, Terry Wallin. Some of her organs had been removed. Stains and residue in a yogurt container suggested that her blood had been collected and drunk. Their baby was missing, and in the bathtub police found traces of brain tissue. A deputy sheriff who examined the scene had nightmares for weeks afterward.

Police contacted the FBI. Profiler Robert Rennsler suggested that the killer was a slender Caucasian man in his late twenties who was a loner, possibly a former mental patient, slovenly, probably a "fetish burglar," and that evidence of the crime would be found in his home.

As for burglaries in the area, there was nothing unusual except that someone was stealing cats and dogs.

That same week, the phantom gunman killed thirty-six-year-old Evelyn Miroth, her six-year-old son, and a fifty-two-year-old family friend, Daniel Meredith. Miroth's twenty-two-month-old nephew was missing and was later found dead.

Police staked out the apartment of a suspect, Richard Tenton Chase, and nabbed him in a foot chase as he carried Meredith's wallet and a box of bloody clothes. In his messy truck, police found three kitchen blenders with the remains of human blood and organs. Chase said he needed to swallow the concoction to keep his own blood from turning into powder.

A look into Chase's background provided hints but no answers for what he did. He was a bed-wetter until he was eight or so, which is sometimes a sign of family strife. His parents always seemed to be quarreling, with Chase's mother accusing his father of infidelity and even of trying to poison her. Some thought she was schizophrenic.

As an adolescent, Chase was considered rebellious. As a teenager and young man, he sometimes tried to have sex but was unable to sustain an erection. His parents divorced but continued to support him because he was unable to hold down a steady job. He was frequently arrested for drunken driving and weapons charges.

Echoing the claims of his mother, Chase came to feel that he was poisoned, but he believed he knew the antidote. When he was caught trying to inject rabbit's blood into his veins, he was sent to a nursing home. Employees there called him "Dracula" because he would capture birds in the bushes and bite off their heads. Although the staff was afraid of him, Chase was released to the general public because he responded to medication, and his mother secured an apartment for him. He was arrested near Lake Tahoe because of blood-stained clothes, but tests showed that the blood had come from a cow or a bull. The murders began a few months later.

Chase was clearly insane, but when he was arrested the public clamored for his execution. While on Death Row, he died from an overdose of antidepressant pills he had saved.

The Trailside Murders

Police referred to the person leaving the bodies of women in some of northern California's most scenic remote areas as the "Trailside Murderer." The killings began on August 19, 1979, with the shooting of forty-four-year-old Edda Kane as she hiked without her husband in Mill Valley below Mount Tamalpais. Dana O'Connell was shot after she was separated from two other women in the fir woodlands of Point Reyes National Seashore, and another woman was killed a mile away. In all, there were eight victims, one of them a man who police assumed had gotten in the way. Some of the female victims were forced into a submissive position before they were killed, but most were not sexually assaulted. A criminal psychologist theorized that the killer derived his maximum excitement from his victim's terror rather than from the murder or sex act.

Clues led to fifty-one-year-old David Carpenter, a neat, well-dressed printer with a severe stutter. Carpenter had served time first for raping a woman while stationed at the sprawling Presidio army base in San Francisco and then for kidnapping and robbery. A psychiatrist found him to be a sociopath, someone without a conscience. Carpenter grew up with strict and demanding parents who supposedly preferred his brother and sister to him. In fact, his mother tried to beat his speech impediment out of him.

As a young man Carpenter would run away to the Santa Cruz mountains, to get away from family life. When he returned, he would act out his hostility, getting into one form of trouble after another. Psychiatrists felt that he took out his anger in the form of sexual attacks. Carpenter claimed he had intercourse—mostly by force—about fifty times before he was eighteen. A psychiatrist who studied him before the murders began warning, "Whenever Carpenter feels hemmed-in his sexual urge climbs, and the only way he can think straight . . . is to rape the nearest female." In prison, his urges might have taken the form of murder fantasies. The killings began just three months after his release on parole and while he was still living with his elderly parents in San Francisco.

In May 1981, authorities used dental charts to identify a victim found in a Santa Cruz County state park as Heather Scaggs, a coworker of Carpenter. But he did not become a suspect until another coworker from many years before reported to the police that a sketch of the suspect vaguely resembled Carpenter. He was arrested, convicted, and sentenced to die in the gas chamber for two of the killings.

The Giant Killer

No one outside of law enforcement knows how difficult serial murder cases are to investigate. The case begins after several victims disappear, but people also disappear who are not victims or who are killed by someone else. Serial killers nearly always have above average intelligence, which can make them more difficult to catch. And usually there is no real motive with which to work; the victim was killed only because he or she was attractive, or because he or she reminded the killer of someone he loved or hated, or simply because he or she was there. Sometimes no clear pattern emerges because the killer goes from state to state.

Most serial killers are men, but a few women have committed similar crimes. There have even been cases where relatives or friends of a suspect have committed copycat crimes to throw the police off the track, and some drug pushers have killed in a way to simulate a sexual attack. The public demand for an arrest in such a case is usually echoed by the news media as well as local politicians. If an investigation goes on for a few months, the mayor and police chief start talking about ways to cut expenses. Meanwhile, the killer keeps stalking.

On May 2, 1972, Mary Pesce and Anita Luchessa—eighteen-year-old roommates from Fresno State College—vanished while hitchhiking. Police assumed the teens were runaways. After all, hundreds of girls were loitering on the Strip or going off with boyfriends or girlfriends, or they were merging with the drug scene, living in communes, or joining utopian or religious groups such as the Hare Krishna, the Rev. Moon's cult, and More House.

In September, fifteen-year-old dancer Aiko Koo dropped out of sight after being seen entering a car at a bus stop on University Avenue in Berkeley. At the wheel was a very tall man with light brown hair. His name was Edward Kemper. The giant of a man stood six feet, nine inches and weighed two hundred eighty-five pounds. For someone so large, Kemper was surprisingly soft-spoken and was generally congenial with strangers, but he did not have any close friends.

His mother was six feet tall, and his father was six feet, eight inches tall. When the boy was seven his parents separated, divorcing a year later.

Kemper's mother made him sleep in the basement for eight months rather than share a room with his older and younger sisters. Kemper, who was his father's favorite, seems to have felt rejected. He liked to suppose that the furnace near his bed was a fiery demon about to wreak destruction on his family.

Kemper vented anger by cutting off the heads and legs of his sisters' dolls. He once prayed that everyone else in the world except himself would be killed. Kemper went so far in fantasizing the killing of his mother's female friends that he kept track of them when they moved away, as if some day there would be a reckoning. Needing a leveling influence to keep from feeling estranged, his thoughts often drifted to death. He rigged up a mock gas chamber to sit in while blindfolded as his younger sister pretended to pull a lever. As an early adolescent, he had thoughts of killing an attractive teacher.

At thirteen, he shot to death a boy's pet dog, and around that time sliced off the head of a cat, supposedly out of curiosity. The six-foot boy lived with his father for awhile, but the man's new wife felt unnerved when Kemper would just sit and stare at her like a zombie. The boy admitted later that he had become aroused when he saw her naked, and he apparently did not know how to handle his feelings. At the wife's request, the headstrong and yet emotionally dependent boy was sent to his paternal grandparents in North Fork, in the Sierra mountains of California.

The fifteen-year-old showed his resentment by shooting to death his sixty-eight-year-old grandmother and then his seventy-two-year-old grandfather. Next, the teenager phoned his mother to tell her what he'd done. When authorities asked him why he did it, he said, "I just wondered how it would feel to shoot grandma." But years later, he admitted that in his mind he was really killing his mother.

Kemper was sent to the Atascadero state mental institution and was released on his twenty-first birthday. He moved in with his mother when she obtained a secretarial job at Cabrillo College, part of the University of Southern California. Working as a highway repair crew flagman, Kemper kept seeing all those bright, attractive young women driving by and decided to have sex with them in the only satisfactory way he could—murder.

The day after killing Luchessa and cutting her open, Kemper kept her head in the trunk of his car as he went to an interview with two psychiatrists in Fresno to show them how normal he was. He hoped they would seal his juvenile record so that he would never be impeded by his past. One psychiatrist reported, "I see no psychiatric reason to consider him a danger to himself or any other member of society."

Kemper was socially awkward but in his leisure moments he sometimes frequented a bar near the Santa Cruz courthouse called the Jury Room. Over a few beers, he would talk to off-duty officers and lawyers from the district attorney's office. He was perfectly at ease.

A month after Luchessa's beheading, twenty-four-year-old Mary Margaret Guifoyle was abducted while hitchhiking to the college. The police responded by issuing this alert to all female college students: "When possible . . . stay indoors after midnight with the doors locked. If you must be out at night—walk in pairs. DON'T HITCH A RIDE, PLEASE." The college helped organize a car pool and provided stickers and ID cards to drivers and riders. But Kemper, with his IQ of 136, found a way to turn these precautions to his advantage. His mother gave him one of the stickers, and he used it to pass himself off to females walking alone as a member of the university police. He was so rational in his method that he would engage his intended victims in a friendly conversation to learn something about them, which was part of his thrill. "Those passions, those fears made me somebody," Kemper would say. "I was making life and death decisions . . . playing God in their lives."

Six teenage girls and young women were killed, some decapitated with an ax or a power saw. Occasionally, Kemper ejaculated as he killed the victims, for in his mind killing was sex.

But Kemper was working up his courage for a final action: freeing himself from his mother's domination.

He chose Easter Sunday of 1973, a time that celebrates redemption and brings families together. At 5:15 A.M., the giant struck his mother on the head with a claw hammer as she slept, then cut off her head, raped her body, and removed her larynx in revenge for her years of ridicule. He dragged her nude and mutilated corpse into a closet and cleaned up the blood. He invited her friend Sara Hallet to come over and join them for a dinner and a movie. When Hallet arrived, Kemper stabbed her and covered her head with a plastic bag. He went out for a few beers and came back to sever her head.

Kemper took Hallet's car to Reno, then ditched it and rented another auto. He drove eighteen hours more and reached Colorado. He had less than one day of freedom, but it was enough for him. He went to a phone booth in Pueblo and called the Santa Cruz police to tell them about his crimes. No one took him seriously, and he had to call several times and wait until Santa Cruz authorities finally asked the Colorado police to pick him up. The officers discovered three guns and about two hundred rounds of ammunition in the car.

Kemper was found sane, convicted of all eight murders, and sentenced to life in prison, where he later cooperated with the FBI in a study of multiple murderers in hopes that others might understand the phenomenon. The interviews were later used in a massive effort to educate the public about serial killers moving through America.

REFERENCES

Associated Press, January 25, 1989.

Biondi, Ray, and Hecox, Walt. *All His Father's Sins*. New York: Signet Books, 1988.

Cahill, Tim, with Ewing, Russ. *Buried Dreams: Inside the Mind of a Serial Killer*. New York: Bantam Books, 1986.

Caputi, Jane. *The Age of Sex Crime*. Bowling Green, Ohio: Bowling Green State University Popular Press, 1987.

Cheney, Margaret. *The Co-Ed Killer*. New York: Walker & Co., 1976.

Chicago Sun-Times, December 4 and 6, 1985.

Cray, Ed, and Hawk, Richard. *Burden of Proof*. New York: Macmillan, 1974.

Douglas, John. *The Mind Hunter*. New York: Pocket Books, 1996.

Falk, Gerhard. *Murder: An Analysis of Its Forms, Conditions, and Causes*. Jefferson, N.C.: McFarland & Co., 1990.

Fawkes, Sand., *Killing Time*. New York: Taplinger Publishing, 1977.

Fosburgh, Lacey. *Closing Time: The True Story of the "Goodbar" Murder*. New York: Dell Publishing, 1978.

Graysmith, Robert. *The Sleeping Lady: The Trailside Murders Above the Golden Gate*. New York: New American Library, 1991.

Hickey, Eric W. *Serial Murderers and Their Victims*. Pacific Grove, Calif.: Brooks/Cole, 1991.

Holmes, Ronald M. and Holmes, Stephen Y., *Murder in America*. Thousand Oaks, Calif.: Sage Publications, 1994.

Howard, Clark. *Zebra*. New York: Richard Marek Publishers, 1979.

Kendall, Elizabeth (pseudonym). *The Phantom Prince: My Life with Ted Bundy.* Seattle, Wash.: Madrona Publishers, 1981.

Larson, Richard W.. *Bundy: The Deliberate Stranger.* New York: Pocket Books, 1980.

Leith, Ron. *The Torso Killer* (originally published as *The Prostitute Murders*). New York: Warner Books, 1983.

Leyton, Elliott. *Compulsive Killers: The Story of Modern Multiple Murder.* New York: Washington Mews Books, 1986.

Linedecker, Clifford L. *Serial Thrill Killers.* New York: Knightsbridge Publishing, 1990.

Los Angeles Times, January 6, 1982.

Lunde, Donald T. *Murder and Madness.* San Francisco: San Francisco Book Co., 1976.

Lunde, Donald T. and Morgan, Jefferson, *The Die Song: A Journey into the Mind of Mass Murder.* New York: W.W. Norton, 1980.

McDougal, Dennis. *Angel of Darkness.* New York: Warner Books, 1992.

McGinnis, Joe. *Fatal Vision.* New York: Signet Books, 1984.

Magee, Dough. *What Murder Leaves Behind.* New York: Dodd, Mead, 1981.

Michaud, Stephen G., and Aynesworth, Hugh. *The Only Living Witness.* New York: Signet Books, 1984.

New York Times, July 6, July 15, and December 22, 1977.

———, January 12, 1981.

———, May 5, 1984.

Newsweek, November 26, 1982.

———, November 24, 1984.

O'Brien, Darcy. *Two of a Kind: The Hillside Stranglers.* New York: Signet Books, 1985.

Olsen, Jack. *The Man With the Candy: The Story of the Houston Mass Murders.* New York: Simon & Schuster, 1974.

Ressler, Robert H., and Schachtman, Tom. *Whoever Fights Monsters.* New York: St. Martin's Press, 1992.

Rignal, Jeff, and Wilder, Rob. *29 Below.* Chicago: Wellington Press, 1979.

Rule, Ann. *The Stranger Beside Me.* New York: New American Library, 1980.

Schechter, Harold, and Everitt, David. *The A to Z Encyclopedia of Serial Killers.* New York: Pocket Books, 1996.

San Francisco Chronicle, August 28 and 29, 1964.

San Francisco Chronicle, April 25 and 26, 1973.

———, April 25, April 26, and November 10, 1973.

Schwarz, Ted. *The Hillside Strangler: A Murderer's Mind,* Garden City, N.Y.: Doubleday, 1981.

Sharkey, Joe. *Death Sentence: The Inside Story of the John List Murders.* New York: Signet Books, 1990.

Terry, Maury. *The Ultimate Evil.* New York: Bantam Books, 1989.

Time, December 15, 1980.

———, February 6, 1989.

van Hoffman, Eric. *A Venom in the Blood.* New York: Kensington Publishing, 1991.

Williford, Charles. *Off the Wall,* Montclair, N.J.: Pegasus Rex Press, 1980.

Wilson, Colin, and Seaman, David. *The Serial Killers: A Study in the Psychology of Violence.* London: W.H. Allen, 1990.

Wilson, Colin, and Wilson, Damon. *The Killers Among Us: Book II. The Motives Behind Their Madness.* New York: Warner Books, 1995.

Winn, Steven, and Merrell, David. *Ted Bundy: Killer Next Door.* New York: Bantam Books, 1980.

Villasenor, Victor. *Jury: The People vs. Juan Corona.* New York: Dell Publishing, 1977.

The 1980s

W hen Washington state authorities tore down the old
Seattle area airport, they had no development plan
for the river valley by Pacific Highway South.
Motorists found the flat land near the Green River a con-
venient place to pick up experienced prostitutes or runaway girls. Business thrived. On August 12, 1982, the body
of a young woman from the Strip was found hanging over a
log in a stream near the Green River, her arms moving
slowly with the flow of the water. A few days later, another
prostitute was found. A third was discovered in the tall
grass along the riverbank. After five victims of the "Green
River killer" were discovered, FBI profiler John Douglas,
assuming the women were attacked by one man, issued a
profile.

The killer probably had a criminal or psychiatric history. There was marital discord between his parents after which the killer's mother took over and became a strict disciplinarian. He probably had average or above average intelligence, was currently married or divorced, was shy, and had feelings of inadequacy. The most likely setup for murder, Douglas proposed, was that the man would become angry when the woman asked for money for sex, causing flashbacks of women who had controlled him. The man was likely to be a laborer or in some sort of maintenance work, because his muddled mind probably kept him from holding down a better job, and he was used to walking in water, such as an amateur fisherman. Because four of the first five victims were Caucasian, the killer probably was also white.

The King County sheriff's department was underfunded and still operating as it did in the 1940s, and investigators were unable to find a clue. Police thought they could catch the killer by staking out parts of the dumping area and waiting. But a TV newscaster flying overhead reported for all his viewers that he could see the police watching certain areas.

Subsequently, all of the bodies were found along highways from Seattle to Spokane, and from Portland, Oregon, to Vancouver, British Columbia. The number of victims reached at least forty-nine. Many observers felt that the later killings were copycat crimes, and that the original Green River killer had moved on, possibly to San Diego, where there were up to twenty-five similar murders in the mid-1980s. The Seattle-area crimes have never been solved.

The Green River murders led the U.S. Justice Department to convene a homicide conference in January 1984. The conference was held largely to inform the public about the seriousness of the situation in every part of the country. A Justice Department study concluded that there were thirty cases in the past decade in which a single person had killed at least six people over a period of time.

Robert O. Heck, who was considered a specialist on the subject, said at the conference that "we all talk about Jack the Ripper. He killed five people. We talk about 'the Boston Strangler,' who killed thirteen, and maybe 'Son of Sam,' who killed six. But we've got people out there now killing twenty, thirty people and more, and some do not just kill. They torture their victims in terrible ways and mutilate them before they kill them. Something's going on out there. It's an epidemic."

At times it seemed as if the early 1980s were a pressure cooker of generalized hate, with a lingering recession adding to the "me too" clamor of conflicting races and lifestyles, the tragic discovery of AIDS, and undercurrents remaining from the Vietnam war.

On Monday, December 8, 1980, amateur musician Mark David Chapman, who had been telling people he was a recording engineer for the Beatles, saw John Lennon walking down the street and asked him to sign an album. Hours later, with a copy of *Catcher in the Rye* in his pocket, Chapman emerged from the shadows of the Dakota apartment building at 72nd Street and Central Park West in Manhattan. While Yoko Ono was unlocking the door, Chapman went into a marksman's crouch and fatally shot Lennon by the entranceway. He didn't attempt to escape.

Emotional isolation was out of fashion. On December 22, 1984, the novel *Death Wish,* intended as a warning, came true when a thin, blonde electronics technician named Bernie

Goetz shot four black teenagers aboard a New York subway train. He said that he assumed they were robbers because they had asked him for five dollars. The wounded youths said they just wanted to play video games.

Goetz was a hero to people who were living with an unvoiced streak of anger; others feared that he was the fore-runner of vigilantism. He was acquitted of attempted murder but served more than eight months in jail on gun charges. Goetz, after all, was just an emanation of the bubbling over animosity seen a few years later with escalating traffic shootings on Los Angeles freeways in a newly recognized type of crime, "road rage." With religion and respect for laws considered less fashionable, and half the country uprooted from somewhere else, people were killed or severely wounded simply because some driver wanted to move a few miles an hour faster.

The mid-1980s also saw an increasing number of women committing bank robberies and violent crimes. Some women, freed from the traditional roles that were forced on their mothers and grandmothers, entered a sort of alienated emotional detachment from their surroundings.

The fact that such crimes were becoming more common suggested an unconscious current running through the decade. No single event triggered such crimes, but one contributing factor was the 1973 U.S. Supreme Court decision legalizing abortions. The decision created rage on both sides of the issue and led to a number of murders—not all of them of abortion clinic workers.

On May 19, 1983, a woman with a wounded arm drove to a hospital in Springfield, Oregon, and tearfully said a shaggy-haired stranger had shot her three young children. Doctors at first thought that all three of Diane Downes's children might die. The staff was unable to save eight-year-old Christie, but seven-year-old Cheryl and three-year-old Danny pulled through. Police were skeptical about the mother's story from the first, but it took months to establish any kind of a motive.

Downes said her martinet father sexually abused her when she was twelve and living in Phoenix. True or not, her relationships with men ran cold and hot. She said she could not stand being touched by domineering males. Her only requirement for a man was that he be married. She had an IQ of 125 but never knew what to do with herself. Downes went from being a wallflower to a compulsively talking flirt. She and her husband, Steve Downes, were married in their teens but it was an on-again, off-again relationship with infidelity on both sides.

The turning point may have been Downes's low feelings after an abortion. She saw pro-life demonstrators and felt an urge to produce a replacement for the child that never was. In her pregnancy, an altered flow of hormones erased her depression and she felt such an exhilaration that she wanted to produce babies forever. But she could not stand the demands of actually raising children. Then her lover left her, and she felt she had to do something to keep from falling apart.

She decided to get rid of her children. Downes shot her youngsters with a pistol while listening to one of her favorite songs on the cassette player in her car. Then wounded herself in the arm. She was convicted, and is in prison.

Also in 1983, twenty-three-year-old Karla Faye Tucker of Houston and her bartender-boyfriend, Daniel Garrett, broke into the apartment of a biker to steal parts for a Harley-Davidson. Tucker had been a heroin user since she was ten, sometimes getting drugs from her mother. When Jerry Dean tried to force them out of his home, Tucker grabbed a pickax and mauled him to death. Seeing Deborah Thorton cowering under a sheet in the bed, Tucker whacked her until her arms hurt, and Garrett finished the job. Tucker eventually found God and married a prison minister being executed in February 1998.

On a gorgeous day in May 1988, former perennial college student Laurie Dann, a professional baby-sitter afflicted by a compulsive disorder and depression, entered a public school in the upscale Chicago suburb of Winnetka and calmly opened fire on the young students. She killed an eight-year-old boy and wounded five other children. The dumpy, once attractive young woman walked out, holed up in a stranger's house nearby, and killed herself as police surrounded the building.

The Children

When a woman searching for cans and bottles found the bodies of two black fourteen-year-old boys in a ravine by Niskey Lake Road near Atlanta, the police shrugged off the crime as another drug killing. This was July 19, 1979, the year the U.S. Justice Department called Atlanta, with two million people in its metropolitan area, "the murder capital of the United States." The officers identified the bodies as Edward Hope Smith, a shooting victim, and Alfred Evans, who died by asphyxiation.

Atlanta had built a trendy downtown at the expense of its neighborhoods, as if to refute the Northern image of a sleepy

South. Visitors came to the city for its nightlife or its *Gone With the Wind*-era homes. They did not want to see the backstreets, where despair had turned many of the once proud poor toward drugs. But there was hope for change: Atlanta had its first black mayor, Maynard Jackson, and its black public safety commissioner, Lee Brown, was a longtime law enforcement official with a Ph.D. in criminology. Residents were confident that the city could contain any crime. But the child killings continued.

On November 8, the remains of nine-year-old Yusuf Bell were found in a maintenance trap at an abandoned school. He, too, died of strangulation or some other form of asphyxiation. A week later, fourteen-year-old Milton Harvey's decomposed body was uncovered among rotting food and broken appliances in a dump near Redwine Road.

But it was not until a girl was killed—twelve-year-old Angela Lanier—that the police realized what was happening. Angela disappeared as she was walking to school on March 5, 1980, so her murder was obviously not drug-related. Five days later, her body was discovered tied to a tree in a weeded lot, a pair of someone else's panties stuffed down her throat, and an electrical cord still around her neck. There was no evidence that the girl was sexually molested.

On March 12, ten-year-old Jeffrey Mathis vanished on his way to a store.

Police were confused because serial killings were considered a white man's crime. But a Caucasian could never roam these streets without being noticed.

Yusuf's mother, Carmine Bell, galvanized the neighborhood by charging that these children were murdered because of the "crime" of being black and poor in America. Dick

Gregory, the stand-up comedian cum African-American activist, claimed a conspiracy involving the Atlanta-based U.S. Centers of Disease Control to take the blood of Negro children in the hope that the sickle cells would cure cancer. Others spoke of a murderous religious cult or speculated that the Ku Klux Klan was committing genocide.

Fourteen-year-old Eric Middlebrook was found fatally stabbed and beaten on May 19 after receiving a telephone call and saying he was going to meet someone. On June 9, eleven-year-old Christopher Richardson disappeared, and his body was not located until early the next year. The killer—if there was only one person—either was getting bolder and playing "catch me if you can" with the police or he was in the meltdown phase of overlooking caution. On June 22, La Tonya Williams was abducted from her own bed in a housing project the night before her eighth birthday; the killer had removed a window pane to enter the room. Two days later, ten-year-old Aaron Wyche's body was recovered from under a bridge a few miles from Atlanta.

The murders affected the community as no other rash of killings had in American history. Many of the victims came from broken homes or had no homes to speak of. A few already had police records, but these were children; they were the only hope their families had that some day things might be better. An entire community was being violated. Each funeral drew more and more mourners. Schools became havens of weeping children as one body after another was found, and teachers could offer kind words and hugs but no explanations.

Test scores declined, some children wet their beds at night in silent terror of what tomorrow might bring, and some slept with Bibles for protection. Children lost their capacity for trust, and more than three thousand volunteers of all races participated in sweeps through vacant lots, dilapidated housing projects, and ravines for children still missing.

And yet the killings continued. On July 6, nine-year-old Tony Carter was found dumped in a grassy area with multiple stab wounds. The families alleged that for every child on the police list of killings, evidently by the same person, another was dead or had vanished.

Mayor Jackson imposed a strict curfew of 7 P.M. to 6 A.M. for children under sixteen and offered a reward of $100,000. Corporate donors, boxing champ Muhammad Ali, and entertainers Sammy Davis Jr. and Frank Sinatra raised the reward or contributed a total of $750,000 to the police investigation.

On July 31, ten-year-old Earl Terrell never reached home after being ejected from a public pool for teasing some girls. That night, his family received several telephone calls from a man claiming to be holding the boy in Alabama and demanding a $200 ransom. The call apparently was a cruel exploitation of the family's grief rather than from the killer, but it officially brought in the FBI after months of their monitoring the situation.

Twelve-year-old Clifford Jones was found strangled in an alley in September, and ten-year-old Darron Glass—a chronic runaway—disappeared that same month. In all, there were thirty children and young men on the list, and thirty-four others whom the parents said should have been added.

Mothers sent out their children to play with whistles around their necks or kept them inside day after day. Volunteers from Atlanta Youth Against Crime, wearing red jackets, helped patrol streets and shopping areas. Police were checking fifteen hundred men with sexual "priors" (prior arrests) in the Atlanta area but were getting nowhere. To test how the killer might have lured the children, undercover police officers offered youngsters on the street $5 to come with them to do a job, and the children went willingly despite all the fear around them.

Behavioral Science Unit profilers John Douglas and Roy Hazelwood determined what type of person the killer might be. They felt that many of the children had something in common besides poverty and race; these children were outgoing and streetwise but naive about the world beyond their neighborhood. The profilers concluded that the killer was a black man in his late twenties, a police buff, possibly driving a police-type vehicle, and that he would try to insinuate himself into the investigation. Because there were no signs of sexual abuse, the killer might be genitally inadequate, either because of his fantasy life or gender confusion.

They believed that the killer might employ a ruse involving music or performing but became frustrated when he could not produce results and the boy or girl wanted to leave. But the profilers felt that only a dozen of the murders were committed by this person. The others might have been coincidental, copycat crimes, or committed by drug dealers to look like part of the series.

More of the most recent victims were older, from fifteen to twenty-eight, and there was another element. Police thoroughly searched the Sigmond Road area, yet afterward the body of fifteen-year-old Terry Pue was dumped there some time after he was last seen alive. It was as if the killer—or one of the killers—was saying to himself, "I can dump a body there if I want to." But he was leaving clues just the same. When twelve-year-old Patrick Baltazaar was found in a neighboring county, hair and fibers removed from his body matched those found on five previous victims.

Douglas thought the man who had killed about a dozen of the victims might start dumping bodies in rivers, and he suggested that police set up stakeouts. The next victim, thirteen-year-old Curtis Walker, was recovered from the South River. Then two more—thirteen-year-old Timmie Hill and twenty-one-year-old Eddie Duncan, who was retarded—were found in the Chattahoochee River.

Two other bodies were later recovered from the same river. One was twenty-one-year-old Jimmie Ray Payne. The other, twenty-three-year-old Michael Cameron McIntosh, was older than the other victims but was small and slender, like a child, and was considered a little slow. The police speculated that the attacker wanted to kill young men all along but perhaps took to abducting children because it was easier or that he wanted to kill children but recently had found them too guarded.

Any number of men generally fit the FBI profile of the killer. One of them was Wayne Williams, a man in his twenties who was something of a "police groupie." Williams lived with his parents, Homer and Faye, both retired schoolteachers, in a middle-class part of northwest Atlanta. Both were in their mid-forties when he was born, and they may have been more like doting grandparents than parents. They raised their only child with what might have seemed to him as a stifling correctness, obeying every law of God and man.

At eleven, Wayne set up a telescope for other children on the night of the first moon walk. All the neighborhood children looked up to him as being brilliant. In high school, Wayne amazed other students by constructing a low-powered radio station in his basement. But then the adulation stopped. He dropped out of college, claiming that the courses were slowing his way to the top, but he never started any career to reach the fame he sought.

He was known for driving a surplus police vehicle and rushing to crime scenes to take photos. Once he was arrested for impersonating an officer after using flashing red lights to go out on a police call; the charge was reduced to the unauthorized use of emergency lights. Williams also organized a singing group named after his astrological sign, Gemini. In the past year or so, he had tried to contact aspiring musicians, falsely portraying himself as a professional record promoter and promising wealth and fame like the Jackson Five. His flyers were distributed throughout the neighborhood, and they were among the possessions of four of the victims.

At 2:30 A.M. on May 22, a police recruit named Bob Campbell was on stakeout at the Jackson Parkway bridge over the Chattahoochee River when he heard a splash and shined his flashlight at the ripples. Another member of the team saw a green station wagon pull off the bridge and drive into a liquor store parking lot. The driver, apparently seeing the squad car, turned around his station wagon and headed across the bridge, slowly at first but then speeding up. An FBI agent in a second car joined the pursuit, and in a few minutes they pulled over Williams. He was friendly and seemed surprised to be stopped. Police looked into his car, saw nothing suspicious, and let him go.

Other officers worked from the riverbank and pulled out the body of twenty-seven-year-old Nathaniel Carter, the second oldest of all the victims. But there had been too much time between the splash and the sighting of Williams's station wagon for authorities to be sure he was involved. The authorities prepared to wait, even though a witness would say he saw Williams and Carter holding hands on a street a few hours before the body was dumped.

Wherever Williams went, the police and the FBI trailed him by car and occasionally by helicopter and small plane. He playfully led them on several wild-goose chases around the city. Once he even stopped in front of Public Safety Commissioner Brown's house, honked his horn, and then sped off. Tired of pussyfooting with the police, he agreed to take a polygraph test. But the results were inconclusive.

Police could not stop Williams as long as he stayed within the law, but they felt he was trying to destroy evidence as they watched him burning photos and washing his car inside and out. He was so bold he gave a press conference to declare that the police and the FBI were slandering him, and explained that he was on the bridge at 2:30 A.M. looking for a woman vocalist he expected to interview in the afternoon.

Convinced they had their man, investigators persuaded a judge to sign a search warrant. On June 3, authorities impounded Williams's car and found hair and fibers that he had missed in the washings. Larry Peterson of the Georgia Crime Laboratory detected even more damning evidence. The green, yellow, and purple fibers found on some of the bodies matched the carpet in Williams's home, and dog hairs removed by tweezers from the bodies came from his German shepherd.

On June 21, Williams was arrested for the murder of Nathaniel Carter, and he was later charged with fatally shooting twenty-one-year-old Jimmie Ray Payne. Because Georgia law allowed prosecutors to mention the ten other murders in the pattern, the district attorney's office introduced seven hundred pieces of hair and fiber evidence. Through it all, Williams sat well controlled, appearing unworried, his thick glasses hinting at his intelligence, and his soft features and delicate hands seeming to proclaim innocence.

Prosecutors sensed that it was this tight self-control that had led to the murders. They decided to drag Williams to the breaking point and let the jury hear his rage. Every question received a soft reply from Williams. But again and again, attorneys for the state badgered him with verbal jabs such as, "What was it like when you wrapped your fingers around the victim's throat, did you panic? *Did you panic!*"

Williams suddenly unleashed a startling outburst against what he called the goons and fools who were trying "to make me fit that FBI profile, and I'm not going to help you do it!" But then he realized he had fallen into a trap. He regained control, but the image he had heretofore projected was shattered.

On February 27, 1982, after a nine-week trial, the jury found Williams guilty of both of the adult murders with which he was charged. No one was ever charged with the murders of the children, and grieving in Atlanta's African-American community continued throughout the decade. There remain many who believe that Williams was only a procurer for the real killer, as Elmer Wayne Henley had been for Dean Corll. After all, no motive was ever brought out. Whatever sexual fantasy may have been involved in the killings, there was also self-hatred, and perhaps hatred for homosexuals and poor blacks.

American Roulette

Day 1: September 29, 1982

Seventh-grade pupil Mary Kellerman of Schaumburg, a quiet Chicago suburb, had the sniffles from a lingering cold but wanted to go to school anyway. Her father heard her go to the bathroom, then collapse. "Mary, are you okay?" he asked. He found her lying unconscious and still in her pajamas. She was rushed to a hospital and diagnosed with a cardiopulmonary collapse.

Ten miles away in Arlington Heights, Adam Janus had some chest pains. The Polish-born young man reached for a bottle of painkillers in his kitchen. In a minute, he collapsed in a coma. At Northwest Community Hospital, Janus's younger brother, Stanley, and his wife told Dr. Thomas Kim that there was nothing in Janus's history to explain what had happened.

The couple went to Adam's home to comfort the rest of the family. Stanley was so upset that he took some of the painkiller he found in the kitchen and fell to the floor from oxygen starvation in his brain. His wife, Teresa, was so disturbed by what was happening to her family that she groped for the painkiller and soon she, too, collapsed. Both were rushed to Northwestern Community Hospital, and Dr. Kim ordered urine and blood tests.

Eighteen miles from the hospital, twenty-seven-year-old Mary Reiner had a headache after the birth of her fourth child a couple of days before. Something happened, and she collapsed.

Within a few hours, all the victims but Teresa Janus were dead, and Teresa was in a coma on life support. Police bagged for analysis anything the victims might have touched just before they became ill.

A few miles away, Mary McFarland told fellow workers at an Illinois Bell Phone Center in Lombard that she had a "tremendous headache." She reached for one of the two bottles of painkillers she had with her, took the pills, swallowed, and collapsed.

Day 2

United Airlines attendant Paula Prince landed at O'Hare International Airport from Las Vegas. She had another flight the next day, but she was bothered by her allergies. Still in uniform, she bought a bottle of painkillers at a drugstore and went to her apartment in Chicago. No one found her body that day or the next.

Two firefighters from neighboring suburbs who happened to be friends, Richard Keyworth and Philip Capittelli, were talking over the cases when they realized that all the victims had taken Extra-Strength Tylenol. Laboratory tests on the bottles collected from the homes showed that some of the capsules were tainted with cyanide. The technicians could tell this because a trace of cyanide shows up as a reddish color, and "this one turned so red you could see it across the room."

The investigation stalled because the case involved different suburbs, different hospitals, and even different counties. But once the link was made, authorities worked hundreds of overtime hours to remove the bottles from shelves, check bottles of other products, and talk to employees and customers in hopes of learning whether anyone was seen acting suspiciously around drug counters. The worst-case scenario was that someone at the McNeil Consumer Products Co. factory in

Fort Washington, Pennsylvania, had tampered with all of the 93,400 bottles shipped to thirty-four states.

Frantic testing showed that the only contaminated bottles were in the area immediately northwest and west of Chicago. This meant that someone was going from drugstore to drugstore in the suburbs, opening bottles on a shelf, adding cyanide with an eyedropper, and then screwing the lids back on in a game of random murder that Dr. Kim called "American roulette." No one had detected the "bitter almond" smell on the breath of the victims, which is a telltale sign of cyanide poisoning, because only forty percent of the population is sensitive to it.

Psychiatrist Donald Greaves of Evanston Hospital assumed that the killer "is probably an ordinary person who feels very ordinary. By this act, he has suddenly managed to catapult to fame." Another psychiatrist in the area suggested that the killer was impulsive yet neat, well-organized, unmarried, and felt that a great injustice had been done to him. Dr. Richard Rappaport, a psychiatrist brought into the Gacy case, surmised that the eyedropper killer had a personal vendetta against someone close to him.

Day 3

McNeil announced the voluntary recall of lot MC 2880, although most stores had already removed the product from their shelves. Eli Lilly & Co. in Indianapolis flew to Chicago one hundred antidote kits for distribution to paramedic units. The largest poison center in the country, at Chicago's Rush-Presbyterian St. Luke's Medical Center, received seven hundred calls in fourteen hours, and drugstores were busy throughout the day accepting returns of Tylenol.

Day 4

As Teresa Janus remained only technically alive on machines, the first of an eventual two hundred copycat crimes began around the country. McNeil offered a $100,000 reward for information leading to the "Tylenol killer." There also began an industry push for the types of sealed containers used today as a result of these murders. Teresa was finally taken off life support, stopping the game of American roulette at seven. An eighth victim became sick but recovered, and the wife of a judge was about to swallow a tainted capsule but then heard about the scare and put it down.

The Associated Press named the Tylenol case the second most important news story of 1982, following the economic recession. The only arrest ever made was of James Lewis, who sent a $1,000,000 extortion letter to a McNeil subsidiary "to stop the killing." Lewis—perhaps by coincidence—matched the general profile proposed for the killer. Police found him in the newspaper reading room of the New York Public Library, and he served a long prison term.

Most Wanted

Police across the country were increasingly ready to believe anything about serial killers. The greatest murder scare in American history followed the July 27, 1981, disappearance of six-year-old Adam Walsh. His mother had left him at the video game department of a Sears store for just a few minutes at a mall in Hollywood, Florida, near Fort Lauderdale. A security guard ushered some older boys outside, and Adam might have gone with them.

Following a search by hundreds of volunteers, the boy's head was found in a canal near Varo Beach about three weeks later. Adam's father, John, was embittered at the failure of the police to find his boy alive and began a national campaign for missing children, which led to placing their photos on various publications and milk cartons across the country. Walsh became such a proponent of public involvement in stopping crimes that he became the host of the TV show "America's Most Wanted."

From October 1975 to January 1982, the FBI's file on missing persons reached 791,403—averaging 10,552 a month. Of these, seventy-six percent were juveniles. In 1982, President Ronald Reagan signed the Missing Children's Act, which requires the Justice Department to keep more detailed records on children who apparently have been abducted.

Many of the children were feared to have been attacked by serial killers, a threat worsened by the FBI practice of assuming that any person found dead in a remote location without a clear motive was a victim of a pattern killer. At the time, few pointed out that most "abductions" were children taken away by a parent who had been denied custody.

Amid the frenzy, along came a pair of drifters, Henry Lee Lucas and Otis Toole. Toole was tall, slim, and not very bright. Lucas, an average-looking forty-seven-year-old man whose dead eye gave him a disturbing permanent wink, realized the time was ripe for a little perverse fun. While being held on a weapons charge and suspicion of murder, he "confessed" to killing sixty-nine men and women alone and nearly twenty others with Toole. In subsequent interviews by Texas Rangers, Lucas kept raising the number.

More than halfway across the country, Toole, who was serving five life terms for arson in Florida, claimed he killed Adam Walsh, and the mass murder story exploded.

Lucas gave ghastly details of torture and random slaughter in small towns and on backroads. "If I wanted a victim, I'd just go get one," he said. "I had nothing but pure hatred." Some were crucified and others were filleted, he claimed. Police believed that he was providing information only a killer would know, unaware of the many hints they were feeding him in the way they posed their questions.

Lucas is believed to have killed only three people, beginning with his elderly, half-Indian mother in their home in Tecumseh, Michigan, in 1960. He reportedly raped her corpse. Lucas spent four years in prison for the crime and was sent to a mental hospital for six years. After his release, he was caught trying to abduct someone and returned to prison until 1975. He met Toole in 1980, and they went around the country in old cars committing burglaries and robberies.

Lucas enjoyed going to murder scenes and walking around until he reached places where police reactions showed him that a victim had been found. Having created a media frenzy about an unprecedented serial murder scare, Lucas pleaded guilty to killing an eighty-year-old woman in a robbery in Ringgold, Texas, and was sentenced to seventy-five years in prison.

When Toole recanted his confession about Adam Walsh and committing fifty other murders, no one paid much attention. After all, killers often recant.

Police from nineteen states held a conference in Louisiana in October 1983 to compare notes and decided they could close the books on two hundred ten slayings by charging Lucas and possibly Toole. The following month Alfred Regnery, administrator of the federal Office of Juvenile Justice and Delinquency Prevention, estimated that of the twenty-one thousand murders across the United States in 1982, several thousand could be attributed to serial killers. The FBI, declining to be specific, said that such psychopaths might be behind some thirty-five death sprees then under investigation.

When Lucas tired of his game, he privately told true-crime writer Hugh Aynesworth that he was elsewhere at the time of the murders he claimed; he even gave Aynesworth ways to verify his alibis. But publicly, Lucas continued his Baron Münchhausen act and eventually told of six hundred killings worldwide. By then, his statements had become so absurd they received little newspaper space.

Lucas was later charged with killing his fifteen-year-old "wife," Becky Powell, whose body parts he reportedly scattered over a field. Lucas, officially linked to only three deaths, was sentenced to die in the electric chair. Toole died in prison from cirrhosis of the liver in September 1996.

The Thirteenth Juror

Despite his slender build and well-defined features, Douglas Daniel Clark probably didn't stand out at the Los Angeles singles bars he frequented. The factory worker from Burbank was the son of a naval officer and lived off romancing women who could support his unfaithful ways. Often, he would slip on designer glasses and frequent night spots on Hollywood's Sunset Boulevard. At least six times, Clark picked up a young woman or a teenage girl, drove her to a remote location, and then shot her in the head as she was performing oral sex on him. He removed the panties of his victims as a souvenir and had sex with some of the bodies before dumping them in remote parts of Los Angeles County. Despite his use of a gun, the police called the killer the "Sunset Strangler" for alliteration. But Clark bizarrely called himself the "king of one night stands."

Clark took up with a heavyset forty-year-old nurse, Carol Bundy, who told authorities that he claimed to have killed forty-seven people since he was seventeen. But, like Lucas, he may have been lying. After turning Clark in to the authorities, Bundy admitted cruising with him once or twice, but she denied taking part in any of the killings.

Bundy reportedly told Clark, "If you're going around killing people, like hookers, you might as well make it as gruesome as possible and do some weird thing like cut off the head, make it look like some psycho did it." But Bundy—a mother of two children—claimed she was surprised when he took her facetious remark seriously and came home laughing with the head of twenty-four-year-old Exxie Lee Wilson, a prostitute whose body he had dumped some time before. They kept the gaping head in their refrigerator for awhile and, as Bundy said, "had a lot of fun with it."

With the grandiose stage serial killers often reach, Clark called a Hollywood woman and told her about his killings and identified himself as Police Lieutenant Douglas Clark. In his boldness, he at least once hunted down a young woman with his car before shooting her. And Bundy became a killer on her own, stabbing and decapitating her Australian former lover, John Robert Murray, because he suspected Clark.

The killings might have gone on for months more but Bundy became upset at work and told her nursing supervisor, "I can't take it anymore, I'm supposed to save lives, not take them." The supervisor called the police, and Clark was soon arrested at the soap factory where he worked. Police found a .22-caliber pistol he used in five of the killings hidden in the boiler room.

Clark smiled when the six guilty verdicts were read. In the next phase of the trial, he presented the closing arguments himself. With bravado, he offered to serve as the thirteenth juror and said, "We have to vote for the death penalty in this case, the evidence cries out for it." The twelve impaneled jurors agreed, and Clark was executed in the San Quentin gas chamber. While Clark was in jail, attractive Veronica Lynn Compton was caught trying to garrote a woman to prove that Clark was not the "Sunset Strangler."

Bundy was sentenced to serve fifty-two years in prison for killing Murray and handing Clark a gun to kill a prostitute known only as "Jane Doe."

Coast to Coast

Intelligent, personable women of beauty would seem to have it all, but beauty can sometimes be a terrible curse. As with the Boston strangler, who turned to murder after fantasizing tape-measuring lovely women, Christopher Wilder expanded voyeurism to a murder spree and a pursuit that took him across the country and back again.

Wilder was born in Sydney to an Australian woman and an American Navy career man. The family—Wilder had three younger brothers—moved to the United States when Wilder was a child. His father's naval service took the family to Alabama, Virginia, New Mexico, and finally Florida. Wilder, who was raised Catholic, was closer to his doting mother and resented the military discipline his father demanded. The boy had no known psychological or physical trauma, but for some reason he was nervous and developed mood swings.

Wilder said that in early adolescence he would spy on partially clothed women. Although he was a good-looking young man, his real interest was in masturbation with magazines such as *Playboy* and adult movies. Because the seventeen-year-old Wilder was so attractive, some of his friends used him to lure a girl to the beach after school; he stood aside and watched while the others violated her. The other teens were charged with rape, but Wilder was only made to undergo psychological therapy, which included electroshock treatment. As he grew older, he included electrical shocks in his fantasies.

His middle-aged parents, not knowing what to do with their troublesome eldest son, left him with considerable money and returned to Australia. Wilder invested his funds sensibly in businesses and Florida real estate. He enjoyed passing himself off as wealthier than he was with rings of zircon that looked like diamonds. By age thirty—having lost much of his hair and put on weight—Wilder's fantasies turned to rape. While living in Tallahassee in 1976, he hit a sixteen-year-old girl he was driving to a job interview and ordered her to perform a sex act. He later sobbed to a psychiatrist that he could not help himself; he was feeling "down in the dumps" and an urge came over him. The doctor found him to be a psychotic who disintegrated when left to his own resources and under stress.

Having all the money he needed, Wilder decided to pass himself off as a carefree photographer. Two years after his attack on the sixteen-year-old, he approached two teenage girls vacationing in West Palm Beach and talked to them about modeling. He raped one of them after lacing her pizza with a "hypnotic drug" (knockout drop). Wilder plea-bargained and was placed on five years probation, provided that he undergo psychological counseling and treatment by a sex therapist. To get around the terms of his probation, he contacted a modeling service rather than picking up women on his own.

Neighbors along Mission Hill Road near Palm Beach became accustomed to seeing pretty teenage girls going to and from Wilder's home. He had a photography studio in his garage as well as a Jacuzzi and indoor and outdoor pools at the house, and he persuaded some of his models to stay a couple of weeks. He loved reading John Knowles's novel *The Collector* so much that he kept several copies of the best-seller around the house. The much-praised book, told from the view of a disturbed young man, chronicles his life with a woman he keeps as a sex slave, her death, and his search for a second victim.

Wilder loved fast cars and competed in the Miami Grand Prix and Sebring races. Many people liked his outgoing personality, and one person called him "the nicest person I know." His net worth was estimated at $2,000,000. However, he began to have blackouts—periods of refusing to accept what he was doing. Wilder would disappear for two or three days and tell his friends upon his return that he could not remember what had happened.

During a visit to Australia in 1982, he attacked two fifteen-year-old girls, stripped them, forced them into pornographic poses, and photographed them, with the photography taking the place of a sex act in his mind. His parents posted $350,000 bail, and he fled back to the United States, where he behaved as if nothing had happened.

On February 26, 1984, lovely Rosario Gonzalez worked at her job distributing aspirin samples at the Miami Grand Prix. Wilder was fuming that day because he had placed only seventeenth in the race. By evening, people were trying to find Gonzalez. Her body has never been found.

Around this time, Wilder had a few dates with stunning Beth Kenyon, who was a finalist in the Miss Florida contest and a teacher of emotionally disturbed youngsters. She assured her parents that although Wilder had a playboy reputation, he was "a perfect gentleman" with her. But in early March, Beth told her family that she had decided to tell Wilder they should not see each other anymore. On March 4, Beth disappeared and a coast-to-coast manhunt began.

A short time later, Wilder kidnapped Terry Ferguson from a Florida shopping mall, and her body was found in a snake-infested creek. She was stabbed repeatedly with something resembling a filet knife.

In Brainbridge, Georgia, a fully bearded Wilder abducted a nineteen-year-old woman from a shopping center and sealed her eyes nearly shut with a super glue in a motel room. He lay next to her nude body on a bed and masturbated while watching female aerobic dancers on television, then subjected her to electric shocks and raped her twice. Although her hands were tied and her mouth taped, the captive was able to scream as he hit her with a hair dryer. Leaving her bound, Wilder ran out of the room and hastily said "excuse me" to the other guests in his light Australian accent.

A sixteen-year-old girl was kidnapped from a mall near Gary, Indiana, and stabbed repeatedly, but she survived by playing dead. Twenty-one-year-old Susanne Logan was taken from a shopping mall in Oklahoma City, and driven to a motel in Milford, Kansas; her body was found in the town reservoir. She had been raped and stabbed, and bite marks were found on her breasts.

The FBI put the search for Wilder at the top of its priority list, but he made the trail easier by using a credit card he had stolen from his business partner.

Michelle Korfman, the daughter of a casino executive, had never tried modeling but wanted to compete in *Seventeen* magazine's cover contest in the Meadows Mall of Las Vegas on April 1. The search for her would end in the Los Angeles County morgue.

While in California, Wilder unsuccessfully tried to entice a young woman in Redondo Beach, one of the hot spots for serial killers. Later, he had a sixteen-year-old girl pose for him near Santa Monica and put a gun to her head when she said she was leaving. "Your modeling days are over," Wilder said. He took her to a motel and subjected her to threats and humiliations but let her live.

Authorities assumed Wilder would try to fly to Australia. After weeks of Wilder's trail getting colder, a pretty Sunday School teacher, thirty-three-year-old Beth Dodge, disappeared in Victor, New York, and her body was found in Rochester. Some police guessed that Wilder might try sneaking into Canada.

New Hampshire State Police in remote Colebrook stopped his car near the border. Four things gave him away: he matched the description of Wilder, his Pontiac looked like

Wilder's, he had a tan in a New Hampshire April, and his cheeks and jaw were pale where a beard had recently been shaved off. When the officers started asking questions, Wilder grabbed a .357 Magnum revolver. One officer threw himself on Wilder, and there was a struggle. Wilder died, and an officer was wounded with a bullet that came within one inch of killing him.

The end had come forty-seven days after a journey that claimed at least five lives. It was Friday the 13th.

"La Doctera"

In the 1980s, pop singer Madonna made herself known as "the material girl," and President Ronald Reagan's trickle-down economy defied gravity and trickled up. First Lady Nancy Reagan preached her "Just Say No" anti-drug campaign coldly in stylish dresses. Scandals threatened the banking industry, the economy was slipping and sliding, junk bond investment schemes defrauded millions across the country, and Jim Bakker's church secretary, Jessica Hahn, exposed how he had used his ministry at the PTL Club to grow rich. And nowhere was "do your own thing" more of a cultural motto than in California.

But there were still many people who showed compassion and worked among the poor, such as Dorothea Montalvo Puente. The elderly Sacramento woman with the fair skin made large contributions to the Mexican-American Youth Association and was affectionately called "La Doctera" for the help she extended to the down and out, and she was lively enough to dance with Governor Jerry Brown at a charity ball.

Puente developed close ties with social workers, who saw her well-kept three-level boarding house with leaded-glass windows at 1426 F Street as the last resort for skid row men and women facing old age in a world of loneliness. The top floor of the white Victorian house served as Puente's quarters and the dining room; all the boarders lived below. She offered them care, good food, and their own color television set. When Puente was not helping others, she was often seen carefully tending her garden.

The garden might have continued to grow, but Judy Moise, a street counselor for the Volunteers of America's Courtesy Outreach program, became concerned about one of her missing charges, shambling Alvaro (Bert) Montoya from Costa Rica. Montoya was a likable man, even sweet, with a bushy white beard although he was only fifty. Ever since he was nineteen, he felt that spirits of the dead were haunting his brain. Moise first saw Montoya as he stood in front of a graveyard saying, "Get out of here, keep away from me!" Montoya helped Moise with little chores in the detoxification center.

Puente was doing so much good for people that no one thought it particularly odd when she took Montoya to the Social Security office and had him make her the payee for his government checks. She said the honey bear of a man was a little retarded and had trouble managing money. On the form, she wrote that she was his cousin. This meant that Puente would receive $637 from the taxpayers of America every month until the government was notified that Montoya had died.

Puente was born Dorothea Gray in 1929 to a low-income family in the Redland Valley of San Bernardino County, California. Her Baptist father was wounded in World War I and suffered from tuberculosis. Everyone in the family worked by following the crops, with Dorothea learning to pick cotton when she was three, the year before her father died. Her mother was often drunk and sometimes spent time in jail for rowdy binges. As a schoolgirl, Dorothea faked illness to get out of work, and she created fantasies in which she had a comfortable living and was admired. When she was nine, she was sent to an orphanage, and then was bounced around among a number of relatives, including older brothers and sisters.

With her good looks, the teenager went from a waitress in a milk shake parlor to prostitution, and not only for the money. She liked the feeling of power over men. She was married in 1945, spent some time in Mexico, had a series of dull jobs back in the United States, and began stealing checks from a woman she had befriended.

From then on, she led a life of cons, name changes, more prostitution, and jail time until she was rich enough to run several brothels in the 1960s. In fact, her quaint boarding house was a former bordello. Her third husband, Roberto Puente of Mexico City, was twenty years younger than she, and he soon had an eye for younger women. Her fourth and final marriage was to Pedro Montalvo, whom she called abusive. In her multiple marriages, she had several miscarriages and one stillborn child, but never a son or daughter who lived.

Having grown heavy and her hair turning white, she decided to enter the mainstream for a final con—cheating the national health care system. She arranged for her lodgers' government checks to be sent to her. To make sure they did not die in a hospital or on the street, thereby ending her checks, she killed them quietly and disposed of the bodies while everyone else was sleeping. One boarder was always replaced by another.

Few of the social workers realized it, but Puente frequented bars near the state office buildings and sometimes paid for the cocktails of reporters, whom she called "the guys with ties." She was always tastefully dressed, often in lavender and pink chiffons, and was a good tipper, sometimes paying a tab with a hundred-dollar bill. She never just swapped stories with the men at the bars; she seemed to be looking for someone who might show up not too shabby but possibly in need of help.

When Judy Moise started asking about Montoya in April 1988, two social workers told her that Puente—the kindly old lady—had angrily refused to speak to them about another man they had placed with her but who was found to be living somewhere else. Moise and the social workers wondered whether Dorothea Puente was the Dorothea Montalvo who had spent some time in prison for victimizing elderly boarders. But Montalvo was dark-haired and weighed two hundred pounds; Puente was white-haired and more slender.

Moise made what she hoped would seem like a social visit to the boardinghouse, and she used the pretext of Puente's fair skin to inquire about whether Puente had any other name. Dorothea hesitated, eyeing Moise closely, and finally answered "Johanson," the name of a former husband. Moise had a lot of questions, but the cleanliness of the house and Puente's simple manner made her think that Montoya must be around somewhere. Moise saw no reason to remove him.

But by October, Moise wondered whether she had made the worst decision of her life. She heard from a coworker at detox that Montoya had visited her in late July and again in

August. Puente told the coworker that he no longer wanted to stay at the boardinghouse because Puente insisted that he take drugs to stop his inner voices. At Moise's suggestion, the coworker called Puente to ask about Montoya. The older woman said that she had taken Montoya to her in-laws in Mexico and left him there. Moise herself called a few days later and was assured that Montoya would be back in a week, then it was in another week, and then by Thanksgiving.

On her way to the office on November 7, Moise received a call from a man claiming to be Montoya's brother-in-law in Utah, although Moise was sure the missing man never had a brother-in-law. The caller said he picked up Montoya in California and that Moise could stop his Social Security checks. When she asked for the caller's number, he said he had to go and hung up. Moise phoned the police department's missing person's office.

Officer Richard Ewing went to the boardinghouse and spoke to a tall, elderly lodger named John Sharp. Sharp told him that Puente really had gone to Mexico with Montoya and that Montoya had returned but left again in his brother-in-law's pickup truck just that Sunday. The police officer accompanied Puente around the house and saw that everything was fine. But when Ewing came downstairs to leave, Sharp pushed an envelope into his hand. On the back was scribbled: "She wants me to lie to you."

Ewing stepped into Sharp's room, turned up the TV to cover their conversation, and then arranged to see him at a corner a few blocks away. When they met, Sharp said there was "something strange going on," and he was not talking about just Montoya. Another boarder, Ben Fink, disappeared last spring. Sharp thought it had something to do with the holes Puente had some ex-convicts dig in her yard. The holes were empty one day and covered up the next. Sharp once worked in a mortuary, and he said there was the "stink of death" in one of the rooms upstairs.

A prostitute the police sometimes used for information reported that Puente had served time for forgery, theft, and drugging and robbing elderly victims. She said Puente had fooled parole officers after her release by taking them upstairs to her "apartment" and not letting on that she had boarders downstairs.

On Friday, November 11, three officers and Puente's newly assigned federal parole agent met with Moise to discuss their leads and what they thought might be happening. With thousands of people lining up for Sacramento's Veteran's Day parade, the officers went to the rooming house with its blue trim and carpenter's lace gingerbreading the columns of the front portico. During questioning, Puente had explanations for everything and admitted her criminal past, but added, "I'm trying to straighten my life out now." With her permission, the police started digging.

In the far corner of the yard, the shovel of the probation officer struck white powdery lime eighteen inches down. The officers carefully removed the dirt until they found pieces of clothing and a leg bone with bits of skin. The body had obviously been there for longer than Montoya was missing, so now there could be two or more victims. The officers turned to Dorothea and saw her with her hands to her face in a withering posture of shock.

Authorities summoned crime scene technicians, heavy-equipment operators, forensic anthropologists, and a deputy coroner. But there was no link that would stand up in court between Puente and the body. She said she poured the lime over the ground to soften the dirt for her gardening. Puente offered to take a polygraph test but asked the investigators to wait until Monday "to give my nerves a chance to settle." The crews returned the next morning, this time with a van in case there were any more bodies.

Puente took her woolen coat and left with one of her tenants, John McCauley, saying she was taking him to the Clarion Hotel to meet her nephew over a cup of coffee. "I'll be back soon," she said pleasantly. She passed calmly through a growing crowd of reporters and onlookers. Detective John Cabrera even accompanied them for three blocks, then waved and watched them walk away.

A short time later, diggers found a second body, that of a petite gray-haired woman. Police who raced to the hotel learned that instead of going there, Puente had called a cab and gone to a bar and to drop off McCauley. Next, she took a taxi fifty miles to Stockton, in the breadbasket of central California, one place where the police would probably not think of looking for her. She boarded a Greyhound bus that afternoon for Los Angeles. Cabrera fumed at himself for letting her get away. He was fooled by her harmless-little-old-lady act, just like everyone else.

By November 14, crews had removed seven bodies, including Montoya's. Most were buried in blankets. Thoughts went to Belle Gunness of La Porte, Indiana, who was never found after poisoning and burying more than ten men at the turn of the century. Would Puente fool everyone as well?

Autopsies found no obvious wounds on the victims, but there was a green substance in all the stomachs and a trace in the lungs. This was found to be the drug flurazepam, sold under the brand-name Dalmane.

Sacramento Police Chief John Kearns was trying to explain the embarrassment of losing the only suspect when Puente, using the name Johanson, checked into the cheap Royal Viking Motel in Los Angeles, hoping for the heat to cool down. She had a blonde rinse and tried to blend in. Feeling restless, she took a cab to a down-in-the-heels neighborhood bar on Third Street, dressing well and wearing perfume and pumps. Puente started talking to a steady patron, Charles Willgues, a thin, balding widower and retired handyman. Speaking as Donna Johanson, she told of being a lonely fifty-five-year-old widow from San Francisco who had just been robbed of all her luggage by a larcenous cabdriver. But Willgues thought she came on a little too strong in telling him she knew how to increase his Social Security payments. Because of the search for Puente, he called the local CBS news bureau, which assembled a film crew and contacted the police.

Los Angeles police went to Puente's room and asked to see her driver's license. Minutes later, she walked to a patrol car in handcuffs. Because of all the publicity about the case, Puente was tried in Monterey County. By then, two more bodies were added to the list of her dead, including Everson Gillmouth, who had written to his sister that he intended to ask Puente to marry him. His body was found in a box on the side of the Sacramento River.

On August 25, 1993, after nearly six weeks of deliberations, the jurors found Puente guilty of killing three of the victims. Because the exhausted jurors could not agree on the sentence, Judge Michael Virga ordered her to life in prison without parole.

The Collectors

Bondage fantasies may be as old as civilization, providing plots for sadomasochistic games in which both partners are willing. But only in the 1980s did there appear multiple cases of men actually having "sex slaves" and killing them or allowing them to die. Several of these men, including Christopher Wilder, were inspired by the novel *The Collector* or the film of the same title. Although the book was written in the 1960s, it stirred images in the minds of teenagers at a time when they were questioning the rest of humanity. But such dark thoughts must be nourished, replenished, and expanded for years before they lead to violence.

Case No. 1

On October 16, 1984, police in pleasant San Jose, California, pulled over a van because the driver was weaving out of his lane. Fernando Velazco Cota then surprised a highway patrol officer by pulling out a revolver and saying, "I'm a very sick man, kill me. If you don't kill me, I'll kill myself." As the officer froze, the thirty-eight-year-old computer programmer drew his gun and shot himself to death. Cota was carrying a fake badge and bogus identification. In the back of the van was the body of twenty-one-year-old Kim Dunham and evidence that Cota may have killed five other women from the area after keeping them chained in his closet.

Case No. 2

Starting in 1984, Robert Berdella invited men from gay circles in Kansas City, Missouri, to his nice-looking two-story house at 4315 Charlotte Street. The exterior was well kept, but the interior was a mess of boxes and bags of clothing and junk— an extension of Berdella's business as a secondhand dealer.

For some reason, Berdella—a fat man with a black mustache—never attacked strangers. His final victim was a young hustler who found himself tied to a bed and being injected with a bizarre combination of drugs. With the victim under his control, Berdella dabbed the man's eyes with bleach or ammonia to cause pain and partial blindness, so that the victim would, in Berdella's imagination, forever be his companion. But the young man was able to think rationally despite the tortures and pretended to be a willing partner. Berdella believed him because he desperately wanted to, and one day he left the house long enough for the captive to escape.

Police found the skull of murder victim Larry Pearson on one of Berdella's shelves and thirteen audiocassettes with sounds that may have come from torture. Two other skulls were discovered upstairs. Additional evidence included photos of the victims, one of them of a body hanging upside down from the ceiling. A crew using a backhoe discovered a decomposed head in the backyard. An investigation revealed six men were killed. Most were cut up and dumped in trash bags, which were then picked up by a regular garbage crew.

Berdella and his younger brother were raised Catholic in Ohio. Berdella said his father would beat them so often that he was afraid of him and looked to his mother for comfort. The closeness increased when his father died young of natural causes. For reasons unknown, Berdella withdrew from any competition with the real world and lived with thoughts of utter violence until he seemed unable to tell which was which.

Being a methodical person, Berdella wrote a log of the tortures he inflicted, including seventy-seven hundred volts of electricity. When investigators asked whether Berdella was attracted to his victims, he replied, "You're looking at what would be some of my darkest fantasies becoming my reality, where I was capturing people, controlling them. You don't necessarily need sexual attractiveness to do that." He explained that his real gratification was the dominance. He claimed the idea for the killings had been with him ever since he saw the movie *The Collector* in 1965 as a teenager. Berdella pleaded guilty to the final murder and was sentenced in December 1988 to life in prison.

Case No. 3

What happened in Gary Heidnik's cellar in Philadelphia is still not entirely clear. But what is known is that Heidnik used the cellar to torture his kidnap victims.

Heidnik's father was a tool and die maker who separated from his wife near Cleveland when the boy was two. That left him in the care of his mentally unstable mother, who married three times more—twice to black men. Presumably to make Heidnik more at ease with her African-American boyfriends, his mother told the boy that his real father was black. Heidnik believed her, despite his pale skin and Caucasian features. He was drawn to black friends. After his younger brother was institutionalized and his mother killed herself, Heidnik carried considerable diffuse rage.

Heidnik served in the Army, was discharged, and settled in Philadelphia. With an IQ of 130, he earned a license as a practical nurse but could not hold down a job. Over the years, he entered mental hospitals twenty-one times, was diagnosed as schizophrenic, was arrested for numerous petty crimes, and made thirteen self-dramatizing attempts at suicide. He also had relationships with a couple of black women who were retarded, and perhaps he craved a need to control their lives. He constantly had an image of holding ten women in his cellar year after year, keeping them pregnant, and raising the numerous children in his home as one big happy family.

Heidnik may have been mad, but he was so rational in other ways that he had become rich. He created a mail-order church and used the money for wise investments until he was worth more than half a million dollars. Yet, he often ignored his personal appearance and continued to live in a run-down neighborhood.

On November 26, 1986, he offered a prostitute money for sex, took her home, and made her the first captive in his narrow, white house in the Tioga section of North Philadelphia. Three days later, he forced a longtime friend of his, Sandra Lindsay, into captivity with the prostitute. The prostitute insisted later that she was a helpless victim. But she offered Heidnik some suggestions on keeping the women, and there is some suspicion that she planned to turn the macabre situation into blackmail or robbery. Whatever was on her mind, the two young women watched as Heidnik dug individual pits for them in the ground of his cellar. There he kept them while he brought in more women. Each captive was forced to lie in her pit with a chamber pot; a plywood lid was held down with sandbags. Heidnik played his stereo loudly, supposedly twenty-four hours a day, to drown out their screams. From time to time, he held a prayer service upstairs for a congregation of a few children and retarded adults.

On December 22, he brought home a teenage girl and locked her in with the others below 3520 North Marshall

Street. On New Year's Day, 1987, he added Deborah Dudley. On January 18, he took a fifth victim to his enforced harem, an eighteen-year-old. The five women were beaten with a utility handle if they committed an infraction, and he found ways of trapping them in violations so that he might play the role of outraged disciplinarian. From time to time, Heidnik's prisoners were forced into oral sex and rape.

Lindsay reacted by refusing to eat and, being force-fed, refusing to swallow. When she starved herself to death, Heidnik cut up her body and reportedly put parts of it into the dog food he fed the others. He was said to have derived the idea from the black comedy film *Eating Raoul.* Dudley was in a water-filled pit when Heidnik gave her an electric shock, and she died. He removed her head and was cooking it on the stove when police came about a foul odor, but he talked his way out of suspicion.

On March 23, Heidnik used his captive prostitute to pick up another woman to add to his cellar. Two days later, the prostitute escaped from his car and notified the police. Instead of being overjoyed at the sight of the police rushing in, the three chained black women were terrified because they thought Heidnik had sent fake officers downstairs to trick them into misbehaving. The officers also discovered a freezer with twenty-four pounds of human body parts. When Heidnik was arrested near his new Cadillac, he had $1,900 in his pockets.

Heidnik grew a biblical thick black beard for his trial, but the jurors rejected his insanity defense and sentenced him to execution for the two deaths.

A few months after Heidnik's arrest made headlines, police in another part of North Philadelphia in August 1987 found six bodies on the third floor of a row house where Harrison Graham had lived. Although not a sex-slave case, the coincidence is interesting. The twenty-seven-year-old lodger nailed his door shut from the outside and disappeared after his landlord told him that neighbors were complaining about a smell. A duffel bag of human bones was later found on the roof. Skeletal remains in the closet appeared to be those of someone who died while tied up. Evidence suggested that women in the drug-infested community were lured by the promise of narcotics. Graham surrendered one week after the discovery and was charged with seven counts of murder.

Case No. 4

Red-haired burglar-rapist Bill Benefiel lived as if in an armed camp in Terre Haute, Indiana. His camp featured guard dogs and a prisoner-compound fence rising twelve feet at some points. Benefiel abducted attractive young women, terrorized them with threats, violated them with objects, slashed them, and raped them repeatedly while they were chained. He grotesquely wore a gorilla mask to conceal his identity and sometimes held more than one captive at a time. In late 1987, Benefiel killed eighteen-year-old Delores Wells by wrapping her mouth and nose with tape, and buried her near an abandoned mine shaft. Occasionally, he would release a victim after donning a stocking mask and driving her away in a van.

Benefiel, who had a number of clashes with his mother when he was a boy, lived with a woman for more than ten years and eventually married her after his arrest. The short, stocky young man claimed he was abused as a child and was made fun of by his classmates. He had bondage-torture dreams and in fact described one assault that really happened in a dream, possibly because he no longer had a clear distinction between them. Benefiel was convicted of the Wells murder and sentenced to death.

Case No. 5

Not many years from now, people will wonder how there could have been a survivalist mania in America in the 1980s. With the shrinking military and the erosion of the Communist threat, these people who built bunkers and practiced target shooting seemed sadly out of touch with reality. They were satirized in several films, but at least one of these survivalist freaks needed to be taken seriously. Leonard Lake, an average-looking man with more hair on his face than on his head, bored acquaintances with talk about the coming war. And he kept a cyanide capsule with him to commit suicide upon capture.

Lake saw two years of Marine duty in Vietnam, serving as a spotter to call in air strikes. His only run-in with authorities as a civilian was stealing some weatherizing material. He lived for awhile in a hippie reservation in the Redwood Valley in northern California. But Lake was thrown out for strange behavior. He went around to fairs for awhile with a supposed unicorn, which was just a goat whose horn was augmented by skin grafts. Lake held a Bible study group primarily because he craved the company. Then he sold some property and was able to avoid work altogether. He swung from the left to the right and began going around in laced boots and camouflage uniforms. He had finally found himself.

Charles Ng (pronounced "Ing"), a good-looking, athletic young man of Chinese descent, was born in British-controlled Hong Kong. While being educated in England, where an uncle was a teacher, he hated being called "Charlieboy" and was considered inferior by his classmates. But Ng let them know through his strength and quick reflexes that he could beat any of them in a fight. He went to Oxford for awhile until his family disowned him for some unknown reason. He then immigrated to America. Ng became a firearms buff and joined the Marines but was caught stealing military weapons from a base in Hawaii and was sent to the brig. There he began a correspondence with Lake, who might have placed an ad or an item in an arms or soldier-of-fortune–type magazine. Ng escaped and was rearrested in April 1982 on Lake's Mendocino County property. A fatal connection was made, but nothing violent occurred until after Ng was released from Leavenworth prison in June 1984.

Despite Ng's intelligence, the best he could do for himself was working for a moving company near San Francisco. Acquaintances called him "kind of creepy." Others said he lived in a fantasy world in which he was a ninja. He once said he was the son of an imaginary genius in the art and that his talents were being wasted. That is why he turned his panther-like swiftness and agility to burglary.

Around this time, a prostitute filed a complaint alleging that a Caucasian man, who may have been Lake, hired her as "an escort," and that a naked Chinese man with him raped her while repeatedly jabbing a knife into the mattress near her head. The man who may have been Lake stood by taking pictures in a ritual that, if true, combined acting out sadism with voyeurism.

Either by himself or with Ng, Lake conceived of "Operation Miranda," named after the unfortunate victim in *The Collector*. Lake first built a cinder-block bunker on his land in Calaveras County, south of San Francisco, and turned it into a prison for his future captives. Next came a plan for brainwashing women into submitting to sexual desires. They were to be lectured, and their baby, boyfriend, or husband threatened. The women were to be ordered to prepare meals until they were conditioned into following orders. Then they would be ready for sex any time the captor so desired it. If they did not submit to this complete depersonalization, their baby, boyfriend, or husband would be killed. Then the plan was carried out.

Lake killed at least a dozen men, women, and children without anyone realizing what was happening, even though some of the victims were his neighbors. As he went about his normal duties, he used the name of one man who had disappeared, Charles Gunnar, and the car of another, Paul Cosner. No one noticed the bullet holes and small blood stains on the car.

A simple burglary by Ng at a South Francisco lumberyard led to Lake's arrest as he waited in a car on June 2, 1985. Although Ng escaped, Lake was brought in for questioning; he slipped the cyanide capsule into his mouth and died after a few days in a coma. Ng flew to Chicago, then made it into Canada and was arrested in Calgary. By then, the police had recovered fifty shopping bags of broken human bones dug up around Lake's retreat. They also found crude videotapes in which some of the women captives were seen undergoing psychological torture that police called "a brain game." On one of the tapes, a woman is seen pleading with Lake to return her baby to her as she is forced to disrobe. Ng was extradited to California to stand trial on charges of participating in twelve murders and as an accessory to a thirteenth.

The sex-slave cases occurred at the same time as several lone killers were on the prowl.

Police near Tampa arrested unemployed X-ray technician Robert Long as he left a movie theater in November 1984 on charges of abducting and raping a seventeen-year-old girl. Soon afterward, Long was also booked for killing nine young women in a six-month lust spree. And he was a suspect in several more killings. The connection to the murders was made from fibers vacuumed up from the floor of his car while he was being held on the rape charge. One of the murder victims was an Asian go-go dancer, and another was a hotel waitress. Attorneys for the six-foot, tanned, good-looking man blamed his errant behavior on brain damage caused by a car that struck Long in West Virginia when he was six and a motorcycle accident that occurred when he was twenty-one.

Long's background was similar to that of several other serial killers: He lived with elderly relatives while growing up because his parents split up when he was young and his mother had trouble earning a living. Possibly because of this, Long was shy despite his size. His voyeurism led him to take unnecessary X-rays of female patients. He was caught and fired, freeing him for a murder spree. After his arrest, Long's mother said, "He's a very sick boy. He has been for many, many years. He was just an unhappy kid. So sad." In May 1985, he was sentenced to die in the electric chair for just one of the crimes, the murder of an eighteen-year-old prostitute.

From 1978 to 1984, someone was picking up male hitchhikers, killing them, and dumping their bodies in different counties from Terre Haute, Indiana, to near the Illinois-Wisconsin border. The gay community in Indianapolis offered to help the police, but the suggestion was rejected. The police officers did not want to associate with "queers."

The Indiana police were so determined to catch the killer that they jumped the gun, seizing possible evidence found in the pickup truck of muscular Larry Eyler after they had seen him acting suspiciously with a hitchhiker. Eyler was only a housepainter but he was clever enough to sue the police, contending that the evidence was seized without a warrant. With a heavy heart, a judge threw out the case. Lake County, Illinois, Sheriff Robert "Mickey" Babcox muttered that Eyler was free to kill again.

Investigators discovered an amazing correlation after the arrest: A young man was killed each time Eyler had a fight with his handsome, blonde male lover. The final arrest came months later when the dismembered body of a teenage male prostitute was found in a dumpster close to Eyler's Chicago apartment. The crime was especially shocking because the victim, Danny Bridges, had been involved in a public crusade against pedophiles. Eyler maintained his innocence throughout his trial, but as he was dying of AIDS in prison he admitted killing more than twenty teenagers and young men.

In Chicago, there is one street that is sacrosanct: the luxury residential district of North Lake Shore Drive just south of Lincoln Park. Violent crime seemed unthinkable on that silent street facing Lake Michigan, but vivacious Rosemarie Ann Beck was abducted outside a nearby night spot on September 7, 1982. She was tortured and left to die near the doorway of a building along The Drive. Beck was the latest victim of a "Ripper gang" led by Robin Gecht.

Gecht—a Midwestern version of Charles Manson—was evil straight through. Gecht's parents were never married, and he lived with his grandmother when he was a boy. Things were all right when his brother was born three years after he was, but the five-year-old resented the birth of a sister. Their house became so crowded that Gecht had to sleep on the floor.

The next year, Gecht wandered off rather than look after his brother. The younger boy was seriously hurt by a car and had to be institutionalized, and Gecht seems never to have gotten over it. Another girl was born into the family, and Gecht hated watching over his sisters. At school, Gecht was taunted by the other boys for being small, skinny, and Jewish. Finally, a third sister was born. At age eleven, Gecht was the man of the family but his rebellion landed him in reform school. The natural deaths of his grandparents occurred within a brief span, and an aunt killed herself. Yet the only hate known in Gecht's background was in Gecht himself.

He used his eyes and hypnotic ways to bind to him several men of limited intelligence. He turned to murder and rituals after persuading his wife to mutilate her breast for him. Following the abduction and butchering of several women in 1981 and 1982, Gecht, despite his Jewish background, presided over a sort of informal Communion in which his disciples ate small parts of the flesh.

At least five women were killed, one lifted out of her shoes at a shopping center and another abducted while waiting for her family on a highway. Another women was hauled into the murder van, forced to take drugs, her breast was mutilated, and she was dumped still alive from the vehicle. She survived to identify the members while still in the hospital. Gecht was convicted and sentenced to serve one hundred twenty-five years in prison. A member of his gang, Andy Kokoraleis, was put on Death Row.

The shopping malls and highways of cities made it easier than ever to abduct someone. But the vast expanse of Alaska made it easy for Robert Hansen to dispose of at least seventeen bodies.

Hansen grew up in Pocahontas, Iowa. The red-haired, stuttering boy had a strict father and an overly forgiving mother, making his emotional balance rather lopsided. After he was accused of torching a bus barn in 1960, he moved to Anchorage to work as a baker. He felt that Alaska was where the jobs were. In his spare time, he visited a small bar on Fourth Avenue, where there were easy pick-ups, and frequented a topless dance club, where he would flash a roll of bills as bait money. If he was interested in a woman, he would stalk her with a rifle. Hansen sometimes forced his prey to walk into his trophy room at gunpoint. Some he lured there with singles ads. He would kill the woman, find a remote location on his aviation chart, and fly the body to the spot in his Piper Super Cub bush plane.

Hansen kept telling himself the murders were the proper thing to do. If he wanted a moral woman, he would find something about her to consider immoral, such as her using a foul word. He apparently became aroused at the topless club but would use a dancer's assumed immorality as a justification to eliminate her. Yet he went to prostitutes because he did not want a wife to engage in oral sex. With his confused morality, Hansen said he killed prostitutes when they failed to please him. And, of course, they never pleased him when he was in a mood to kill.

His ten years of hunting humans ended when a seventeen-year-old prostitute broke away from him and ran for help while still in handcuffs. Hansen pleaded guilty to four of the killings and was sentenced to serve four hundred sixty-one years plus life in prison.

A Case that Reopened Itself

On March 19, 1985, officers from the sheriff's department in Orange County, California, were called to a well-furnished house on Ocean Beach Drive in Garden Grove. The short, stocky owner, David Brown, said with tears in his eyes, "I think my wife's been shot." Off to the side, his wife's young blonde sister, Patti, cried as she held her sister's screaming baby.

"I'm afraid to look," Brown told the officers, explaining that he had a bad heart and other medical conditions.

Brown and his teenage sister-in-law waited on a couch as the officers—careful not to touch anything that might disturb any fingerprints—went past a partly opened door and found Linda Brown lying on her bed in her nightgown amid a pool of blood. Her lungs were still gurgling from two shots through the chest. She would later die after being rushed to a hospital.

Brown and Patti told the officers that someone resembling Brown's fourteen-year-old daughter, Cinnamon, was seen leaving through the back door just after three shots were fired. They added that Cinnamon was going through a moody period and had even talked of suicide.

The officers found Cinnamon curled up in the fetal position in a large doghouse. She was lying in her own vomit and was apparently ill from what appeared to be a suicide attempt. One of the officers pulled Cinnamon from the narrow enclosure. Her skin was cold, and she was barely conscious. Beside her was a note: "Dear God, please forgive me. I didn't mean to hurt her."

Other officers bagged possible evidence, including Brown's bottles of prescription medicine found in the laundry room.

Patti told the police that the family's two cocker spaniels did not bark before or after the shots, meaning that whoever wounded Linda was likely no stranger to the house.

At the police station, Cinnamon complained of a terrible headache and regurgitated a bright orange substance into a wastepaper basket. But she said she would be all right. She told the investigators that she held the gun and fired it twice because her cruel stepmother had kicked her out of the house and forced her to live in a trailer. Cinnamon contended that she was so upset by what she had done that she swallowed some pills from her father's medicine.

Still drowsy and light-headed from the overdose, Cinnamon asked, "Is my Dad all right? How's Linda?" She seemed not to fully realize what she had done. After hours of questioning, Cinnamon lapsed into unconsciousness and was rushed to a hospital, where she was hooked up to an IV and a heart monitor. A female officer who accompanied her in the ambulance said the girl muttered phrases such as "had an accident . . . killed my stepmother . . . she wanted to kill me . . ."

Although the gunpowder test on Cinnamon came back negative, the result was not surprising given that the test was taken after she had been lying in her vomit. When Cinnamon recovered, she claimed to have no memory of what happened. A psychiatrist diagnosed her with psychogenic amnesia.

The case seemed open and shut. But Detective Fred McLean and district attorney's investigator Jay Newell had lingering concerns about the case. First, teenage girls seldom use a gun when they are angry. Second, there was something about Cinnamon herself. She did not have the aloofness, the remorse, the distance, the anger—the one thing or another that killers usually exhibit. And her psychological tests showed no tendency toward violence.

Despite Brown's efforts to present an insanity defense for his daughter, Cinnamon was convicted and sent to the Ventura School for Girls. There, she was a model prisoner and began taking college courses. Legally unable to requestion her because she was a juvenile, McLean and Newell decided to take a long, hard look at David Brown.

The father was thirty-two but looked older, his face pitted from teenage acne. He quickly became successful with the computer information-retrieval business he ran with his wife, Data Recovery. But could he have had a reason for wanting to get rid of his young, attractive second wife?

Because Linda operated the business, if she left her husband she would take half his remaining assets, and Data Recovery would collapse. The officers talked at length with Brown's first wife, Brenda, to see if there might also be a personal motive.

Ex-wives are seldom disinterested observers, but most of what Brenda offered was secondhand. But she brought up something interesting: Linda was afraid her husband might want to leave her for her pretty seventeen-year-old sister, Patti. Brenda also mentioned that Brown asked her to describe Cinnamon to the police as flaky, suicidal, and out of control, even though she was not. In addition, Brown's ex-sister-in-law claimed Cinnamon was made to live in a trailer outside the family home because pretty, shallow, materialistic Patti wanted a room of her own.

The more the investigators heard, the more the relationships in the Brown family thickened. Brown took Patti out of school, saying she was not learning enough and that he would hire a tutor for her. He never did. Patti stayed in the house with him day after day—first with Linda there and then with no one else. And from Linda's death, Brown received about $850,000 from several insurance policies, allowing him to buy a Tudor-style home with a swimming pool near Anaheim.

Digging deeper, the investigators discovered that Brown really did have heart trouble and allergies, as he said. But he was also in seventeen auto accidents for which he had filed insurance claims. He apparently used the money to replace the wrecked cars or to purchase fancier ones. In less than three years after Cinnamon was found guilty of Linda's murder, Brown bought fourteen expensive vehicles, including a $70,000 Mercedes convertible. Brown seemed to renew cars, wives, and homes as his ego expanded.

But the investigators wanted to know why Cinnamon would cover for her father? She had sometimes quarreled with her stepmother, but there was no long-standing hatred. McLean and Newell found the answers in the very nature of her clever and manipulative father.

Brown always loved to be the rescuer, someone admired for his ability to use compassion and intelligence to solve the personal problems of others. He was an attentive father, and Cinnamon grew up thinking that he was the funniest, most powerful, and most wonderful man in the world. In fact, wanting to be admired was one reason why Brown had a penchant for teenage girlfriends; more mature women could see through him.

Patti still seemed years away from sophistication. Despite all that happened, on July 1, 1986, she secretly married Brown in Las Vegas. But having learned something from his past,

Brown had her sign a prenuptial agreement entitling her only to a classic 1955 MG British-made sports car if they split up.

Newell met with Brown's father, Arthur, who told of overhearing Linda talking to her twin brother over the phone about doing away with her husband to take over the business. As Arthur and the investigator were speaking, Brown pulled up in one of his fancy cars. Newell instructed Arthur to introduce him as a real estate agent. Arthur went along, but he later informed Brown as to the true identity of the visitor.

Brown yelled at his father for endangering the whole family by talking to the authorities. He told his teen bride to burn any sign of their marriage and not to leave the house unless he was with her. But some things were not so easy to hide: Patti was pregnant. Brown decided to invent a husband, a man named Doug who drove around in a Camaro and delivered flowers to his "wife." In September 1987, Patti had a daughter and gave her the fashionable Valley Girl name of Heather. Then she learned something about her husband; he stopped being wonderful and caring. For once a wife became a mother, she could no longer be the adoring teenybopper playmate Brown craved. Trying to make the best of a bad situation, Brown tried to take out insurance on his baby but was turned down because the amount he sought was suspiciously large.

By now, Data Recovery was nationally known, and he moved into an even larger home in Anaheim. Newell meanwhile kept checking on Cinnamon, now seventeen. The girl still claimed to have no memory of the events, but she dropped perhaps unconscious hints to a doctor at the Ventura home that she might be innocent. Newell could not legally speak to her without her father's consent until she was eighteen, but he thought he could get her upset enough to confide in the staff parole officer. Using psychology rather than sleuthing, Newell took photos of Brown's new home and gave them to the parole officer.

Hearing about the baby and seeing pictures of the glamorous home, Cinnamon felt betrayed by the man she once adored. In July 1988, just after turning eighteen, she called Newell from Ventura and said, "I know now that it's time for him to take responsibility for the crime that's taken place."

Cinnamon said the plan was set in motion seven or eight months in advance. Her father told her that he had overheard Linda plotting with her twin brother to kill him for his business—the same story he later told his own father—and that she had to be stopped, but he did not have the health to do it himself. He said Cinnamon and Patti should kill her, and he told Cinnamon that she would do this "if you love me." Otherwise, Brown said, he would have to leave the family for his own safety, which Cinnamon could not bear to think about.

Over the next few weeks, Brown helped Cinnamon and Patti accept the idea, and the three of them held discussions about ways to kill Linda. One plan fell through, but they still had a suicide note Cinnamon had written to be found near her stepmother. On the fateful night, after the family played a card game, Linda left to take a shower and go to bed. Brown told the teenage girls, "We have to do it." After the murder, Brown took his daughter to the kitchen and asked her to swallow some harmless, over-the-counter pills to make her appear remorseful.

But Newell wondered if the pills were not an attempt by Brown to kill his daughter. The drugs she took were not the medicine she was told she was being given. Doctors said that if she had not vomited so much she would have died from excessive amounts of the painkiller Darvocet-N and the diuretic Dyazide.

Cinnamon said her father took her to the doghouse and assured her that as a juvenile she would receive only a light penalty and could return to a home without Patti. In the hospital, her father told her that a lawyer was urging her to claim she could not remember anything about the killing. Her story was convincing and seemed complete, except for who pulled the trigger.

Newell and McLean arranged for Cinnamon to wear a wire as she spoke to her father. Cinnamon called Brown and asked him to come to the Ventura home because the parole board was demanding that she tell about the murder or be sent to prison, and she did not know what to do.

Sitting on the lawn outside the building, Cinnamon, following suggestions from the investigators, asked her father why her stepmother had to die. He spun stories about how the Mafia wanted to take over their business and that Linda wanted to kick Cinnamon out of the house. The lies overlapped and contradicted each other. He then started talking about how Patti might be planning to kill him.

The tape and the previous evidence were enough to charge Brown and Patti with murder and murder conspiracy, even though there was still no evidence about who fired the gun. Patti, who also was betrayed, obtained her own lawyer and agreed to talk about that night. Cinnamon then came forward with the moments she was leaving out.

Cinnamon said her father told her to put a pillow over the muzzle to muffle the sound. She added that Patti gave her the .38 caliber revolver and showed her how to hold the pillow. Cinnamon went to the bedroom and shot her stepmother, but the pillow became stuck in the mechanism and she could not fire again. Panicking, and with Linda still alive, Cinnamon ran to Patti's room. Patti removed the pillow covering, but the gun went off again, sending a slug into a wall. Cinnamon returned and fired a second shot into her stepmother, then took the pills and went to the doghouse.

Seeing that Patti was about to testify against him, Brown tried to arrange for a hit man to kill her and the two investigators, Newell and McLean. But the intended hit man, who was being held in jail as a material witness in another case, went to the authorities instead. The authorities arranged to make it seem as if all three targets were dead. The supposed hit man then wore a body microphone as he spoke to Brown. "You did great," Brown said, "I love you!"

No testimony was more damning than Brown's own words on the two tapes. Sentencing him to life in prison, Judge Donald McCartin said, "You're a scary person . . . Mr. Brown, you make Charlie Manson look like a piker." Patti pleaded guilty and received a life term. Cinnamon, with support from Newell and others, was paroled at the age of twenty-one.

The Night Stalker

Los Angeles County Deputy District Attorney Philip Halpin faced a jury and outlined the crimes of the infamous "night stalker." Richard Ramirez was charged with thirteen murders in addition to numerous counts of burglary, robbery, and rape. The attacks began on March 17, 1984, when Dayle Okazaki was fatally shot and her roommate was wounded. That same day, thirty-year-old Tsai-Lian Yu was dragged from her car and shot to death. March 27 began a series of home invasions in which the man in the house was shot and the woman raped, beaten, then shot or stabbed, and left to either die or to survive.

The tall, gaunt, good-looking young man with intense features sat motionless as the horrors unfolded before those sitting in judgment. Halpin told them that one dying man called 911 and said "Help me." A teenage girl died when her head was crushed. An eight-year-old boy was sodomized after his father was killed and his mother raped. An eighty-three-year-old woman was bludgeoned to death, but her seventy- nine-year-old sister survived the attack. Many of the scenes and some of the bodies had Satanic markings.

Soon after the home invasions revealed a pattern, newspaper people brainstormed for a nickname for the unknown killer and decided to use the title of a 1971 made-for-TV movie, *The Night Stalker.* Richard Matheson's tongue-in-cheek story was about a reporter who discovers that the killer he is tracking is a vampire. The film led to the TV series "Kolchak." The victims of the real "night stalker" seemingly were picked at random but generally were attacked in upscale middle-class areas. Some were of Asian descent, especially the first ones.

Most of the buildings the killer entered were single-story homes in pastel colors, such as faint yellow or beige, and near freeway ramps. But people everywhere in Orange and Los Angeles counties were terrified, keeping locksmiths busy while the price of security systems shot up. People who would never before touch a gun kept one in their bedroom.

Police believed the deadly intruder killed the male first because he was a coward, leaving open the question of why he preferred attacking groups of two in the first place—two female roommates, two elderly sisters, and several couples. In fact, the arrest and prosecution of Ramirez left a lot of questions unanswered.

Ramirez was born in 1960 in El Paso, Texas, and grew up with a lot of rage that has not been understood. His father was a hard-working Mexican alien, and the boy was raised Catholic. He and the four other children in the family were brought up well in a small stucco house on Laredo Street. If anything, former neighbors said his parents were too lenient with the boy. He was given to seizures, possibly as attention-getting devices.

By age nine, he was a loner and soon started using drugs and living almost exclusively on junk food. A lot of boys in the El Paso barrio joined sometimes violent gangs, but Ramirez instead would spend evenings at video arcades and slip into homes at night to steal what he could. For most thieves, there is nothing strange in such behavior. But for serial killers such as William Heirens and perhaps Ramirez, the break-ins were apparently a substitute for sex, just as attacks on two people at a time may have stemmed from childhood voyeurism.

Ramirez spent some time in a reform school, came out unreformed, and dropped out of junior high school. He was then six-feet, one-inch tall. Following arrests on drug and other charges in Texas, he moved to California and did not do much of anything. His biggest job was as a street sweeper for a short time.

Ramirez entered a Bible study group sponsored by Jehovah's Witnesses and came away fascinated with Satan as a sort of father figure. He drew a personal message from the Satanic element in some hard-rock music. A year before the murders began, he had a Satanic pentagram tattooed on his palm. Rather than repeating a fixed fantasy, Ramirez may have set out to do everything he could think of to become evil. Living off cash he stole and stashing most of the valuables away at his sister's home, he seemed intent on continuing attacks until his once real self disappeared into a blur of unreality.

He appeared oblivious on the already hot morning of August 31, 1985, when he returned on a Greyhound bus from a trip to Arizona and passed stands of newspapers with his photo splashed on the front pages. Because he did not care to read newspapers or listen to the news—possibly amusing himself from time to time with news stories of his own imagination—Ramirez was unaware that he had been identified from a fingerprint. Walking down a street in East Los Angeles, Ramirez decided he needed a car. With the bold stupidity of meltdown, he pulled a woman from her auto and demanded her keys. Neighbors started running after him, some of them yelling in Spanish, "It's him, the killer!" Ramirez jumped over a fence, only to find others chasing him. The citizens, with outrage overriding any fear of this monster, grabbed him and beat him until the police could arrive.

In a holding cell, Ramirez told his keepers, "You got me. The Stalker." He also gave a guard a reason for his crimes: "I love to kill people. I love watching people die." While being held in jail, he used a photo of a mutilated woman to keep other inmates from getting too close. Although he looked grim during his trial, the mask came off when he was convicted on September 20, 1989, of thirteen counts of murder and thirty other felonies, from oral copulation to attempted murder. While Ramirez was being led in handcuffs to a sheriff's police car for return to jail, reporters asked him what he thought of the decision. He flashed a smile under his dark sunglasses—looking like a rugged movie actor—and gave them a Satanic gesture by making a fist while extending his index and little fingers. Then he said, "Evil."

When the jury later recommended that he die in the gas chamber, he remarked to reporters that "death always went with the territory." At his sentencing, Ramirez told the judge that "Lucifer lives in us all." He was then given twelve death sentences.

REFERENCES

Baden, Michael M. *Unnatural Death: Confessions of a Medical Examiner.* New York: Ivy/Balantine Books, 1989.

Blackburn, Daniel J. *Human Harvest.* New York: Knightsville Publishing, 1990.

Cox, Mike. *The Confessions of Henry Lee Lucas.* New York: Pocket Books, 1991.

Crockett, Art, ed. *Serial Murderers.* New York: Pinnacle Books, 1990.

Detlinger, Chet, with Prugh, Jeff. *The List*, Atlanta: Philmay Enterprises, 1983.

Discover, April 1981.

Douglas, John. *Mind Hunter.* New York: Pocket Books, 1996.

———, and Olshaker, Mark. *Journey into Madness.* New York: Pocket Books, 1997.

DuClos, Bernard. *Fair Game.* New York: St. Martin's Press, 1993.

Egger, Steven A. *Serial Murder: An Elusive Phenomenon.* New York: Praeger, 1990.

Englande, Ken. *Cellar of Horrors.* New York: St. Martin's Press, 1989.

Fido, Martin. *The Chronicle of Crime.* New York: Carroll & Graf Publishers, 1993.

Fletcher, Jaye Slade. *Deadly Thrills.* New York: Penguin Books/New American Library, 1995.

Fox, James Alan, and Levin, Jack. *Overkill: Mass Murder and Serial Killing Exposed.* New York: Dell Publishing, 1994.

Gibney, Bruce. *The Beauty Queen Killer.* New York: Pinnacle Books, 1984.

Harrington, Joseph. and Burger, Robert, *Eye of Evil.* New York: St. Martin's Press, 1993.

Hickey, Eric W. *Serial Murderers and their Victims*, Pacific Grove, Calif.: Brooks/Cole, 1991.

Holmes, Ronald M., and Holmes, Stephen T. *Murder in America*, Thousand Oaks, Calif.: Sage Publications, 1994.

Jackman, Tom, and Cole, Terry. *Rites of Burial.* New York: Pinnacle Books, 1992.

Jeffers, Paul H. *Who Killed Precious?* New York: St. Martin's Press, 1991.

Jenkins, Philip. *Using Murder: The Social Construction of Serial Homicide.* New York: Aldine de Gruyter, 1994.

Kaplan, Joel, Papajohn, George, and Zorn, Eric. *Murder of Innocence: The Tragic Life and Final Rampage of Laurie Dann.* New York: Warner Books, 1990.

Keppel, Robert D. *Signature Killers.* New York: Pocket Books, 1997.

Kolarik, Gera-Lind, with Klatt, Wayne. *Freed to Kill: The True Story of Serial Killer Larry Eyler.* New York: Avon Books, 1992.

Lang, Roger. *Murder in America*, Columbus, Ohio: Columbia University Press, 1997.

Leyton, Elliot. *Hunting Humans: The Rise of the Modern Multiple Murderer*, Toronto: Seal Books, 1986.

Linedecker, Clifford L. *Thrill Killers.* New York: Paperjacks, 1988.

———. *Night Stalker.* New York: St. Martin's Press, 1991.

Los Angeles Times, January 29, 1983.

Lyons, Arthur, and Truzzi, Marcello. *The Blue Sense.* New York: Mysterious Press/Warner Books, 1991.

Mackenzie, Drew. "Daddy's Girl," *Sunday Bloody Sunday.* London: Blake Paperbacks, 1992.

Marriner, Brian. *On Death's Bloody Trail: Murder and the Art of Forensic Science.* New York: St. Martin's Press, 1991.

Masters, Brian. *Killing for Company: The Case of Dennis Nilsen.* New York: Stein & Day, 1985.

New York Times, January 21, and October 17, 1984.

Newsweek, July 6, 1981.

Noel, Joel. *Serial Killers*, Garden City, N.Y.: Doubleday, 1988.

Norris, Joel. *Arthur Shawcross: The Genessee River Killer.* New York: Windsor Publishing, 1992.

Norton, Carla. *Disturbed Ground.* New York: William Morrow, 1994.

Odell, Robin. *Landmarks in 20th Century Murder.* London: Headline, 1995.

Olsen, Jack. *Misbegotten Son: A Serial Killer and His Victims.* New York: Dell Publishing, 1993.

People, April 30, 1984.

Ressler, Robert K. and Schachtman, Tom, *Whoever Fights Monsters.* New York: Warner Books, 1995.

Rubin, Lillian B. *Quiet Rage: Bernie Goetz in a Time of Madness.* New York: Farrar, Strauss & Giroux, 1986.

Rule, Ann (writing as Andy Stack). *The I-55 Killer.* New York: New American Library, 1984.

Rule, Ann. *Small Sacrifices.* New York: New American Library, 1988.

———. *If You Really Loved Me.* New York: Simon & Schuster, 1991.

Schultze, Jim. *Cauldron of Blood: The Matamoros Cult Killings.* New York: Avon Books, 1989.

Singular, Stephan. *A Killing in the Family.* New York: Avon Books, 1991.

Smith, Carlton, and Guillen, Thomas. *The Search for the Green River Killer.* New York: Penguin Books/New American Library, 1991.

Tampa (Fla.) Tribune, September 4, 1982.

Wilson, Colin. *Written in Blood: Detectives and Detection.* New York: Warner Books, 1989.

Wilson, Colin, and Seaman, Donald. *The Serial Killers: A Study in the Psychology of Violence.* London: W.H. Allen, 1990.

Wilson, Colin, and Wilson Damon. *The Killers Among Us: Book I. The Motives Behind Their Madness.* New York: Warner Books, 1995.

Wolf, Marvin J., and Mader, Katherine. *Perfect Crimes.* New York: Ballantine Books, 1995.

Wood, William P. *The Bone Garden.* New York: Pocket Books, 1994.

The 1990s

The Ring of Truth

My wife's been shot, I've been shot!" The call came from a cellular phone to the Massachusetts state police on October 23, 1989. The wounded caller could not tell the police where he was except that it was somewhere in Boston. When the dispatcher asked what happened, the man replied in a panicky voice, "I don't know. He drove us . . . he made us go to an abandoned area." The dispatcher kept the wounded man on the line, getting more and more specifics, until he heard a siren in the background and knew the man was found.

Officer Wayne Rock reached the blue Toyota Cressida and saw a woman who was about seven months pregnant slumped over and bleeding from her head. Her husband, wounded through the intestine, sat beside her. Moments later, an ambulance arrived and Carol Stuart was rushed to the Brigham and Women's Hospital. A second ambulance took Charles Stuart to Boston City Hospital. His arrival was taped by a crew from the TV show "Rescue 911," which was following the paramedic team that night.

The police could tell that the Stuarts were a suburban couple not familiar with the crime rate in the Mission Hill area, where many blacks committed holdups to support their drug habits. Charles managed a prestigious furrier, Kakas & Sons, and his wife was a tax lawyer. They were on their way to a Lamaze childbirthing class at Brigham hospital. Stuart said he had stopped at a traffic light when a black man with a raspy voice threatened him with a gun, climbed into the car, and ordered him to drive to an area near the Bromley-Heath housing project. When Charles stopped the car, the robber grabbed the car keys, their money, and their jewelry; then he shot them and fled.

As Carol lay dying in a surgery room, the doctors delivered her baby by Cesarean section two months before its due date. Charles underwent two emergency operations to save his life. The story made national news at a time when many people were pushing for laws against handguns. The robbery stirred outrage among Bostonians: Many whites blamed the high crime rate on blacks, and the NAACP charged that the city had done little to stop crime in black neighborhoods until two white suburbanites were shot.

The news media presented the Stuarts as an ideal couple. Acquaintances portrayed Charles as a Horatio Alger figure, born to an Irish family and rising through his ambition from hotel cook to manager of Boston's premier furrier. His boss told of how Charles always organized drives for orphans and the needy around the holidays, and how he and Carol were looking forward to having a Christmas baby. Eight hundred mourners attended Carol's funeral, including Boston Police Commissioner Francis "Mickey" Roache and Massachusetts Governor Michael Dukakis. When doctors soon afterward told Stuart they could not save the baby, he asked to be taken to the other hospital so he could cradle his dying Christopher in his arms at least once.

Police were encouraged when Stuart said from his hospital bed that he had a "strong physical reaction" to a mug shot of a robber being held on $50,000 bail in an unrelated case. But Stuart said he could not be sure that was the man. At the time, Stuart was getting nearly daily calls from one of his coworkers, Debbie Allen, who went to Brown University most of the year and worked at Kakas during summer vacations.

Allen could be just a supportive friend, but some officers had their doubts. Crime crosses racial boundaries all the time, but it is also common for someone faking a crime to describe the attacker as someone from another race. However, the skeptical detectives were won over by the doctors' findings. Because of the angle of the bullet, it would have been almost impossible for any person to shoot himself that way. There almost certainly was an outside gunman.

On December 5, rather than going back to his split-level home in Reading, Stuart moved in with his parents in Revere. He still needed a colostomy bag because of his wound. While there, he signed the papers on a life insurance policy that Carol had taken out through her employer, and he eventually received $82,000. He tried to fight police requests to attend a lineup for the prime suspect, but a court ordered him to participate. On December 28, he looked over eight black men in the lineup room of police headquarters. He pointed to the prime suspect and said, "He looks most like the guy." Then he walked out without speaking to reporters. The case seemed closed.

But a new decade dawned on January 1, and events related to the case began to happen quickly. To put these developments in perspective, it is necessary to go back to three days after the shooting. Stuart's brother Matthew—a paint mixer with a reputation for drinking—made allegations to their brother Michael that Charles had something to do with his wife's murder. Then Matthew took a trip to California. Michael said nothing to the authorities. When Matthew returned from his trip around Christmastime, he made similar allegations to his girlfriend; her family contacted a lawyer on his behalf. Michael learned of this and called a family meeting on New Year's Day to discuss damage control.

The next day, Charles, drawing on his wife's insurance money, traded in the Toyota and bought a new Nissan Maxima as well as $1,000 earrings for his mother and a $250 gold brooch to celebrate Debbie Allen's twenty-third birthday.

On January 3, Michael, accompanied by his lawyer, notified the district attorney's office that Charles caused his wife's death. This is the story he gave: About four years ago, Matthew had broken into an acquaintance's home as a lark after a bout of drinking. A few weeks before Carol was shot, Charles ended two years of not talking to Matthew by offering him $5,000 to pull the same kind of prank by removing insured items from his own home.

But while Matthew was doing this, Carol came home sooner than expected. Matthew hid in a bathroom until he could slip away. Michael told the district attorney's investigators that Charles later offered him $10,000 to help him steal something from Kakas & Sons. Charles supposedly told Matthew that he would throw something out the window of his car in the Mission Hill area at about 8:20 P.M. on October 23, and Matthew was to run away with it like a robber.

But Michael said Carol appeared to have been shot when Matthew arrived and picked up the package. Matthew later opened it and found a nickel-plated .38 revolver, a purse, makeup, an engagement ring, and some other jewelry. Matthew and a friend reportedly threw away everything but the ring, which they kept in case Charles might want it. To dispel any doubt about the story, Michael held up the engagement ring.

There were holes in the story—it had the look of something patched together to be least damaging for Matthew, especially given that someone had apparently shot Charles— but the district attorney's office accepted the account. Michael then claimed through his lawyer that he was protected by a 1784 Massachusetts law holding that a person cannot be prosecuted for harboring a blood relative or even helping him conceal a crime.

Somehow Charles had learned that his two brothers were going to the authorities against him. Rather than hiring a lawyer, he drove across Boston to Braintree, where he checked in without any luggage at 10 P.M. on January 3 at the Sheraton-Tate hotel. He made one call to Boston. At 2 A.M., he showed up at the hotel convenience store in a seemingly good mood. Charles left the hotel at 4:30 A.M. and drove his new car to the Tobin Bridge over the Mystic River. That was where a state police officer found the Nissan with its hood up and the emergency lights flashing. Charles's driver's license was on the front seat along with a scribbled note saying he loved his family, he had been through hell, and he did not have the strength to continue. His body was found at the bottom of the river. In the end, police concluded that Stuart had killed his wife for personal profit. A murder of greed had touched off issues of race discrimination like never before. The Stuart case was a wake-up call to the chilling truth about racism and prejudice at home.

The Loneliness

In the early morning of May 27, 1991, a fourteen-year-old Asian boy sprinted naked from an apartment building in Milwaukee. Bruised and bleeding, he ran until he fell. While some neighbors dialed 911, two others flagged down a squad car. A tall, blonde man with a mustache came out of an apartment building and grabbed the boy, saying, "Here he is!" Then, looking at the people staring at him, the man said, "We've been drinking Jack Daniels, and I'm afraid he's had a little too much."

One of the police officers who arrived asked the mumbling boy his age, and the blonde man said for him, "Nineteen." Suspicious, both officers asked more questions and went with the tall, young man, Jeffrey Dahmer, to his apartment at 924 North 25th Street. They saw nothing amiss and left the Asian boy there. The boy never came home.

As warmer weather arrived, neighbors complained of an odor coming from the building. On July 22, just before midnight, a black man was seen running with a set of handcuffs around one wrist. Two officers stopped him, and he said a white man with a big knife claimed he was going to cut out his heart. The thirty-year-old Dahmer was drinking beer when the officers asked if they could enter his home. There was not much to see, just two rooms. There was a knife under the bed and, in a dresser, dozens of photos of homosexual acts along with pictures of apparently dead male bodies and body parts. On a shelf in the refrigerator was a human head.

The officers handcuffed Dahmer and led him away, and soon his apartment was filled with detectives with rubber gloves and hazardous material technicians with breathing masks. The more they looked, the more body parts they found: in closets, drawers, coolers, boxes, and a large plastic drum.

Police across northern Wisconsin and in Chicago returned to missing persons reports and questioned patrons in gay bars about Dahmer and any men who might be missing. One by one, the victims in Dahmer's photos were given names. Most were in their late teens to thirty years old, and they were white, Laotian, American Indian, and Hispanic, but most of the seventeen were African-American. All they had in common was that they had gone off with Dahmer, some for sex and some just for the money. Three were killed in his grandmother's pleasant-looking home in the Milwaukee suburb of West Allis.

Dahmer was born in Milwaukee but reared in Ohio in a fundamentalist family. Neighbors remembered his mother as being easily excitable and given to histrionics. Perhaps jealous of his younger brother, Dahmer tried to win his father's love. After Dahmer's arrest, his father said Dahmer was sexually abused by another boy when he was eight and never got over it. Unable to relate to other boys, he sought his own world of finding dead animals, perhaps killing some, and using his chemistry set to remove flesh from their bones. But apparently his rage was not misdirected; being with death merely comforted him.

When in high school, Dahmer would down several beers before going to class, and sometimes he would drink from a bottle of Scotch in class. His parents were going through a divorce as he was graduating. After dropping out of college, his family persuaded him to join the army. He was discharged for drunkenness.

As a young man, Dahmer often expressed hatred for homosexuals. Just by denying his feelings, he created a loneliness that kept him from any kind of human relationships. He said after his arrest that he fought his sexual urges until one day when he was in the West Allis public library. A stranger dropped a note on his table saying that if he wanted an encounter he should go to the second-floor washroom. Although Dahmer did not act on the note, it disturbed him enough to start visiting bathhouses and gay bars. But, as if afraid of rejection, he found himself looking for victims instead of friends. Often before he went out, he would prepare a sleeping pill to slip in the young man's drink.

His choice to live amid his victims is reminiscent of the British serial killer Dennis Nilsen, a handsome former police officer who kept the bodies of some of the fifteen derelicts he killed under his floor until his arrest in 1983. At least once, Nilsen reportedly ripped up the boards to remove a specific victim to relive a moment they had shared. Dahmer created his own world by working at a chocolate factory by day, and by night living under the artificial calm of lorazepam, an antianxiety drug used as a sleeping pill, and the antidepressant doxepin. His reality was not our reality.

Dahmer received fifteen life sentences in Milwaukee at a hearing in which a relative of a victim had to be restrained by guards, and a sixteenth life term in Akron for fatally beating his first victim, eighteen-year-old Steven Hicks, in June 1978.

Then Dahmer was returned to his home state. Although Wisconsin does not have executions, this sentence was. On November 28, 1995, he was fatally beaten along with wife-killer Jesse Anderson as they were cleaning a washroom and shower area in Columbia Correctional Center in Portage. The inmate charged with wielding the metal club that killed them was Christopher Scarver, who was serving a life term for the execution-style murder of a man in a Milwaukee robbery.

Even in death, people were so terrified of Dahmer that his shackles remained on during the autopsy as if he could rise up and kill again. Dahmer's brain was removed for forensic study, but not until science finds a way to illustrate thoughts can it ever answer all the *whys* that go into murder.

———◦—◦———

In late January 1993, sixty-nine-year-old Jean Harris was released after serving not quite twelve years of her prison sentence of fifteen years to life. Harris had headed the prestigious Madeira School for girls in McLean, Virginia, one of the most selective schools in the country. The blonde Harris, who still had attractive features although she became stocky in middle age, had maintained a life of propriety while carrying on a fourteen-year relationship with Dr. Herman Tarnower, famous for his book *The Scarsdale Diet.* Depressed when he took up with a younger woman, and possibly refusing to accept that her own youth was going, Harris drove to his home in

Purchase, New York, on March 10, 1980. She maintained that she just wanted to say good-bye to him before she killed herself. In a crime that made a nationwide sensation, she fatally shot Dr. Tarnower. In her version, she pulled out a gun to use on herself and he was killed when it went off in a struggle. Harris portrayed herself as a victim of an abusive relationship and suffering from the withdrawal of prescription amphetamines. Harris experienced heart problems in prison, and her sentence was commuted by Governor Mario Cuomo.

Lawyers continued to use a drug or insanity defense although it is seldom successful, even when the defendant may actually be insane. In former decades, jurors were aghast at senseless crimes. But so much has been shown about the rational side of these killers that a plea of insanity virtually concedes defeat, as with Joel Rifkin of New York state.

The thirty-four-year-old unemployed landscape gardener from East Meadow was being chased for a traffic violation near Farmingdale on June 28, 1993. Rather than pull over, he led the police on a twenty-mile chase until his pickup truck hit a utility pole. Officers looked in the back of the truck and saw the strangled body of twenty-two-year-old Tiffany Bresciani. Rifkin readily claimed that he killed sixteen other women, most of them prostitutes and drug addicts from Manhattan and three neighboring counties. One victim was found in a cardboard box floating in the Hudson River off Pier 45.

He said that after killing Bresciani, he gave his mother a ride while the body was in the trunk. Afterward, he placed the victim in the garage of the home he shared with his sister and seventy-year-old mother, then when decomposition became too great he moved it to his truck by wheelbarrow. Two or three of the bodies he cut up for easier disposal. Rifkin always saved a souvenir, such as clothes or a driver's license, which he stuffed in a closet.

The defense claimed that Rifkin was a paranoid schizophrenic who lost control of himself after his father died in 1987. The story his lawyer told the jury was a familiar one of abuse, low self-esteem, and a loner who could not relate to others. Rifkin in fact had avidly read books on serial killers, and he studied police procedures for tips on disposing of bodies without detection. One method was putting them in metal drums and rolling them into waterways. Like David Berkowitz and Richard Ramirez, Rifkin set out to play the role of a terror rather than acting out of compulsion. The beefy man with glasses and a mustache even fell asleep during his trial. The outcome was a foregone conclusion. He was sentenced to twenty-seven years for the murder of his final victim, and on August 23, 1995, he pleaded guilty to two other killings.

The Rifkin murders came at a time when New York City finally saw its murder rate decline, reflecting a trend other major cities had seen for several years. The year before, 1992, saw an all-time high of twenty-two hundred and sixty-two homicides in the city. But something else deadly had begun—domestic terrorism and the merging of survivalist groups with doomsday cults.

The Bombers

Case No. 1

On September 1, 1992, Ramzi Yousef, declaring that he was seeking political asylum, left Kennedy International Airport to live with a New York City man named Mohammad Salameh.

They opened a bank account and received funds from a bank in Germany, where many Palestinians and other Islamic immigrants had settled. Salameh, using a fictitious name, rented a storage locker in New Jersey. The two men used that address in ordering bomb parts, including compressed hydrogen to add power to explosives. When they were ready, Salameh rented a van from Ryder.

On Friday, February 26, 1993, Salameh drove a pale yellow van with a twelve hundred-pound bomb into the underground garage of the one hundred ten-story World Trade Center. The place was well chosen because on any given day the twin towers saw fifty thousand workers and eighty thousand visitors. At about noon, someone flicked a cheap lighter and set the flame to each of four fuses. Minutes later, steel beams snapped, cinder blocks became a shower of powder, a woman sitting at her desk was flung thirty feet, and automobiles in the parking level were crumpled like tin cans. A firefighter who forced open the doors of an elevator discovered a tomb. The ten seconds of hell killed six people and injured more than one thousand.

The terrorists made their point: No one in America was safe anymore. An anonymous letter later claimed the act was to punish the United States for siding with Israel on Palestinian issues. But there was nothing really to be gained but self-satisfaction, because the crime would do nothing for the Palestinian cause. The terrorists had not even thought out the details very well. Salameh was arrested on March 4 when he returned the van for his $200 deposit. Soon, someone gave the New York City police information that led to a raid of five suspects found with what was called a "witch's brew" of explosives that were to have been placed in tunnels, under bridges, and at landmarks in the New York City area.

In March 1994, a federal judge sentenced Salameh, Nidal Ayyad, Mahmud Abouhalima, and Ahmad Ajaj to serve two hundred forty years each in prison. In January 1998, a judge called Yousef an "apostle of evil" for masterminding the bombing and sentenced him to life in prison, with a rare recommendation that it be spent entirely in solitary confinement. The sentence included the penalty for a 1994 deadly bombing of a Philippine Airlines plane. Yousef, who was captured in Pakistan, had intended the World Trade Center attack as a test run for blowing up dozens of airliners in America.

Case No. 2

A musician claiming to be Jesus Christ—Vernon Howell, better known as David Koresh—headed a sect called the Branch Davidians near Waco, Texas. The Branch Davidians were an offshoot of the Seventh Day Adventists that moved to Texas after a break with the mother church in 1935. An Australian private detective who investigated the members claimed that Koresh abused children and had at least fifteen "wives," and that he believed all women in the world belonged to him. Rumors had the group stockpiling weapons such as AK-47 rifles, Israeli assault rifles, and nine-millimeter handguns.

On February 28, 1993, a hundred law enforcement officers headed by agents of the Bureau of Alcohol, Tobacco, and Firearms (ATF) exchanged shots with the members for an hour following a thwarted attempt to search the compound for weapons. Then seven hours of tense silence ended when three members came out shooting. In all, four federal agents and a two-year-old child living in the compound were killed, and sixteen agents were wounded. The shootout caused the greatest loss of life in the history of the ATF, but the repercussions were even worse.

On April 19, the FBI fired tear gas canisters into the compound and smashed holes in the walls with armored vehicles. A rush of flames killed eighteen children and forty-nine adult members of the cult. In addition, a body removed with a gunshot wound in the head was later identified as Koresh's.

Following the Branch Davidian raid and the World Trade Center bombing, it seemed that the decade was ripe for apocalyptic criminality. In fact, any crime as inhuman as the World Trade Center bombing was bound to inspire copycats. The question was when and where.

The answer came with a roar on April 19, 1995, with the explosion of the Alfred P. Murrah Federal Building in Oklahoma City. The blast murdered one hundred sixty-nine people, nineteen of them children. One rescue worker who was comforting a dying woman asked a companion to turn off a dripping faucet, only to discover that it was not water but blood.

Timothy McVeigh was arrested an hour and a half later on a firearms charge after a traffic stop near Billings, Oklahoma. McVeigh was brought up in a good family in Lockport, New York, near Buffalo. As a teenager, he earned money by babysitting, and the families for which he worked thought he was wonderful. He joined the infantry and won the Bronze Star during the Gulf War and was a crack gunner in Operation Desert Storm. But for some reason, he and possibly one or two others built a bomb in the cargo compartment of a twenty-foot Ryder truck rented in Junction City, Kansas.

McVeigh's defense was that the bombing was a political statement for the deaths of the Branch Davidian cult in Waco and the

FBI killing of a separatist's wife during an eleven-day siege at a mountain cabin near the northern Idaho town of Ruby Ridge in 1992. After a trial in Denver, he was convicted of murder, conspiracy, and weapons charges and sentenced to die by lethal injection.

Just hours after the Oklahoma City explosion, McVeigh's army buddy Terry Nichols was seen dusting his lawn in Herrington, Kansas, with the same fertilizer—ammonium nitrate—that was used to make the bomb. Some of the other materials were stolen from a quarry months before. Nichols surrendered to authorities on April 21, 1995, when he heard that they were searching for him. In December 1997, Nichols was convicted of conspiracy and involuntary manslaughter.

Case No. 3

The sketch used for years in the search for the Unabomber was of a dashing half-hooded figure from some exotic background. The reality was far different.

The first explosion occurred on May 26, 1979, when a cigar box packed with thousands of match heads exploded in the hands of security officer Terry Marker and also injured graduate student John Harris at Northwestern University in Evanston, near Chicago. "It scared the hell out of me," Harris would say later. But the professor to whom the package was addressed was not the target. In fact, no one in particular was ever the target, although three were to die when they opened harmless-looking packages. They were Gilbert Murray, a lobbyist for the California Forestry Association, in Sacramento on April 24, 1985; Hugh Scrutton, owner of a Sacramento computer rental store, on December 11, 1985; and Theodore Mosser, a New Jersey advertising executive, on December 10, 1994. In addition, twenty-nine people were injured.

The bomber was Theodore Kaczynski, a student who lived at the time of the university bombing in the Chicago suburb of Evergreen Park. A brilliant mathematician, he entered Harvard at age sixteen. He became an assistant math professor at the University of California in Berkeley but abruptly quit and turned his back on the world. Feeling out of place, he blamed his mental confusion on a world gone mad from technology.

Possibly suffering from paranoid schizophrenia, Kaczynski became a hermit and lived in a ten-foot by twelve-foot cabin in the mountains near Lincoln, Montana. He had no furniture, just a potbellied stove. He maintained polite occasional contacts with his few neighbors, slept on a wooden platform, and used his own waste as fertilizer in a small garden. He wrote a diary of sorts partly in Spanish and partly in mathematical code. His only outside activity was building bombs with virtually impossible to trace items, such as match heads, flashlight batteries, and pieces of lamp cord. Because the sending of bombs to airlines, professors, and computer stores showed no pattern, the person responsible was called the "unabomber" as the attacks seemed universal.

In June 1995, Kaczynski sent a long manifesto to the *New York Times* and the *Washington Post,* claiming the bombings would stop if it were printed. Both papers complied, and there were no more attacks. But when his family was about to move from the Chicago suburb of Lombard, they came across papers with similar phrasing to the manifesto and shuddered in horror at the possibility. Kaczynski's younger brother, David, consulted a lawyer first and then went to the authorities.

The seventeen-year nationwide search, the most expensive in American history, ended quietly when Kaczynski was quietly arrested in his plywood home. His shack was carried by trailer to a warehouse in Sacramento for his trial. In custody, he suffered from insomnia and thought his heart would burst. He quarreled with his lawyers over whether to use the insanity defense and insisted on pleading guilty, pointing out once again that those who refuse to plead insanity are often less sane than those who do. The tall, lean man with a shaggy beard, now fifty-five, was sentenced to life in prison on January 23, 1998.

The decade saw the emergence of the first documented female serial killer. Eileen Wuonos, a prostitute, was charged by Florida law enforcement with murdering six johns. When a jury convicted her of the first murder, Wuonos swore at them and insisted that she had been raped. She was sentenced to die by execution.

The decade also saw a continuation of death at the hands of caregivers. In the 1970s and 1980s, Marybeth Roe Tinning of Schenectady, New York, killed nine of her own children.

A few angels of mercy at hospitals around the country were angels of death in the 1980s and 1990s. Texas nurse Genene Jones killed several babies. Gwendolyn Graham, a nurse at the Alpine nursing home in Walker, Michigan, smothered five elderly victims with some help from her female lover in 1987. The other woman, Catherine Wood, pleaded guilty to second-degree murder and testified against Graham. Prosecutors say the murders were part of a pact to bind the women together.

Male nurse Orville Lynn Majors may have been involved in the deaths of dozens of patients at the Vermillion County Hospital in Newport, Indiana. Officials said one hundred forty-seven patients passed away while he was on duty from 1993 to 1995, whereas a normal number might have been no more than forty-seven.

Not a Tear

Derry was one of those New England towns that could pose for a toy railroad setting. The place was so quiet you had to be thirty before you could buy a drink without showing an ID card for scrutiny. The faculty at Winnacunnet High School instilled small-town values to its students while other parts of the country were fighting crack cocaine use and street gangs.

On the night of Tuesday, May 1, 1990, Frank Lombardi was hosting a party for his son when he heard a woman screaming in a cluster of town houses occupied by young couples just the other side of a hill from a shopping center. Lombardi ran toward the sound and encountered twenty-two-year-old Pamela Smart, who hysterically said, "It's my husband, he's been killed!" Lombardi motioned for his son to call the police.

The officers found the body of Greg Smart shot in the head and lying in a hallway of his simple condo. His empty wallet was nearby, and the place had been ransacked. A small shaggy dog was cowering in the basement. Greg's parents, William and Judith, ran to the scene from their home just a block away. Soon, two representatives from the New Hampshire attorney general's office arrived to supervise the investigation.

Pam, who looked like a teenager rather than a married woman, was taken to the small police station. She told the officers that there did not seem any reason for someone to kill her husband because they did not earn that much money. Greg was an insurance salesman, like his father. Pam, who grew up in Florida, was a media director for the school board. She said she discovered the body when she returned from a routine board meeting. Although not a teacher, she had an office across from the school for producing educational videos used in the district. She and Greg were married for a little less than one year. They were an ideal couple in that both were party animals and loved hard rock. Pam even had her own once-a-week radio program and called herself the "Maiden of Metal."

At first glance, the killing seemed like a burglary gone wrong, but doctors removed from the body several fragments of hollow-point bullets. Also, there were no splatter stains, so perhaps a pillow was used to muffle the shot. The neighbors did not recall hearing the dog barking at any time that day, although he usually yapped at strangers. The killer also left without taking Greg's diamond ring or credit cards. And the detectives noticed that Pam was calm; she did not express the blankness of someone refusing to accept a death. It was as if she did not care. Her in-laws told the detectives that at mournful gatherings of relatives the night after the killing, Pam did not shed a tear, and consequently, relatives started calling her the "ice princess."

Looking for a motive beyond robbery, the police learned that Greg sometimes gambled in Atlantic City, New Jersey. They also suspected drugs, but search dogs found no trace of narcotics in the home. Pam was cooperative with the police and even reporters. Yet the officers learned from other students that Pam was having an affair with a student, Billy Flynn, starting the year before, when he was fifteen, to make up for the many hours Greg was away from home.

Flynn—looking a little like a young Paul McCartney—was one of several student facilitators who helped with her video production, and he shared with Pam a fondness for hard rock. Flynn was not the only teenager who loved to spend time with Pam. Another was shy, overweight Cecilia Price, who went from student intern to personal friend. The fifteen-year-old girl seemed to think that being with Pam, she could absorb some of the woman's confidence and friendliness.

Despite Pam's infidelity to her husband, she was upset when she learned that Flynn had sex with another woman. She reseduced him by watching the steamy film *9½ Weeks* with him in her home and putting on a blue negligee. Price stayed behind watching the film.

With $140,000 from her husband's life insurance, Pam bought a new Trans Am and moved into a rented condo in neighboring Hampton. All the while, she told reporters she felt frustrated because the police had not made an arrest. Detectives were sure they knew who was responsible for the killing, but they needed something more substantial than the silence of a dog and tears that were never shed.

The more officers talked to students, the more incriminating information they picked up, such as Flynn's supposedly saying "We're gonna go do Greg." Finally, a twenty-year-old school dropout, Danny Blake, said he had heard from a boy named Ralph Welch that Pam offered Flynn and a friend, Pete Lattimore, $500 each to help her kill her husband. The teens were going to slit his throat, Blake said, but

Flynn shot the man with a gun belonging to Lattimore's father. Blake added that the teenage killers sang in the car on the way home. Lattimore's father, hearing of this, checked his gun and told police the .38 caliber revolver was in like-new condition even though he had neglected to clean it the last time he fired it.

The teens knew that the police were onto them. Pam at first planned to drive Flynn, Lattimore, and another boy, J.R., to her condo to decide what to do, but then she ordered them out of the car and told them to stay put. The boys got their motorcycles out of her garage just as Flynn dropped by to tell Pam that if ever arrested, he would never tell on her. Flynn, Lattimore, and J.R. went to Connecticut but returned as the police made arrangements to put Welch, the snitch, in protective custody.

Because the boys would try to cover for themselves, detectives decided to learn how much young Price knew about the killing. At first, the girl denied knowing anything. But after Flynn was charged with murder and Lattimore and J.R. were charged as accomplices, she admitted overhearing Pam discussing the murder plot with Flynn. Price also said she tried to find a gun for the boys but could not.

To the jurors and the news media, Pam presented herself as an innocent victim caught up with three teenage thrill-killers who betrayed her trust and murdered her husband, yet she seemed concerned only about preserving her image. The jury convicted her on March 22, 1991, and she was sentenced to life in prison without the possibility of parole. The three boys were also sentenced to life, but their terms were reduced to twenty-eight years in exchange for their cooperation, and Price was never charged.

Dead Week

At the University of Florida in Gainesville, "Dead Week" is the period when students move into their dorms and off-campus apartments before classes begin. In that week in August 1990, it was also the period that a disturbed convicted criminal was lurking about the woods, living off the land, and looking into student homes, watching young women dressing, undressing, getting into showers, and just moving about with their windows open or unlocked.

The first to die were Sonja Larson and Christi Powell. Larson was stabbed multiple times. Powell was not only stabbed in the back but her nipples were also removed with a knife as part of a ritual that would be the killer's "signature." The killer found the door to Apartment 13 unlocked, wrapped tape around Larson's mouth to keep her quiet, killed her, crept downstairs, killed Powell in a similar way, and then returned to Larson's body. He removed her panties, spread her legs although he had no sex with her, and then went back to Powell's body. He removed the knife, cleansed her vagina with liquid detergent, then cut off her nipples and put them in a lunch bag. Having possessed both young women in his mind, he felt comfortable and ate an apple and a banana in the apartment before leaving.

The same man watched the small rectangular duplex apartment of Christa Hoyt for at least two days before breaking in while she was away. He moved some furniture to make it easier to grab her, then watched through a window as she approached with a tennis racquet over her shoulder. Once the door opened, he grabbed her, taped her mouth, and raped her on her water bed. He stabbed her in the back, removed her tape, and cut her from her hips to her breasts. He next removed her nipples as souvenirs. He left but returned an hour before sunrise and cut off her head, which he placed on a shelf in the front room. As if to deny her death, he propped up the body and left.

On another night, he intended to attack just Tracy Paules, but when he broke in he discovered that she had a muscular young man as a roommate, Manny Taboda. The killer stabbed him without ritual as Taboda slept and finished him off in a struggle. Paules opened her door, saw the killing, and slammed it in terror. The killer kicked the door open, taped her mouth, raped her, and with his knife transformed her from a human being into one more fantasy he would carry around in his head. Then he cleansed her vagina with a liquid detergent. For a souvenir, he took a shirt from Taboda's dresser. He cleansed himself of all that blood in a swimming pool outside a student apartment complex.

The five murders occurred within a seventy-two-hour period. But they were not the first killings by Danny Rolling, a six-foot, two-inch, thirty-six-year-old self-made loser.

Rolling's macho father, John, was a police officer in Shreveport, Louisiana. True or not, Rolling said his father did not want children and resented any kind of independence in a son as a threat to his authority. His father flew into rages and once had his son jailed for fighting with him. His mother over-reacted and became so protective that Rolling became awkward in his relationships with girls. He was in the Air Force for nearly two years, attended Pentecostal services, married, and had a child. Before long, his wife left with their baby when Rolling threatened her with a gun. He became furious—

not for himself, he claimed, but because the incident upset his mother.

Rolling went through a drug period and tried robbery while in a depression just before his twenty-fifth birthday. He was caught and paroled in 1988. He took up with a country singer in her fifties, Lillian Mills, in a mother-son relationship and, under her inspiration, wrote a few songs. He robbed again and became embittered when he could not find a job upon his release. He blamed his record, and employers blamed his immaturity. The more the disparity increased between his thoughts and the rest of the world, he took to Rambo-type costumes, even with a knife strapped to his leg. It was as if he were unconsciously identifying with his father. Neighbors thought he was having a mental breakdown.

On the day he was fired from a low-paying job, he worked off his anger by invading a home and fatally stabbing twenty four-year-old Julie Grissom, her father, and her eight-year-old nephew in Shreveport on November 4, 1989. Rolling drifted to Florida, leaving behind Mills, the only positive relationship he ever had as an adult.

The tall, almost handsome, young man was said to hate women. But he hated only the sexual element in young women, believing that their vaginas needed cleansing, as if distancing himself from his own sexual desires. A woman who had sex with him said Rolling kept looking down rather than at her, as if he were having sex with himself. Always compulsively clean, Rolling became obsessed with thoughts of impending nuclear destruction and went to movies like the *Friday the 13th* series.

Rolling returned to Shreveport and had such a violent family quarrel that his father fired a threatening shot, and

Rolling shot him in the face, but the older man recovered. There was now a final break from his family. He camped out in the woods near the University of Florida at Gainesville and Santa Fe Community College. Although he tried opening doors and windows in a number of homes while wearing the black clothes and ski mask of a burglar, all four of the young women he attacked were generally like his wife: young, moderately pretty, petite, brunette, and innocent-looking.

After the final murder, Rolling went to Tampa and began a series of burglaries—perhaps, as with DeSalvo and Heirens, as a substitute for killing—and that was what led to his arrest. He gave the police details of all the Gainesville crimes, leaving the experts to wonder why he did them. Some said he was manic depressive and others that he was paranoid schizophrenic. A psychiatrist who studied him after his arrest found no sign of overriding delusions.

While awaiting sentencing, Rolling wrote to his judge: "I am not the keeper of time, only a small part of history and the legacy of all mankind's fall from grace. I am sorry, your honor." In April 1994, he was sentenced to die in the electric chair. Rolling, then thirty-nine, was earlier sentenced to three life terms plus one hundred seventy years for the burglaries and robberies committed after the slayings.

Whether a copycat was involved or whether it was just coincidence, an intruder wielding a knife killed twenty-six-year-old Gina Langevin and critically wounded her roommate at an off-campus apartment in Gainesville in September 1993, just a little after "Dead Week."

An advancement in the investigation of sexual crimes had a separate development from the rest of criminology when scientists discovered phosphoglucomutase, an enzyme involved in the production of cellular energy. It is found in blood, hair, and semen. This helped rule out suspects, but a positive match was not strong enough for the courts. That was why the development of DNA comparisons was such a breakthrough. As an example, the process was used to eliminate an early suspect in the five Gainesville murders of Danny Rolling.

In 1984, Dr. Alec Jeffreys of Leicester University in England devised chemical typing of "genetic fingerprints." He was studying the gene coding for certain types of proteins that carry oxygen to muscles called myoglobin proteins when he discovered a building block made up of repeated sequences of ten to fifteen sections within the DNA. He cloned and isolated two of these building blocks and made them radioactive to follow their movement. He noticed that similar blocks were drawn to others with the same pattern. This let Jeffreys isolate the DNA from the protein surrounding the nucleus. He chopped the DNA material into tinier pieces and analyzed them under radio-sensitive film so he could see marks identifying each piece of DNA. This meant that the only people on earth with identical DNA "bar codes" were identical twins.

After working on paternity cases, Jeffreys personally applied his technique in 1987 to determine the guilt of Colin Pitchfork, who had raped and strangled teenagers Lynda Mann and Dawn Ashforth three years apart. Pitchfork, a baker, knew something was up as authorities obtained blood samples from nearly forty-six hundred men in one of those sweeps for evidence with which the British comply but over which Americans file suits. Pitchfork arranged to have someone stand in for him. When police learned of the deception, they arrested him and he admitted the first killing. Because England had abolished the death sentence after an innocent man was hanged in the late 1940s for two of the murders committed by John Christie, the judge sentenced Pitchfork to double life sentences.

DNA has also shaken some faith in the legal system of America as it is used to free dozens of men convicted of rape or murder. In the Chicago area, Rolando Cruz underwent three trials and spent a dozen years on Death Row before DNA evidence cleared him in the rape and fatal beating of a ten-year-old girl. But a "dream team" of attorneys in Los Angeles persuaded a jury to disregard DNA evidence submitted in the O.J. Simpson murder trial by showing how it could be possible to misuse the evidence.

Handsome Simpson was likable as a football player, in commercials, and then as a supporting actor in the *Naked Gun* films. On June 12, 1994, his beautiful blonde former wife, Nicole Brown Simpson, and her friend Ronald Goldman were savagely knifed to death at 875 South Bundy Drive in Brentwood. The evidence suggested that Goldman was killed first, then Nicole. Los Angeles police followed Simpson's car in what was called a "slow speed chase" that was televised live across the country.

The defense attacked Detective Mark Fuhrman's contention that he found a glove containing blood carrying the DNA of Simpson as well as the victims. The lawyers suggested that the white officer had a grudge against the African-American defendant stemming from a 1985 incident in which Simpson bashed the windows of his wife's car with a baseball bat. The hints being given to the jury were that Fuhrman might have used drops from a blood sample Simpson had given the day after the bodies were found.

Possibly wanting to give Simpson every chance because of memory of the 1991 videotaped beating of black motorist Rodney King by white Los Angeles police officers, Judge Lance Ito allowed the case to go on for a full year despite questionable actions on both sides, and the defendant was found innocent. Simpson, like Lizzie Borden a century before him, may have to live under the conviction of public opinion unless there is an unexpected development.

Simpson's behavior after the murders suggested to some that he showed guilt, or at least concern about his career. But guilt in murder cases is more pliable than some experts might think. Many pathological killers are considered psychopaths or sociopaths—people without a conscience. Yet sometimes they do have a conscience.

One example is Richard Macek, who killed several women in Illinois and Wisconsin in the 1970s. He sometimes grabbed a victim and slammed her against a wall, beat her, and then strangled her with a terry-cloth towel. In one attack, he killed a child in order to murder a woman, and it was this child's murder that haunted him and apparently led to his suicide in prison. Killing the child had not been part of his fantasy, and it stayed real in his mind. The murders of women were more like dreams.

A more recent case involved the Canadian Paul Bernardo of the Niagara Falls area of Ontario. He was a rapist who caused the death of his girlfriend's teenage sister, Tammy Homolka, by drugging her to rape her. After Homolka's death, Bernardo and his girlfriend—eventually his wife— drugged several other women, and Bernardo killed two other women in the early 1990s. When a neighbor saw a photo of Homolka in Bernardo's home and asked who she was, Bernardo broke down crying, hit himself several times on the head, and said, "She fucking died in my arms, right in my fucking arms." But he had no remorse whatever for the women he intentionally killed. Bernardo is serving a life term in prison.

Racing with the Devil

Andrew Cunanan's middle-class father was born in the Philippines but lived in Rancho Bernardo, California, near San Diego. He tried being a stockbroker but failed. In shame, his dark-haired son claimed to be the scion of a Filipino plantation owner who had fled from the Ferdinand Marcos regime and bought a large tract of land in New Jersey.

Andrew grew up something of a show-off with glasses and the fair skin and features of his European-descended mother. As a student at an expensive prep school, he would whistle at boys on the water polo team. Flashiness and lies were part of his charm, and no one took him seriously for long. His father embezzled $106,000 from his company and fled the country in 1988. His mother eventually was reduced to living in public housing in Eureka, Illinois. Cunanan, too good in his own mind for steady work, took to selling prescription drugs like Prozac and Xanax on the street. With more money in his pocket, he could rise to better circles.

He lived off rich older men, smoked large cigars, and was generous and friendly. That was his public appearance. The twilight in his soul involved leather straps, sadomasochism videotapes, and black latex masks with just a nose opening, for bondage. The darkest side of him he kept to himself.

In 1990, he was part of the crowd of partygoers in the VIP room of San Francisco's Colossus club that greeted fashion designer Gianni Versace for work he had done on Richard Strauss's opera *Cappricio*. Versace seemed to recognize the twenty-one-year-old from a casual meeting, although the designer's family insisted later that he had mistaken the attractive young man for someone else. When Cunanan met Versace again, it was after leaving a trail of bodies across the country.

Cunanan was not so much a hustler as a compensated companion. He added a touch of class to the men he accompanied, with a running knowledge of current events, etiquette, and fine wines. He had taught himself to hide his insecurities.

In the mid-1990s, he lived with an elderly arts patron in the elite La Jolla part of San Diego. The millionaire gave him expensive gifts and took him on a trip to Europe, but they are said never to have slept together. While still with the millionaire, another wealthy man he knew—sixty-one-year-old Lincoln Aston—was beaten to death apparently by a mentally disabled drifter. As with a number of pathological killers, being close to murder may have set Cunanan's thinking in a certain order.

Cunanan remained comfortable in his dual role of being an almost feminine companion of the millionaire, and on his own time being the more masculine life of the party with surfers and other young men at gay bars. Then he overdid it. He accused the millionaire of not spending enough on him, and this made Cunanan look like a cheap hustler rather than a loved companion. The elderly man ordered him to leave, and Cunanan never got over the rejection.

Something we may never know happened in early 1997 that made Cunanan, who had no history of violence, suddenly act like a desperate man. At a talk about safe sex, he made an outburst that indicated he may have thought that he was infected with AIDS. He might just have been joking, and he was found never to have been infected. On April 25, Cunanan had drinks in San Diego with a Minnesota friend, smiling, blonde, young architect David Madsen. But Madsen wanted to break up the relationship because he suspected Cunanan of some unknown "shady dealings." At the time, Cunanan had overextended his credit cards, but he managed to buy a one-way ticket to Minneapolis.

After Cunanan arrived in Minnesota, Madsen took him to dinner, and the unstable companion annoyed everyone by talking about driving a Rolls-Royce convertible. Two nights later, Cunanan asked Madsen's strong yet boyishly handsome friend, Jeffrey Trail, to Madsen's loft apartment, although the two men did not get along well. It is not known whether Madsen was there. Trail always objected to Cunanan's drug use, and neighbors on this night heard one of the men tell the other to get out. Cunanan killed Trail with a claw hammer and rolled his body in a carpet and stayed with it for two days. On the second day, he and Madsen were seen walking a dog. Leaving the body behind, Madsen and Cunanan drove to a lake north of Minneapolis. Using Trail's pistol, Cunanan shot Madsen and dumped the body to be discovered later by fishermen.

Something drew the twenty-seven-year-old gigolo to Chicago's Near North Side, and he decided to kill wealthy Lee Miglin, who had risen from being the son of a Czech coal miner to one of the city's best known real estate developers.

Miglin, who happened to resemble the millionaire who had jilted Cunanan, was threatened with a fake gun and then his throat was cut with a bow saw in the garage of his home on Scott Street. Stranger still, the elderly man's head was wrapped in masking tape with holes left in for the nostrils, similar to the bondage masks Cunanan had once mentioned to a bartender. Miglin's body had shallow wounds from a gardening tool, possibly from being tortured to reveal the location of his money and car keys.

Feeling at home, Cunanan packed $2,000 in a briefcase, shaved, and ate half a sandwich in the row house. Then he left Madsen's red Jeep nearby and took Miglin's dark green Lexus, possibly the only thing for which Miglin was killed.

For some reason, Cunanan was next known to have been in a Civil War cemetery in Pennsville, New Jersey, a little south of Philadelphia. Caretaker William Reese was shot to death in his office. Cunanan left Miglin's Lexus in the graveyard, stayed in Manhattan for at least two days, drove through Florence, South Carolina, and was in Miami Beach in mid-July. By then, police across the country were wondering where he would strike next. And although not all the victims were homosexuals, gays everywhere in America became a little tense about casual meetings with slender, dark-haired young men. Canadian authorities were apprised of the situation, and Interpol was notified because of Cunanan's family in the Philippines. Responding to possible sightings in Florida, the FBI distributed leaflets in English, Spanish, French, and Arabic.

Knowing what we do now, there seems only one reason Cunanan went all the way to Miami: He was going to kill Versace because—there seems no other explanation—he admired him yet had no way to enter his circle of friends.

Insiders have said that Cunanan might have made an impression in San Diego, but in Florida he could never expect to join the elite homosexuals, the "A-gays."

He checked into a low-budget hotel where Marilyn Monroe and Clark Gable once stayed during its better days. The manager said that some of the guests who came in were a little scary, "but not him." Cunanan was never known to have pushed his window curtain back to watch the ocean. He never made a phone call. He just waited. And, from the way his bed linen was angrily rolled up, it looked as if he had been trying to sleep but could not.

Versace went on with his life apparently unaware his spacious grounds in South Beach were being watched. The quiet, temperate middle-aged man liked walking alone. On Tuesday morning, July 15, he unlocked his gate, bought some publications at a newsstand, turned around, and walked back. As he was inserting a key into the lock of the gate, Cunanan stepped up to him while wearing a black cap, gray T-shirt, black shorts, and white tennis shoes. No words may have been spoken. Cunanan fired twice and, as the designer fell, he swiftly walked away.

Cunanan left enough fingerprints and other clues for the authorities to track him. Now he made the search even easier by leaving newspaper clippings about the manhunt for him along with his clothes in a garage where he had kept the pickup truck he had stolen from the New Jersey cemetery. Hundreds of police officers and federal agents spread out across the Miami area. Some authorities speculated that Cunanan might be dressed as a woman to escape detection or that he had evolved into a classic, Ted Bundy-style serial killer who would continue a murder spree until caught.

No one ever understood Cunanan, and certainly not the experts. He quietly sat out the manhunt while living in a houseboat he had found moored across from the luxury hotels and condos on Collins Avenue, allowing himself to maintain a final illusion of wealth and leisure. The white and blue boat did not look like much on the outside, but the interior was well furnished by its owner, a Las Vegas club owner. Here the most wanted man in North America lay in bed as thousands of tourists' cars, buses, limousines, and taxis passed him every day. Having accomplished all that he wanted to in life, and tiring of the game, he shot himself.

A caretaker arrived for a routine inspection, saw signs of a break-in, and called the police. A SWAT team cautiously moved in and found Cunanan's body propped up on two pillows in the bedroom of the master cabin on the second level, the gun in his lap. His body was removed, and the houseboat remained moored there until it was demolished in January 1998.

It is only a coincidence, but when you draw a line following his journey, it generally forms a question mark. That is how Cunanan will be remembered by those who knew him and the millions who followed his story in the news.

The Question Marks

On a chilly, clear day, January 8, 1993, workers arrived at the Browns Chicken & Pasta restaurant in the quiet Chicago suburb of Palatine and could not find the overnight crew. They looked around and discovered seven bodies stacked in the coolers. Five employees and the two owners of the franchise were shot in one of the most vicious and baffling robberies ever committed in the United States. There must have been telltale evidence left behind, but whatever it might have been was smudged over or trampled by the eager but inexperienced police. In a rush to file charges, an innocent former employee was detained at length and grilled. By the time a task force of experienced officers from other communities took charge, it was too late to solve the murders.

One of the most talked about killings of the decade was that of JonBenet Ramsey, the six-year-old beauty pageant queen from Boulder, Colorado. Her father, John, reported his daughter missing. He discovered a handwritten ransom note, and later found the girl's body in a windowless basement storage room the day after Christmas, 1996. JonBenet was beaten and strangled but, contrary to early reports, there was no indication of sexual assault. The Ramseys said they often left their doors unlocked at night, which is common in the area. The family had an alarm system but seldom set it because JonBenet or her brother had accidentally set it off a few times.

After following up a number of leads, detectives kept going back to the family because there was no one else to investigate. In early 1998, more than a year after the killing, John and Patsy Ramsey turned over the clothing they were wearing the night before their daughter was found dead. District attorney's investigator Lou Smitt said he was sure the case would be solved, "But it's going to be solved in its own time."

Another case waiting to be solved involved the sometimes commingled worlds of crime and rap music. The crime happened at 11:30 P.M. on a Saturday in 1996 in the land of midnight neon. Las Vegas was bustling with gamblers, tourists, and boxing fans returning from the Mike Tyson and Bruce

Seldon slugfest at the huge MGM Grand Hotel. Suge Knight of Death Row Records was driving a new, black BMW sedan. His passenger was rap star and occasional movie actor Tupac Shakur. They were heading for a benefit party at Knight's Club 662. Shakur had bred a number of enemies living the kind of life he did in New York, and then Marin City and Oakland in northern California. His mother, Afreni Shakur, was one of the founders of the New York branch of the Black Panther Party. His father was once a suspect in a plot to blow up department stores and police stations. When the boy was ten, he told a minister he wanted to be a revolutionary when he grew up. His stepfather was convicted of masterminding a 1981 Brink's armored truck robbery in which two guards were killed. With such a background, it was no surprise that Shakur was convincing in his gangster role in the 1992 film *Juice*.

Hip-hop music blared from the speakers as the BMW led a convoy of friends and bodyguards in a Lexus, a Miata, and a Mercedes-Benz. Knight stopped for a red light at the intersection of Koval Road and Las Vegas Boulevard—a mile from the Strip. A light-colored Cadillac with three or four men inside pulled up to the right. A man from the backseat thrust the barrel of a semiautomatic pistol out a window and quickly squeezed off at least thirteen rounds, five of the slugs tearing into Shakur and one grazing the back of Knight's head. Two other bullets exploded the BMW's right-side tires.

The Cadillac roared away as Shakur lay slumped over under shards of shattered glass. Dozens of witnesses on the street, both sidewalks, and in cars were horrified by what they had just seen and heard. At least half a dozen drivers sped after the Cadillac, but it outdistanced them in the Las Vegas traffic.

Investigators came up with some possible motives: street gang revenge from someone with whom Shakur and Knight had quarreled after the boxing match, because the suspect was aligned with the Crips and Knight was friends with the Bloods; retaliation by a rap group Shakur had accused of setting him up for a 1994 shooting at Quad Records in New York; or money, as Knight had recently taken out a $1,000,000 policy on Shakur's life. Most likely, there was some other motive, but it never surfaced.

Sometimes no amount of police questioning resolves a crime. But police departments are becoming more sophisticated every year. The Seattle-area county police department was a holdover from another era until the Green River victims began piling up. By 1990, the King County sheriff's police were skilled in gathering even obscure evidence, physical leads were processed with the latest technology, and the department's permanent computer bank had become a national resource for information about sexual predators.

Since the 1980s, police across the country had used the Violent Criminal Apprehension Program, or VICAP, for information about criminals who cross jurisdictions. Police add to this store of knowledge by submitting a nearly two hundred-item questionnaire for each major case on which they work. The Behavioral Science Unit of the FBI also supervises the National Center for the Analysis of Violent Crime, or the NCAVC, and several experts in uncommon fields fly across the country to help solve major cases.

Crime by late in the decade was also being fought in new ways on an individual level. A San Francisco prostitute fought off three men who were trying to kill her. She joined with the police in 1995 to cut down sex trafficking and its sometimes violent consequences by going after the customers. Other cities have adopted similar programs.

In the past, sex offenses were treated as impartially as any other crime. But by the mid-1980s, legislators were agreeing with psychiatrists that such crimes by their nature are repeated, and that special laws were needed to protect the public. In New Jersey, a public outcry arose over the murder of seven-year-old Megan Kanka of Hamilton County by a twice-convicted sex offender who lived across the street. The state legislature in 1994 passed "Megan's law," allowing the notification of community members, school principals, school coaches, and Scout troop leaders about the presence of any convicted sex offender classified as "high risk." This was the most specific of the notification laws now in effect in forty seven states. In fact, Alaska in late 1997 posted a list of all of its sixteen hundred paroled sex offenders on the Internet.

Another cause of violent crime is mental illness. Schizophrenia and its often violent parallel form of paranoid schizophrenia are being studied as a chemical imbalance that might be remedied. The National Alliance for the Mentally Ill is looking into the possibility that the imbalance is a result of viral infections or mild brain damage from birth complications, or a genetic predisposition. The goal is a world in which there are no more Unabombers.

The century-old battle between whether there are born criminals or they are "made" by their upbringing is easing into the belief that a person's development is a give-and-take between genes and social environment for approximately the first twelve years. That is, we may inherit a certain disposition rather than one completely blank and that our thinking is molded by responses to where our disposition leads us. As has been suggested, the temperament that might make one person a criminal could, under more favorable circumstances, make him a hot-shot test pilot. If this is true, killers who said they were denied affection when they were children might have been demanding more attention than anyone could give.

Whether this concept of development is valid or not, a study of murderers in the twentieth century reveals a few common elements. Most break down into one of several root causes: hatred of a family member, sometimes from incest, and sometimes when another child is viewed as the favored one, as with Edmund Kemper; material gain, and feelings of inadequacy, such as the serial killers of the 1960s and even such good-looking and intelligent men as Christopher Wilder and Ted Bundy.

We now know more about human behavior than ever before in the history of the world. This places the ultimate crime-fighting weapon, disciplined love and understanding, in our hands.

REFERENCES

Baumer, Ed. *Step into My Parlor: The Chilling Story of Serial Killer Jeffrey Dahmer.* Chicago: Bonus Books, 1991.

Clarkson, Wensley. *Hell Hath No Fury: The True Story of Women Who Kill.* London: Blake Paperbacks, 1991.

Daily Southtown, March 17, 1995.

Douglas, John, and Olshaker, Mark. *Journey into Madness.* New York: Pocket Books, 1997.

Douglas, John. *Mind Hunter.* New York: Pocket Books, 1996.

Englade, Ken. *Murder in Boston.* New York: St. Martin's Press, 1990.

———. *Deadly Lessons.* New York: St. Martin's Press, 1991.

———. interview with the author, 1997.

Fido, Martin. *The Chronicle of Crime.* New York: Carroll & Graf Publishers, 1993.

Fox, James Alan, and Levin, Jack. *Overkill: Mass Murder and Serial Killing Exposed.* New York: Dell Publishing, 1994.

Fuhrman, Mark. *Murder in Brentwood.* New York: Zebra Books, 1997.

Holmes, Ronald M., and Holmes, Stephen T. *Murder in America*, Thousand Oaks, Calif.: Sage Publications, 1994.

Jenkins, Philip. *Using Murder: The Social Construction of Serial Homicide.* New York: Aldyne de Gruyter, 1994.

Jones, Aphrodite. *Cruel Sacrifice.* New York: Pinnacle Books, 1994.

Kappel, Robert D. *Signature Killers.* New York: Pocket Books, 1997.

Kennedy, Dolores. with Nolin, Robert, *On a Killing Day.* Chicago: Bonus Books, 1992.

Lane, Roger. *Murder in America.* Columbus, Ohio: Columbia University Press, 1997.

Levy, Harlan. *And the Blood Cried Out.* New York: Basic Books, 1996.

MacKenzie, Drew. "Presumed Innocent," *Sunday Bloody Sunday.* London: Blake Paperbacks, 1992.

Newsweek, July 28, 1997.

Paul, Annie Murphy. "Do Parents Really Matter?" *Psychology Today*, January–February, 1998.

Philpin, John, and Donnelly, John. *Beyond Murder: The Inside Account of the Gainesville Student Murders.* New York: Onyx Books, 1994.

Publications International, *Murder and Mayhem.* Lincolnwood, Ill.: Publications International, 1991.

Ressler, Robert K., and Schachtman, Tom. *Whoever Fights Monsters.* New York: St. Martin's Press, 1992.

Sawicki, Stephen. *Teach Me to Kill.* New York: Avon Books, 1991.

Scott, Cathy. *The Killing of Tupac Shakur.* Las Vegas: Huntington Press, 1997.

Sheindlin, Gerald. *Blood Trail.* New York: Ballantine Books, 1996.

Vibe, *Tupac Amaru Shakur: 1971–1996.* New York: Crown Publishers, 1997.

Wambaugh, Joseph. *The Blooding.* New York: Bantam Books, 1989.

White, Armond. *Rebel for the Hell of It: The Life of Tupac Shakur.* New York: Thunder's Mouth Press, 1997.

Williams, Stephen. *Invisible Darkness.* New York: Bantam Books, 1998.

Wilson, Colin. *The Killers Among Us: Book II. Motives Behind Their Madness.* New York: Warner Books, 1995.

Index